El Malpais, Mt. Taylor, and the Zuni Mountains

El Malpais, Mt. Taylor, and the Zuni Mountains

A Hiking Guide and History

Sherry Robinson

University of New Mexico Press
Albuquerque

To Dad, who taught me persistence

year   printing
11 10 09 08 07 06 05 04   2 3 4 5 6 7

Library of Congress Cataloging-in-Publication Data

Robinson, Sherry.
    El Malpais, Mt. Taylor, and the Zuni Mountains : a hiking
guide and history / Sherry Robinson.—1st ed.
        p. cm.
    Includes bibliographical references and index.
    ISBN 0-8263-1527-5
    1. Hiking—New Mexico—El Malpais National Monument—
Guidebooks. 2. Hiking—New Mexico—Taylor, Mount—
Guidebooks. 3. Hiking—New Mexico—Zuni Mountains—
Guidebooks. 4. El Malpais National Monument (N.M.)—
Guidebooks. 5. Taylor, Mount (N.M.)—Guidebooks.
6. Zuni Mountains (N.M.)—Guidebooks.   I. Title.
GV199.42.N62E567 1994
796.5'1'09789—dc20   94-18694
                                                    CIP

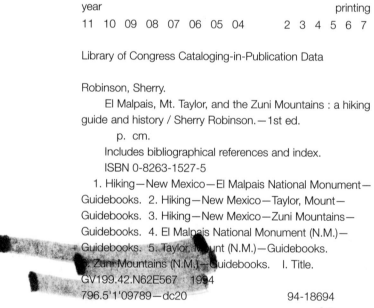

Designed by Mary Shapiro
Cartography by Carol Cooperrider and Mary Shapiro

Contents

$17.95

List of Hikes

List of Hikes (by difficulty)

Challenging

Moderate

Easy

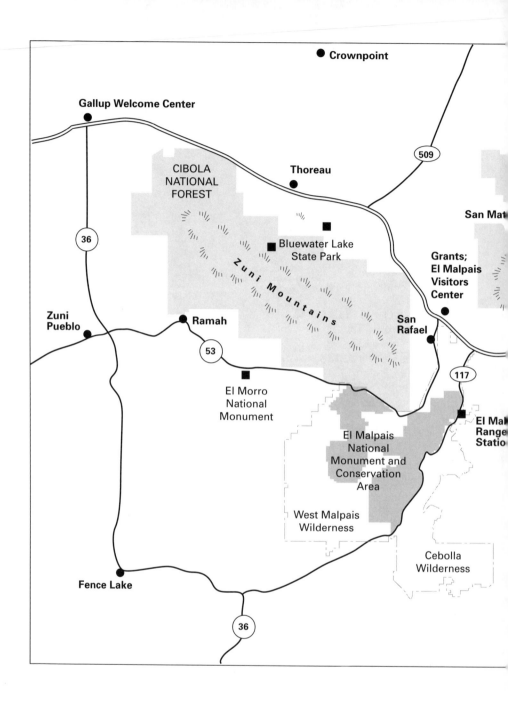

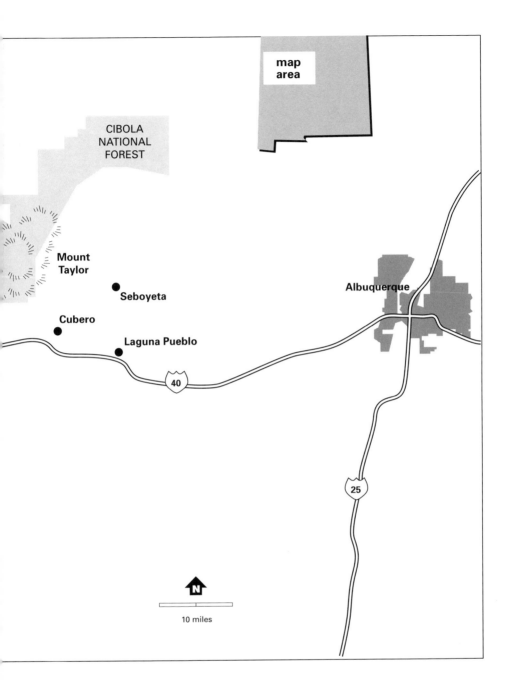

map area

CIBOLA
NATIONAL
FOREST

Mount
Taylor

Seboyeta

Cubero

Laguna Pueblo

Albuquerque

40

25

N

10 miles

Preface

In July 1975 I drove into a stringy town called Milan, the little sister of Grants, New Mexico. The two towns were then in the sweaty grip of a uranium boom, and there was plenty of almost everything—money, jobs, opportunity. Everything but housing. My three-year-old son Eric and I slept in the office of the *Uranium Empire Reporter,* where I'd landed my first newspaper job. It was the craziest place I'd ever lived, and I felt instantly at home.

In those days newcomers hoping for jobs pulled into town daily, with everything they owned in a U-haul; in a boom economy, if they knew how to do anything, somebody would hire them. In much the same fashion, I arrived in a borrowed car with a few possessions and little to recommend me— no degree, no résumé, no references, just a handful of newspaper bylines. The *Gallup Independent* had just bought the paper from its longtime editor, but their first hire fled after a few weeks on the job. My strong suit was my willingness to stay.

My second day on the job, I photographed a Navy jet the size of two Greyhounds buzzing Acoma Pueblo. My lucky shot resulted in a Pentagon investigation and the Navy's apologies to Acoma, which had been hounded by curious but intrusive pilots. I took it as a sign that I should stick around.

It was hardly forced duty. I loved the place. Western New Mexicans, so far from the beaten path, have always enjoyed a refreshing live-and-let-live tolerance. Half the population was new, so Grants and Milan didn't harbor any negative attitudes toward strangers. And it has been my experience in two states that underground miners are a forgiving bunch—maybe because mining people have typically worked and lived all over the country, maybe because they face death every day on the job.

The land was as inviting as the people. My second day in Grants I discovered Mt. Taylor and not long after that, El Morro, the malpais, and the Zuni Mountains. I've wondered ever since why people put up with crowds in the Sandia, Jemez, and Manzano mountains, when they could make the short drive to Grants.

As you might have guessed by now, this is a personal book. In part, it's a thanks to the people who welcomed a young reporter and her little boy nearly two decades ago; I hope it encourages the tourism they so dearly want. The book was also a lark that turned serious. Like most newspaper reporters, I wanted to write something with a life beyond the next day. As I sank deeper into my research and saw how little was devoted to this part of the state, the project soon became a mission—to tell the mostly untold stories of a little-understood corner of New Mexico. To welcome the visitor to the lands of Manuel Chaves, Gus Raney, Stella Dysart, Silvestre Mirabal, Lucy Jane Whiteside, Paddy Martinez, and Cecil Moore.

Western New Mexico is more than mountains and rimrock. It's magic. It's an attitude. And it's different. The land has been used—used hard, sometimes. Its canyons and *cerros* are beautiful and unique, but they're not pristine, and the locals don't apologize. They needed the timber, grasslands, and minerals to stay alive, they will tell you. In the same vein, my history of the area includes mining and logging, which may annoy some outdoor enthusiasts, but it's also part of the picture. Hiking here means getting used to some tailings piles, some logging scars. If that bothers you, stick to the Pecos. If you accept the area and its many dimensions, it will reward you a thousand times over.

Acknowledgments

I now understand what authors mean when they say a book takes on a life of its own. As this book grew and expanded, I often felt there were four members of the family—my husband, my son, myself, and The Book, all requiring care and feeding. I thank my family for putting up with the adopted member these last few years. My husband, Steve Fischer, was also a major source of information, as manager of the U.S. Bureau of Land Management's portion of El Malpais.

Much of the detail in my hike descriptions would not be possible without the wealth of knowledge of Kathleen Havill, my friend and hiking partner, and her husband Steve. Kathleen can walk fifty yards and identify six birds, twelve plants, and three kinds of pottery shards. The Havills introduced me to the real Zuni Mountains, and for that I can never thank them enough.

Other valued hiking partners were my husband, Steve, my son, Eric Robinson; and my friends Lee Schupach, John Roney, and Charlie Donaldson. I also enjoyed many hikes with the good people of Los Amigos del Malpais, a volunteer group.

All three federal agencies in the area were wonderfully helpful and supportive: at the U.S. Forest Service (USFS), John Caffrey, Mark Catron, and Rita Siminski; at the National Park Service (NPS), Doug Eury, Kent Carlton, Cindy Ott-Jones, and Lola Henio; at the Bureau of Land Management (BLM), Pat Hestor, Peg Fleming, and Rick Jones.

I must also thank some people who prepared the way. These are the local historians, homesteaders, and long-time residents who valued their histories enough to write them down. Some of these small, self-published volumes were invaluable, especially those of Gary Tietjen and Josephine Barela. Many other gems of information were available because unknown dedicated souls spent time taking oral histories and leaving them in the library, where somebody like me could make use of them. And although most journalists are more concerned with the present than the past, my fellow journalist Sue Winsor realized that some of her interviews and notes for the Grants Beacon were important and likewise donated them to the library.

Thanks also to the Bright and Savage families, Wolf

Elston and Frank Perry of the University of New Mexico, Bill Laughlin of Los Alamos National Laboratory, John Gruener of Lockheed Engineering and Sciences Co., Fred Wilding-White of the NMSU Grants branch library, and Matthew Silva.

I am grateful to Orville Moore for permission to use his father Cecil Moore's poetry and to Robert Gallegos for use of his miner poetry.

About This Book

This is a different sort of hiking guide. It is, in fact, the hiking guide I always wished I'd had in other places. I'm a curious person. When I hike I want to know what's gone on in a place, who lived in that sagging cabin, what happened to the land. For that reason there's more background and history in this book than in any similar guide I've seen.

Another difference is that hiking guides are usually written by men—young men—and reflect their preferences. I wanted a book that offered outings not just for hot-dog hikers but also for older visitors, as well as for people with small children. You will find in these pages everything from car tours to challenging treks. Keep in mind when reading the hike descriptions that the author is a forty-something woman in pretty good shape, with occasionally sore knees. If I say a hike was "difficult," it was difficult for me.

Finally most writers of hiking books have the luxury of developed trails. There are few in western New Mexico, and so I've described hikes that rely largely on land features such as arroyos, human byways such as logging roads and old railroad beds, and sometimes even cattle trails. This means that a topo map is essential, and common sense is a requirement.

You should carry the following maps with you in west-central New Mexico: Cibola National Forest/ Mt. Taylor Ranger District (U.S. Forest Service) for Mt. Taylor and the Zuni Mountains, El Malpais Recreation Guide Map (U.S. Bureau of Land Management and National Park Service) and topographical maps as indicated in hike descriptions. Also helpful are the Grants Quadrangle and Chaco Mesa Quadrangle (U.S. Geological Survey).

Keep in mind that El Malpais is still being developed; road and hike distances, conditions, and logistics could change, so check with NPS and BLM offices.

Important information appears on pages 38–39 concerning precautions you should take before hiking or entering areas described in this book.

Update 2004

When this book was published in 1994, El Malpais National Monument and Conservation Area was new and still evolving. Not surprisingly, the two federal agencies that manage El Malpais have made some changes. The U.S. Forest Service also reports changes in access for Mt. Taylor and the Zuni Mountains.

Visitors have two more facilities for information. The new Northwest New Mexico Visitor Center (exit 85 from I-40 in Grants) is staffed by National Park Service, Bureau of Land Management, and Forest Service personnel and is open seven days a week from 9 a.m. to 6 p.m. during daylight savings, 8 a.m. to 5 p.m., standard time. For information call 505-876-2783. The NPS also opened El Malpais Information Center 23 miles south of Grants on NM 53. It's open seven days a week from 8:30 to 4:30. Both are closed Thanksgiving, Christmas, and New Year's Day.

The National Park Service has new regulations for caving, camping and fire use in its portion of El Malpais. Only Junction Cave (p. 73), Big Skylight Cave (p. 70), and Four Windows Cave (p. 75) are open year round and accessible without a permit. Braided Cave (p. 77) is open without a permit from October through April but closed from May through September to protect a colony of Townsend's big-eared bats. All other caves require a permit well in advance from the chief ranger.

The agency asks campers to get a permit, and some areas, such as trailheads, are off limits to camping. Ground fires are not permitted. Grills can be used at a few trailheads, if there are no fire restrictions at the time.

The National Park Service has made some changes in trails and roads. At Braided Cave, hike along the closed road until you see cairns. The El Calderon area (p. 58) has changed from a single trail to El Calderon to a three-mile loop that also includes Lava Trench, Bat Cave, Double Sinks, and Junction Cave. The road to Bat Cave is closed. In the area of Little Hole in the Wall some roads are closed; the rest are numbered for better directions.

A new feature is Lava Falls, at the southern tip of the monument. Here you see not just the falls itself, like a small, frozen waterfall, but a great natural amphitheater formed by a lava wall. Here you're in the McCartys flow, the newest in the monument at 3,000 years. Access is over a one-mile loop trail 36 miles south of I-40 on NM 117.

The BLM has also changed some regulations. Camping is allowed in the BLM's portion of El Malpais except at the BLM Ranger Station on NM 117 and La Ventana Natural Arch. Camping and parking are not allowed within 300 yards of springs, water holes, wells, tanks, or structures.

Narrows Rim (p. 45) now has a trail (7.6 miles round trip), which ends overlooking La Ventana. The primitive camping area at Narrows Rim is closed, replaced by a picnic area at the trailhead. A developed campground is planned about two miles south of the BLM Ranger Station on NM 117. And the entrance to Cebolla Canyon and Sand Canyon (p. 94) has been moved south about ¼ mile.

The Continental Divide National Scenic Trail (p. 219) morphed from possibility to reality. In this area it crosses the Zuni-Acoma Trail, El Calderon, and the Chain of Craters. It's still developing. See information centers for latest route descriptions.

On Mt. Taylor a Forest Service land exchange has eliminated checkerboard land ownership in one area and changed access to Guadalupe Canyon (p. 132). From the end of the pavement, take FR 239 about 34 miles, turn on FR 194, and proceed 6.5 miles to FR 194A. Vehicles are allowed only on designated routes from April 16 to June 30 and August 31 to November 29. Horses and bicycles have unrestricted access.

At Rinconada Canyon (p. 134) a change of land ownership has eliminated parking and previous access. Instead drive to the end of the pavement on Mt. Taylor and take FR 193 to the Big Springs spur and reach the canyon from the top down.

In the Zuni Mountains, the Forest Service rerouted FR 483 around private land. To reach Cottonwood Canyon (p. 196), take FR 50 to the new FR 483 exit at Twin Springs, which ties into the old route north of the private land to reach Cottonwood Canyon or continue on the new route to the Dugway, which takes you to Lookout Mountain and Long Park.

And the Forest Service no longer provides water at Coal Mine Campground on Mt. Taylor or the Quaking Aspen Campground in the Zuni Mountains.

Sherry Robinson
May 2004

1

El Malpais

*Lava field near
Bandera Crater.*

El Malpais

*You wonder just how long this unbelievable bit of New
Mexico will remain unexplored, unexploited and wildly
free.*

New Mexico Magazine, *1946.*

When Captain E. F. Dutton and his party rode into
this glorious country in the 1880s to survey it
for the U.S. Geological Survey, he found the
terms of his own language—"hill," "valley,"
"mountain"—too puny to describe what he saw. And for
some features, such as the flat-topped hills that stretched
before them, there were no words at all. But Spanish,
with its rich and precise lexicon of landforms, came to
Dutton's rescue. He was moved in his 1885 report to
express his debt to the Spanish language. I too am
indebted for words like *mesa, malpais, canyon, rincon,
arroyo, caldera,* and *cerro,* not to mention the musical

and colorful names given to places in the area: La Ventana, El Banquito, Cebolla.

The earliest Spanish explorers, encountering the jagged, black rivers of lava, called it El Malpais, "The Bad Country." Unwilling to risk boot leather or horses' hooves, they rode around it. Pueblo people, whose ancestral fields lie nearby, built trails through the malpais and bridged crevices by piling up lava rock level with the rim. Today travelers on Interstate 40 look out car windows and remark on the sight. They may even stop and let the kids pick up a chunk. What they probably don't know is that this badland—forty miles long and from five to fifteen miles across—is one of the most significant volcanic areas in the United States, comparable to those of Hawaii and Japan.

Until recently El Malpais remained a mysterious, forbidding place that invited wild stories. In 1933 a traveler wrote, "So bleak and deserted is the volcanic country that we could easily fancy that we had landed on the face of the moon. Black rock, full of gas holes, like the slag of a blast furnace, covered the ground." As late as 1964, one travel writer was lamenting the lack of study, "which falls into the lot of the daring, zealous adventurer."

In 1969 the U.S. Bureau of Land Management began to awaken this sleeping giant. There followed eighteen years of studies for various official designations. On December 31, 1987, with considerable politicking and support from a community whose mining economy was on the wane, Congress established El Malpais National Monument and El Malpais National Conservation Area. It totaled 376,000 acres, bounded by I-40, State Roads 53 and 117, and County Road 42. (Additional volcanic flows lie outside these official boundaries in the San Jose Valley and in the Zuni Mountains.)

One of four natural arches in the area, this one at Sandstone Bluffs.

The National Park Service manages the 114,000-acre monument, which includes many craters, ice caves, and other lava features. The Bureau of Land Management oversees the 262,600-acre conservation area, which includes La Ventana natural arch, the 39,600-acre West Malpais Wilderness Area, the Chain of Craters, and the 62,800-acre Cebolla Wilderness.

El Malpais holds a wealth of sights for the visitor looking for something different. Here are a few of the major features (described in detail in the hiking sections):

■ Bandera Crater—the area's largest and most accessible cinder cone. It's a half-mile across and 650 feet deep, and the view from the top is well worth the short hike.
■ Candelaria Ice Caves—one of the nation's only easily accessible, perpetual ice caves. The temperature even in the summer is never above freezing.
■ Lava tubes—tunnels in the lava that occur alone and in series. Collapsed tubes look like canyons or may form

3

bridges. Some contain elaborate ice crystals, others sulfur crystals. At least two are home to bats and blind crickets.

■ Sandstone Bluffs—an overlook of El Malpais and some of its features.

■ La Ventana—the second-largest natural arch in New Mexico, with a span 125 feet high and 165 feet across the base.

■ Chain of Craters—a series of thirty volcanic cones stretching twenty miles from Bandera Crater to Ramah Navajo lands.

■ Archeological sites—these include Anasazi ruins and homestead cabins.

Taken together, such an unusual and abundant combination of features offers the serious hiker or caver, as well as the casual sightseer, a unique outdoor experience.

Geology

It is true that there are in this area a great many rivers of a sort not to be found in the East—and such strange rivers! They are black as coal, and full of strange, savage waves, and curious curling eddies, and enormous bubbles. The springs from which they started ran dry centuries ago . . . There lies the broad, wild current, sometimes thirty feet higher than its banks, yet not overflowing them . . . a current in which not fishes but wild beasts live—often even one river on top of another!
Charles Lummis, 1908

Crevices split the lava.

El Malpais lies in the southeastern portion of the Colorado Plateau, in the Acoma Embayment, the sag between the Zuni Uplift on the west and the Lucero Uplift on the east. Geologically speaking El Malpais is new. And contrary to persistent misinformation, Mt. Taylor is not the source. Captain Dutton, of the USGS, was the first to declare that vents in the plain and not Mt. Taylor poured out the lava flows of the malpais. "In the immediate foreground, and indeed, under our feet and spreading over all the lowlands and plains in front, is a chaos of black, rough lava of peculiarly horrid aspect," he wrote in his 1885 report. "Its freshness betokens great recency of eruption . . . Many have presumed that it came from Mount Taylor; but this is a mistake . . . This rough clinkery lava is called by the Mexicans 'malpais'."

Mt. Taylor is a volcano; flows from nearby vents capped the surrounding country, which then eroded into skirtlike mesas encircling the mountain. El Malpais was laid down much later, by about seventy-four vents that periodically erupted. The first flow was an estimated two hundred thousand years ago, the last three thousand years ago; only moments, in geologic time. The three oldest volcanoes are Cerro Encierro, Cerro Bandera,

*The clinkery side
of Cerro Rendija.*

and Cerro Rendija, although even older volcanoes lie under some flows. The most recent flows came from Bandera and McCartys Crater.

University of New Mexico volcanologist Wolf Elston once jokingly called El Malpais "the poor man's Hawaii." The label stuck because you can find in a small area all four kinds of volcanoes—basalt cones, cinder cones, shield volcanoes, and composite volcanoes—and other features typical of basalt volcanoes in Hawaii.

Basalt lava cones are the smallest. Rapid-fire, they spit out lava that spread easily. They left broad craters with steep sides, which can be as large as two miles across and hundreds of feet deep. Lava Crater is a basalt cone.

Cinder cones, which are larger than basalt cones, are responsible for most of the flows in the malpais. They formed from foamy cinders accumulating around a vent. Bandera Crater is a cinder cone; so are most of the cones in Chain of Craters. They're typically several hundred feet high. Because cinder cones were loose structures the consistency of shaving cream, most of their lava eased out of the base or side, rather than rising in the throat.

Shield volcanoes are named for their shapes—broad and flat, with a slight peak in the rim. Gentler eruptions and multiple flows from the same vent or several closely spaced vents created these volcanoes. There are four of them in El Malpais: Cerro Rendija, Cerro Hoya, McCartys Crater, and an unnamed volcano west of Bandera Crater. (Some geologists consider McCartys a cinder cone.)

Composite, or stratovolcanoes, are the largest and most dramatic volcanoes. They rose gradually and in a final furious explosion filled the air with steam, cinders, ash, and lava. The center may have collapsed to form a caldera (cauldron). Mt. St. Helens and Mt. Taylor are composite volcanoes.

From whatever source, as molten lava oozed, tumbled, and broke over the landscape, the drama of its progress froze in place. The flow's surface cooled and crusted over, but the push of still-molten lava underneath cracked and buckled the hard crust, pushing up pressure ridges and building up spatter cones (small,

pointed minivolcanoes) and fiery fountains. In places hotter and faster-flowing lava dragged the cooler surface into wrinkles, like the folds in a throw rug left by a skidding child. These wrinkles are called by the Hawaiian term *pahoehoe* (paHOYhoy), or ropy lava, and point in the direction of the flow. Cooler lava, possibly moving more slowly, hardened into a jagged, broken mass called *aa* (AHah), another Hawaiian term.

The malpais flows have a variety of features. Blocky flows were created by chunks of hardened lava carried along and then piled up. Squeeze-ups resulted from fractures in an outer crust that filled with molten material. *Kipukas* are islands of land surrounded by lava; the biggest is called Hole-in-the-Wall. And collapse depressions, sometimes called sinkholes, formed where the solidified surface caved in. Lava tubes, or caves, took shape where a current of molten rock flowed underneath a hardened surface, leaving behind a tunnel. El Malpais contains the longest known lava tube in North America, sixteen miles long. Because of their similarity

(Left) Spatter cones, many the size of Pueblo bread ovens, are minivolcanoes. (Right) Pahoehoe, or ropy lava: Its folds indicate direction of the flow.

Lava bridges were created when tubes collapsed, leaving narrow bands.

to the moon's sinuous rilles, these tubes have drawn NASA scientists, who have studied their potential for providing shelter on the moon.

The rock itself is varied. As the lava solidified into basalt, some gases escaped and others were trapped, forming bubbles in the rock. As a result some lava may even float in water. Trapped minerals formed crystals. The basalt takes its dark red and black colors from minerals containing magnesium and iron. In places the iron (oxide mineral magnetite) may confuse compass readings for both hikers and pilots. The volcanoes also left behind some interesting debris—huge blown-out blocks that shattered when they hit the ground and half-molten material that became bullet-shaped as it hurled through the air, bending and curling on impact. Rounded missiles are called bombs; some have cores of material from the earth's mantle, miles below the surface.

Using aerial photography, geochemistry, and field checks, geologists have identified multiple flows in El Malpais. Five are most familiar:

■ McCartys flow is one of the largest volumes of lava produced in recent times and, at about three thousand years old, is the youngest in El Malpais. Its 119-square-mile surface, with pahoehoe and aa, resembles Hawaiian flows. This mass originated in a small cone about twenty miles south of I-40 and moved south for a short distance; mostly it flowed north in a narrow stream along the eastern edge of the Hoya de Cibola flow, then east toward present-day McCartys. Apparently lacking the violent explosions that build cones, McCartys crater is little more than a vent.

■ Bandera flow, the next youngest, poured from Bandera Crater and moved south and east, around the Zuni Mountains, and then north toward present-day Grants.

■ Hoya de Cibola is the name given to a shield volcano and its neighboring crater on the west side of El Malpais. Both are the source of multiple older flows that moved south, east, and probably northeast. They are partially covered by the McCartys and Bandera flows.

■ Several overlapping flows originated from neighboring cinder cones: Twin Craters, Lost Woman, and Lava Crater (the latter is also called La Tetra or La Tetera). Because of their similarity, they're classed as one flow unit, called Twin Craters. They flowed south and east around the Zuni Mountains, near State Road 53.

■ El Calderon crater (and possibly others covered by the McCartys flow) is the source of the oldest flows in the monument. They moved east and north, but much is covered by soil and other flows. Far older vents were buried by the Chain of Craters and their flows. About 600,000 to 700,000 years old, they're the source of the Fence Lake flow and North Plains basalts, which are largely covered by soil.

Outside El Malpais are four other volcanic flows. Bluewater flow erupted from El Tintero ("inkwell") crater, near Haystack Butte west of Grants, and flowed southeast along the Rio San Jose bottom. In the Zuni Mountains, one flow started from a lava and cinder cone on Oso Ridge, northwest of Bandera Crater, flowed east to Agua Fria Creek, and then south, nearly to El Malpais. On top of it is the Paxton Springs flow, which poured from a cinder cone near Paxton Springs. It flowed two miles down Agua Fria Creek and then seventeen miles through Zuni Canyon to the San Jose Valley, south of Milan. Finally there is the Fence Lake flow, southwest of El Malpais.

Scientists have been debating the flows' ages for years. Most recently Bill Laughlin, of Los Alamos National Laboratory, has dated flows using potassium-argon and carbon-14 methods. The large amounts of argon-40 in these rocks at the time of eruption skewed previous dates, so that the lava appeared to be many times older than it actually is. The Bluewater flow, previously believed to be about a million years old, is about one-tenth that age. The Hoya de Cibola flow is 110,000 years old. Chain of Craters and the south Rendija area are between 110,000 and 200,000 years old. The Bandera flows are less than 10,000 years old. Mount Taylor, its plugs, and the basalts on mesa tops are 2.5 to 3.7 million years old.

An older geological tale is told by the stunning sandstone ridges and mesas that frame El Malpais for miles along State Road 117, on the east side, and by the Zuni Mountains to the west. During Permian times, 290 million to 240 million years ago, an arm of the sea, advancing from the south, reached toward the area of El Morro. Its fluctuating shoreline left marine limestone and gypsum in alternating layers with red muds and sands, to form the Abo Formation of dark red shale and sandstone and the Yeso Formation of light red sandstone and shale with light grey limestone. One final lap of the sea, extending just north of the present Zuni Mountains, deposit-

Sandstone ridges frame NM 117.

ed the thick, cream-colored sandstones of the Glorieta Formation and the light gray limestone of the San Andres Formation.

For the next 100 million years, the area was above sea level and changed from forest to desert as the climate varied; meandering rivers deposited silts from the south, and hot, dry winds created sand dunes. These were the sources of the dark red shale, sandstone, and conglomerate of the Chinle formation and the banded red-and-white Zuni Formation. Jurassic formations, the Zuni, Todilto, and Morrison, nearly ring the Zuni Mountains and are most spectacular from El Morro to Zuni Pueblo.

In late Cretaceous time, about 138 to 63 million years ago, the sea moved back and forth across the Zuni Mountains, leaving dark, fossil-laden shales and buff-colored sandstone. Periodically slow-moving streams built deltas. The lagoons and marshes bordering the sea became coal deposits. The water retreated for good around 70 million years ago. At about the same time, the dome of the Zuni Mountains was pushed out of the earth's crust, and erosion began its timeless sculpture, ultimately exposing Precambrian granite and carving the colorful Zuni sandstones into fanciful shapes. Sandstone ridges along State Road 117 are a sandwich of Zuni sandstone and shaly siltstones, followed by other sandstones, siltstones, and muddy shale.

Creation Stories
Acoma, Navajo, and Zuni people have their own explanations for the rivers of fire.

Acomas blame it all on KauBat, a gambler who lived near Acoma. The ruthless KauBat seduced a girl and left her in the woods, where a kind badger took her in. She had two sons, who grew up in two years and wanted to find their father. The badger tried to discourage them, but they were determined. So the badger gave in, warning that KauBat would gamble everything until he bet his fellow gamblers they couldn't guess what was in a buckskin bag hanging from the ceiling. She gave them the answer.

In two days the boys found KauBat, who fed them. KauBat's mother liked the boys and scolded her son for not bringing their mother home. As usual KauBat was gambling, and the boys watched until they learned how to gamble and then challenged their father. Soon they won everything KauBat owned—his house and even his mother. KauBat bet his heart against their winnings that they couldn't guess the contents of the buckskin bag. After several guesses, they said, "Stars!" The boys had won KauBat's heart, but they didn't want to kill him. So they took his eyes and left Kaubat's mother to care for him.

Furious, KauBat built a fire and started to sing. He asked an evil one to help him destroy everything. He added some pitch to the fire, and it boiled over and spread across the countryside. The boys ran, and the Rain Maker of the North called the clouds and rain. After four days and four nights, the pitch hardened.

When the boys returned home, they showed their mother and the badger KauBat's eyes and then threw them into the southern sky. They lived with the badger a long time, but finally returned to Acoma. They kept the bag of stars and became great gamblers.

Twin boys also figure into Navajo legend. In their creation story, Navajos tell of the time people were trying to settle in the fifth world, having emerged from four worlds below. But monsters of every kind beset them, killing them off until they despaired of surviving in this place. Finally the Hero Twins, two young men who were supernatural beings, appealed to their father Johonaa'ei, the Sun, for help. He supplied them with weapons, and they began slaying monsters.

They began on Tsoodzil, the Blue Bead Mountain (Mt. Taylor), where Ye'iitsoh the Big Giant lived. Ye'iitsoh, they learned, appeared each day to drink from a lake at the spring To Sido (Ojo del Gallo), leaning against the mountain as he drank. As the Twins watched, Ye'iitsoh took four gulps, emptied the lake and laughed.

The Twins approached the giant, and when he saw them, he felt hungry. They taunted and insulted him, and he threw lightning bolts at them. But they stood on a rainbow and maneuvered it so the bolts missed them. Just then a more powerful bolt from the direction of the sun struck the giant, and he reeled. The brothers fired their own bolts of lightning, until Ye'iitsoh collapsed and died. Then they cut off his head and threw it into the hills, where it remains as Cabezon ("big head") Peak.

Blood from the giant's body poured down the valley. Nilch'i, the Wind, warned the twins that if the blood reached the houses of other monsters nearby, the giant would come back to life. One brother drew lines across the valley with a knife his father had given him, and the blood stopped. As the blood dried and hardened, it turned dark and covers the valley to this day. Navajos still sing of the twins' victory over Ye'iitsoh.

Zuni people say that in the beginning, the Sun created the Earth Mother and Sky Father. They had twins who led humanlike creatures in search of a home. But the earth's surface was marshy, and monsters came from underground. With help from the Sun, the twins struck the surface with lightning, which hardened it and blasted the monsters. Their blood hardened into black rocks.

Flora and Fauna
Here, among the up-turned cakes of lava, piled and shoved over each other in every conceivable form of gigantic disarrangement, one is surprised to see pines, spruce, quaken aspen, juniper and oaks growing out of the lava.

Evon Vogt, scholar and homesteader, 1924

You might wonder what could live or grow here, but this unique environment supports a surprisingly rich variety of plant and animal life. The average summer temperature is about 70 degrees, with a high of 105 degrees; the average winter temperature is 25 to 30 degrees, with a low of minus 20 degrees. The climate has been stable for the last two thousand years. The area gets just 10 inches of rainfall a year—local ranchers say it rains more in the malpais—mostly in afternoon showers between July and September.

However, the porous lava holds scarce water. In addition lava tubes, crevices, and sinkholes trap water or hold colder or warmer air, creating small ecosystems where unusual animals or fragile plants can survive. Sensitive species include grass fern and maidenhair spleenwort. The area also has substantial areas of mixed conifer forest as well as vast grassy islands (kipukas). Along the edges of flows, where water collects, are "ecotones," where trees, shrubs, and grasses are thick and richly varied. In other areas are "inverted lifezones," where trees that would otherwise never be neighbors grow side by side. Aspens may grow alongside piñons and junipers, and both may keep company with ponderosa pines and Douglas firs.

In even the most severe-looking lava flows, the plants

may be small and the trees stunted or twisted, but they're generally healthy. Trees that grow in the lava are junipers, piñons, and ponderosa pines, with some Douglas firs and alligator junipers. This is the northeastern extension of the alligator juniper's range. In 1992 University of Arizona researchers found the oldest known living Rocky Mountain Douglas fir, northeast of Cerro Rendija. The tree sprouted in the year 1062, four years before William the Conquerer invaded England. Researchers also found other nine-hundred-year-old firs and logs dating to A.D. 599.

Trees growing in the lava may be twisted, but they're healthy.

The malpais area is one of the top five tree-ring sites in the world. Scientists have found such distinct rings in some Douglas firs that they almost have a seven-hundred-year rain gauge. With one tree-ring history to A.D. 111, El Malpais has the longest tree-ring chronology in New Mexico and the third longest in the Southwest.

Shrubs that grow here are Apache plume, New Mexico privet, currant, oak, rabbit brush, California brickellbush, skunkbush sumac, Wright sagewort, rough golden aster, wax currant, mountain mahogany, raspberries, and gooseberries. Big sage in areas bordering the lava is the result of overgrazing, the most significant impact on the local environment. Shrubs in the surrounding area are snakeweed, rabbit brush, yucca, bear grass, saltbrush, greasewood, and winter fat.

Grasses are Arizona fescue, mountain muhly, june grass, blue grama and mutton bluegrass. In the kipukas are virtually undisturbed stands of big and little bluestem and Arizona fescue grasses. In the Cebolleta Mesa area, on the east side of the lava, are blue gramma grasses as

(Left) Plants and grasses flourish in the folds of lava. (Right) Tracks near Sandstone Bluffs were probably left by a badger and her young.

well as galleta, hairy gramma, sideoats gramma and, at higher elevations, Indian rice grass. Wildflowers include globe mallow, bee plant, daisies, and sunflowers. And the rocks harbor more than 75 varieties of lichen.

The lava flows and their forests and shrublands are the habitat for about 150 species of wild animals. Adaptation is visible here in the number of black creatures—lizards, frogs, horned toads, squirrels, and other rodents. Some 39 species of mammals live in the malpais. Most common are the mule deer, elk, porcupine, striped and hog-nosed skunks, long-tailed weasel, black-tailed jackrabbit, desert and mountain cottontails, and a variety of rodents. The Zuni prairie dog inhabits the monument's eastern boundary, while pronghorn antelope can be seen on the North Plains, an area generally south of the lava flows. The coyote is common; occasional predators include black bear, badger, gray fox, bobcat, and mountain lion.

In both summer and winter, El Malpais provides the habitat for a variety of bats, including the Mexican free-tailed, Townsend's big-eared, hoary, pallid, big brown, and myotis. Myotis includes long-eared, fringed, long-legged, and small-footed. A colony of Mexican free-tailed bats lives in Bat Cave, and their flights can be seen at dusk from June through October. The estimated population of eight thousand is a fraction of the forty thousand counted in the 1950s, probably because of pesticides. In the winter a smaller population of Townsend's big-eared bats lives here.

Bighorn sheep once grazed here. Navajos used to trap them in Bandera Crater, and Zunis may have domes-

ticated them for wool. Park ranger and rancher Evon
Vogt wrote in 1924 of finding skulls with giant horns
weighing twenty pounds. Homesteaders have said
bighorn rams killed domestic rams in the night and stole
entire flocks of their ewes. In 1930 the *Grant Review*
reported that Frank Sanchez found horns and skulls of
bighorns of "immense size" in malpais caves. Over the
years, remains of some one hundred bighorns have
been found in the malpais, some as late as 1988. Dating
by accelerator mass spectrometry tells us they lived here
as recently as the early 1950s. Biologists believe they were
desert bighorns. Within the twentieth century, bighorns
were eliminated in El Malpais because of disease and
livestock grazing. State and federal agencies have considered this area for reintroduction, but ruled it out, because
bighorns have no immunities to the diseases of domestic
sheep. Other species no longer seen here are the gray
wolf and the black-footed ferret. For awhile in 1993 and
1994, the eastern side of El Malpais was home to twenty-
five American bison moved from Fort Wingate. The buffalo did what they do best, which is to roam, sometimes
to neighboring counties. The BLM and state Game and
Fish Department removed them in 1994.

There are one hundred species of birds, according to
government reports. The most common are Stellers,
scrub, and piñon jays; robin; mourning dove; downy and
ladderbacked woodpeckers; rock wren; white-breasted
nuthatch; mountain and western bluebirds; rufous hummingbird; horned lark; western meadowlark; cliff swallow; mountain chickadee; and scaled quail. The turkey
vulture and raven are also common, and turkeys have
been seen in the East Rendija area. Hawks include kes-
trel, prairie falcon, goshawk, red-tailed, Cooper's and
rough-legged; and great-horned, pygmy, long-eared, and
burrowing owls are also found here. The sandstone
escarpment along NM 117 is prime habitat for golden
eagles, red-tailed hawks, prairie falcons and great horned
owls. Peregrine falcons migrate through the area, and
golden and bald eagles sometimes forage here. Raptors
prefer the sandstone cliffs framing the east side of the
monument, while owls are fond of cave entrances and
lava collapse structures. For unknown reasons, nesting
has declined in recent years.

There are nine species of snake, including the black-
tailed, western diamondback and prairie rattlesnakes;
western black-necked and western terrestrial garter
snakes; bull snake; mountain patch-nosed snake; regal
ringneck snake; and night snake. A variety of lizards and
amphibians also live here. Playas, stock ponds and small
springs host tiger salamanders, toads, and frogs. Not
surprisingly, there are no fish.

Like most other places, El Malpais bears the signs of
human interference. In 1981 Alton Lindsey, a Purdue

University ecology professor, compared the malpais ecology of that year with what he had photographed and studied from 1944 to 1948. He found that construction of I-40 had eliminated a number of ponds at the edge of the malpais. One of those missing had been an opening in the lava that became a well with an island. "On this island was the finest (practically the only) growth of the fern *Asplenium trichomanes* in the entire malpais." The highway also destroyed a series of spectacularly colored ponds with "rose-purple bottoms caused by redsulfur bacteria . . . partly obscured by clouds of bright green filamentous algae and/or stonewort algae." He also found that water levels were shallower in the remaining ponds and that tamarisk, an introduced tree, had invaded many ponds. "I believe there was no tamarisk anywhere in the malpais area in the '40s," and aspens were "far more prevalent and conspicuous" at lava edges and higher elevations. "To me, the most interesting change is the recession of ice in the ice caves." The icy mass in Candelaria's cave had shrunk from fourteen feet in 1926 to nine feet in 1981.

On the rim of Bandera Crater, Lindsey found a piñon he had previously photographed. The tree was more dead than alive, but given the ever so slow processes in these parts, he concluded, "I think this tree considers itself alive." Not so the bats, which were "drastically decimated by human disturbance and doubtless by pesticide chemicals in their prey insects." But he also had good news: " . . . my strong impression is that mammalian life is more prevalent now, especially cottontails. I saw many more ground squirrels, chipmunks and jackrabbits. I never saw a snake or shed snakeskin on the lava during 1944–48, but we found a couple of the skins and one ring-necked snake with all-red belly right out on the lava."

History

South of Mt. Taylor, breaking along the mass of out-poured lava . . . there are craters of comparative newness, where the lava edges cut like glass and the strains and flaws of cooling look as if they had happened yesterday. There are cones too steep for climbing, and craters so deep that the Indians of that country used to drive mountain sheep into these gateless encierros to kill them at their leisure. In one of these the Apaches, who claim the malpais immemorially, used to hide their women and their horses while the men went a-raiding . . . Here are said to be the sacred places of the Apache, still so sacred that I have heard that four men of their nation have joined the Navajo in whose reservation the malpais lies, to see that they are kept unviolated . . . (T)he pathless terror of desertness will keep the malpais for a long time, safe in its wildness. For he who does

not understand that the wildness of mountains serves
us far more than their tameness, understands very little.
Mary Austin, 1924

The great Chaco civilization had become a spectacular network of ruins, replaced by other civilizations at
Zuni and Acoma pueblos when the first Spanish horse
left a hoofprint in their soil. Well-used trade routes tied
Acoma and Zuni to the Rio Grande Valley, the Hopi
mesas, the Pacific Coast, and Mexico. One branch led
directly across the malpais between the pueblos. Spaniards encountered the southern branch of this network
in 1539, when an imaginative priest beheld the play of
sun across the adobe and stone houses of Zuni and
convinced himself and the explorer Francisco Vásquez
de Coronado that he saw cities of gold. Spaniards would
later send soldiers and missionaries over the same
routes to claim land for the crown and the cross.

Early on, Spaniards called the tortured black rock
El Malpais. Rather than tear horseflesh on the Indian
shortcut, they rode north of the flows near Rio San Jose,
or south and west across the Chain of Craters. The
first non-Indian to see the malpais was probably Her-
nando de Alvarado, a member of Coronado's party
sent to visit Pecos Pueblo and report back. Historians
aren't sure he crossed the lava, but he probably passed
through portions and may have traversed the Chain of
Craters, a line of extinct volcanoes on the southern tip of
the lava flows. The first to record his passage through El
Malpais was Diego Pérez de Luxán in March 1583, who
wrote that he traveled "four leagues in waterless malpais."

Historians would record several more expeditions
across the unforgiving rock. During his expedition to the
west in 1604, Don Juan de Oñate crossed the malpais.
When Don Diego de Vargas reclaimed New Mexico in
1691, after the Pueblo Revolt of 1680, his reconquest
took him over the malpais and probably through Zuni Canyon. After that Spanish parties traveled the Zuni-Acoma-
Cibola routes more often and even found the malpais
more inviting, because of water trapped in the lava and
tall ponderosa pines. They named one fork of this trail,
which skirted the Zuni Mountains to Zuni Pueblo, Camino
Obispo ("bishop's road") for the bishop of Durango, who
traveled the route to visit his missions at Zuni. It became
State Road 53.

The last of the great Spanish expeditions, the two-
thousand-mile trek of the friars Francisco Domínguez
and Silvestre Vélez de Escalante, in 1776–77, included
the malpais. The Franciscan brothers camped at El
Morro, passed the malpais on their way to the spring at
what is now San Rafael, and then crossed the lava and
camped at present-day McCartys.

Colonists

The earliest Spanish outpost in the area began in 1746
as a mission to the Navajos. Franciscan priests had
entertained thousands of Navajos in Santa Fe and after
gifts and food, had talked the Navajos into settling per-
manently at a mission they would build in western New
Mexico. In 1748 the Navajos, together with forced labor
from Acoma and Laguna, built a mission on the southeastern flank of Mt. Taylor, at a place called Cebolleta
(later Seboyeta) for the tender onions that grew there.
The church stood in the center, surrounded by a *conven-
to* with long corridors and recessed chapels, a kitchen,
and store houses. If their reluctant fellow laborers weren't
enough to discourage the Navajos, the mission's hanging gallery and whipping post probably were. Within a
year the restless Navajos left, and the mission was
abandoned.

In 1767 King Carlos III issued a land grant west of
Mt. Taylor to Bartólome Fernández and the next year to
Ignacio Chávez, just north of Cebolleta. In the same
years, grantees moved to lands to the northeast, in the
Rio Puerco valley. For a time the colonists lived and traded peacefully with Indian people in the area. Spaniards
recognized Indian land claims and instructed grantees to
treat Indians "with love, fidelity and kindness." But
Navajos, furious at the intrusion, linked up with Apaches,
and together they raided the remote settlements. Spanish colonists asked for arms to protect themselves,
beginning a century of attacks and counterattacks in
which both sides took captives for slaves. Navajos in
those years were as fierce as Apaches; the colonists
took equal pride in their skills as warriors. It was one of
the most brutal periods of New Mexico history.

Cebolleta and the Navajos

In 1800 thirty families arrived from Chihuahua to colonize Cebolleta, then deserted for more than fifty years.
For the first five years, the settlement was under nearly
constant siege by Navajos. For protection the colonists
built a ten-foot stone wall; the only entrance was a narrow gate of ponderosa planks two feet thick, fastened
by a heavy bar. Navajos then added hand grenades of
flaming pitch to their armory of arrows, lances, and
clubs.

During one epic siege in 1804, five hundred Navajos
(or five thousand, depending on the story teller) attacked
the village. As the men returned fire, women and children scrambled to extinguish fireballs lobbed over the
wall. Women brought water and food, tended wounds,
and buried the dead. Doña Antonia Romero was surveying the battle from a rooftop, when she saw a Navajo
climb over the wall and try to open the stout gate, as an
army of Navajos waited outside. She hoisted a stone

Our Lady of Sorrows Catholic Church at Cebolleta: Portions date to 1820. Nuestra Señora de los Dolores was the patron saint of Cebolleta from the founding of the land grant.

metate (grinding stone) and cracked his skull. Another hero of the battle was Don Domingo Baca, who sustained seven wounds in hand-to-hand combat. With one slash across his stomach, his innards tumbled out. He grabbed a pillow, tied it around his middle, and continued fighting. During a lull he stitched up his own wounds with a needle and thread.

The Cebolleteños' only allies in those years were the people of Laguna Pueblo, who hated the Navajos. When things got desperate, a messenger would climb to the top of Cerro de la Celosa, a nearby volcanic plug, and wave a red blanket or build a fire to signal the Lagunas for help.

The Spanish government attempted treaties with the Navajos. One from 1804–05 called for the Navajos to make restitution for "robberies of stock," which then totaled 4,000 sheep, 150 cattle, and 60 horses and mules, or be "deprived of a greater amount (of) possessions than they have stolen." In 1805, however, the weary settlers gave up and began the journey back to Mexico. At Laguna they received word that the governor was sending fifty soldiers to protect them and turned around. (Another melodramatic account says they reached Chihuahua, where the authorities insisted they return and fulfill their contract.) As the settlers grew in strength and numbers, they began retaliatory raids, with slaves as prizes. A Navajo girl was then worth $500 to a Rio Grande rancher.

In this same period, the Spanish founded Cubero, named for the Spanish governor Don José Cubero. It became a Spanish military post, Navajo trading post, and stopping point for travelers on the Zuni-Acoma road. Domínguez and Escalante included it on their map. By the 1830s Cubero was drawing Hispanic settlers.

After Mexico claimed the region in its 1821 revolt against Spain, Cebolleta and Cubero prospered, as trade routes opened. Cebolleta had become a lawless outpost by the time New Mexico became a U.S. territory in 1848, with the Treaty of Guadalupe Hidalgo. Spanish and Mexican renegades had been using Cebolleta as a base

Cubero as it looked in 1885 with Mt. Taylor in the background. (Photo by Ben Wittick, courtesy Museum of New Mexico, 15758.)

for trading whiskey and guns to Indians, in exchange for slaves and stolen horses. The Americans stationed troops at Cebolleta and for a time at Cubero, beginning a long struggle to control the Navajos and contain their raiding.

Preparing the Way

In 1849 an army expedition set out to protect emigrants in the new territory and to survey a wagon road. With that expedition was Lt. James H. Simpson of the military department's topographical engineers, who would have the most lasting impact on the area of any white man to pass through. Simpson, then thirty-six and a graduate of the U.S. Military Academy, was a skilled and reputable surveyor. Traveling through the Zuni Mountains, he detoured to see a sandstone bluff at the insistence of a local trader, found El Morro and its ancient inscriptions, and scratched the first English into the rock. Simpson then crossed the Zuni Mountains and caught sight of a distant mountain, which he named Mt. Taylor, for then-president Zachary Taylor. He would also be the first white man to investigate and mention the ruins of Chaco Canyon and Canyon de Chelly.

Riding out of Zuni Canyon, Simpson camped near the site of what would become Fort Wingate. There he first saw "some unseemly piles of blackened scoriaceous volcanic rocks." Farther on they encountered more malpais. "These piles look like so many irregular heaps of stone coal," he wrote. As they rounded the expanse of the malpais and proceeded into the San Jose Valley, Simpson tried to find the source of the flow. The Cañon del Gallo, Simpson wrote "is quite interesting, both as an object of vision and because of the blackened volcanic scoriaceous rocks which crop out from its bottom." The valley of the Ojo del Gallo near present-day San Rafael was "broad, beautiful and fertile . . . one of the richest I have seen." The party continued east, and at a point near present I-40 and NM 117, Simpson described a hill "where a few picks, crowbars and spades could, with no great labor, in a short time make it practicable for wagons."

Four years after Simpson passed through, the government began a survey for railroad routes along the thirty-fifth parallel. Its leader, Lt. Amiel Whipple, seriously considered the Bishop's Road as a railroad right-of-way, but ruled it out because it would require a tunnel. Whipple wrote of the malpais, "The whole length of the valley followed today has been threaded by a sinuous stream of lava. It appears as if it had rolled down a viscous semifluid mass, had been arrested in its course, hardened, blackened, cracked and in places broken, so as to allow the little brook to gush from below and gurgle along by its side." Whipple noted that a northern route, through Campbell's Pass and along the Rio Puerco, had gentler grades. Hardly used before 1850, the northern route by 1880 was dominant, as emphasis shifted from Indian country to a link between the cities of the East and West. The railroad would follow this route in 1881, as would Route 66 and Interstate 40.

In 1855, David Meriwether, plainsman and then governor of New Mexico Territory, traveled west over the same route Oñate had followed in 1598. Listening to the music of the Rio San Jose, he wrote, "This was the most tantalizing place that I ever visited. The water flowed under this bed of lava, and we could hear it gurgling beneath, and where there were cracks we could look down and see it, eight or ten feet below, but without a possibility of getting a mouthful." Meriwether's party followed the San Jose west to what he called Agua Azul, or Bluewater, and then crossed the Zuni Mountains. He decided to hunt ducks and stumbled over a human skeleton, its bones bleached white. Shocked, he returned to camp.

The last military survey was the most novel. In 1857 Lt. Edward F. Beale passed through with his famous United States Camel Brigade—seventy-seven camels herded by Turks, Greeks, and Armenians, in an experiment to test these ships of the desert in the Southwest. The spectacle drew thousands of curious Indian people to the Bishop's Road, where camels ambled down the San Jose valley and camped at Ojo del Gallo and El Morro. On his return trip, Beale wrote, "Crossed many streams of lava, which appear to have rolled in a fiery torrent just as a mountain stream from the hills." Beale returned in 1859 with government money, to build a wagon road west from Albuquerque over the northern route proposed by Whipple and others. One member of the party noted "quite large masses of lava, apparently having run down the valley . . . All the mountains here are bare and look as if they had been thrown up from beneath and scattered from above."

Fort Wingate and the Navajos

The following year the army authorized the first U.S. fort in the area, Fort Fauntleroy, thirty-five miles west of the malpais; but with Confederate soldiers threatening the Rio Grande Valley, the army abandoned it in September 1861. A quartermaster store at Cubero became the only military presence in western New Mexico, and it was soon seized by Confederate sympathizers. After two memorable battles, the army chased Confederates from the state and turned its attention again to the Navajos.

In October 1862 the army decided to build a new fort on the western edge of the malpais, at Ojo del Gallo ("spring of the rooster," named for abundant wild fowl in the area). The lush valley offered good pasture for horses, and the location was on the old road to Fort Defiance and the Spanish route to Zuni Pueblo. Fort Wingate was named for a Brevet Major Benjamin Wingate, who had fought in the Civil War battle of Valverde and died of his wounds earlier that year. The commander of the new fort was Lt. Col. Jose Francisco Chavez. Most of the officers and enlisted men were Hispanic. Using what was left of Fort Fauntleroy, 25 carpenters and masons and 225 soldiers hurriedly built a wooden stockade 4,340 feet long and 8 feet high, using a million feet of lumber from the Zuni Mountains. The buildings were adobe, 13 feet high and 2 feet thick. Another 8-foot adobe wall surrounded the officers' quarters. The commissary was one of the best in the territory. They also planted a row of sycamores around the borders for shade. When the work was done, soldiers celebrated with a party and invited all the women from Cubero and Cebolleta. In their spare time, soldiers experimented with crops and found that wheat, onions, and beans grew well there.

Navajo raiding continued, however. One territorial official complained to Washington that in one year the human toll of raids was 125 deaths, 32 injured, and 21 taken captive; livestock losses totaled 3,557 horses and mules, 13,473 cattle, and 294,740 sheep. The estimated cost was $1.4 million. In 1863, after a frustrating series of meetings with Navajo leaders, the military sent Col. Kit Carson and 750 soldiers on a summer campaign against the Navajos. They prepared for their foray at Fort Wingate.

(Above) Fort Wingate in 1885. (Photo by Christian Barthelmess, courtesy Museum of New Mexico, 86931.) (Left) Navajo scouts waiting to be paid at Fort Wingate in 1886. (Photo courtesy Museum of New Mexico, 28535.)

Carson's grim success is history, and Fort Wingate became a stopping place on the infamous Long Walk of 1864, in which 2,000 half-starved, ragged Navajos made a forced march from Fort Canby to Bosque Redondo for four years of confinement. Many died on the way. Fort Wingate continued as a center for Navajo surrender and processing—the renegade Chief Manuelito gave himself up here in 1866—and then became a stopping place for their return home, in 1868. In July of that year, the army moved the fort to its present site near Gallup, closer to the resettled Navajos.

One Navajo band living on the slopes of Mt. Taylor cooperated with the army against other Navajos, but still was forced on the Long Walk. When they returned many settled in their traditional homes, and the satellite Navajo settlement of Cañoncito began. Other Navajos returned to their homes near the Zuni Mountains, west of El Malpais, and founded the Ramah Navajo community.

San Rafael

No longer threatened, settlers moved in around the abandoned fort, making use of anything left behind, including
adobe bricks. They even adapted the army's acequia. A
mile away the village of San Rafael grew quickly; by 1870
its population of 678 surpassed Cubero's 581 people and
Cebolleta's 630. However, the new residents of San
Rafael and Acoma Indians both claimed lands in the area.
In 1876 liquor and trickery settled the dispute in favor
of the newcomers, and in 1885, 115 residents sent a

*San Rafael's roots
are in ranching.*

manifest to Washington, claiming the land around San
Rafael. (Acomas filed a claim with the Indian Land Claims
Commission in 1951 and later accepted a settlement of
four dollars an acre for 1.5 million acres of land. Since
then the pueblo has bought some of its lands back at
market price, but protested the creation of El Malpais
National Park and Conservation Area on their aboriginal
land.)

Sheep raising became the economic staple of the area.
Under the *partido* system, a small operator could graze
one hundred head of a big rancher's cattle or sheep and
return twenty calves or lambs a year as payment. At the
end of five years, they had to return the original
one hundred head. Many a rancher got his start this
way; the unlucky ones lost their homesteads and water
rights, which were pledged as security.

In this century a landowner removed the last of the
old fort's standing walls and leveled and plowed the field
for crops. The site today is discernible only to the trained
eye of an archeologist.

The Railroad

*No part of the Southwest is more interesting than the
great lava region lying south and southwest of Grants
. . . So rough and rugged is this immense waste of
"mal pais" that travel is possible by horse only by a
few marked trails. For the most part, those who have
penetrated the wilderness at all proceeded on foot and
then with the greatest caution. During storms, natives
have lost their way and their lives, while many have
worn out their shoes on the ragged edges of the lava*

and came out with sore and bleeding feet.
The country is so vast, so rough and rugged, so very
inaccessible that it . . . will remain wild for many years
to come.

Evon H. Vogt, 1924

As the army was trying to make the frontier safe for settlers, lawmakers concentrated on speeding up their arrival. In 1866 Congress chartered the Atlantic and Pacific Railroad to build from Springfield, Missouri, to Albuquerque, across the thirty-fifth parallel to the Colorado River and then to the Pacific. As an incentive the government gave the railroad alternating sections of land for twenty miles on either side of the track in states and forty miles in territories; more than fourteen million acres of land from Isleta to Needles. The railroad became the largest seller of land in New Mexico and Arizona territories, next to the Federal General Land Office.

In 1880 the Atchison Topeka & Santa Fe Railroad reached Albuquerque, and the two companies agreed to build west together. Construction began in July 1880, with four thousand workers and two thousand mules. Despite its wealth of land, competition and economic conditions ultimately drove the Atlantic and Pacific into bankruptcy. In 1894 the Santa Fe took over the A&P's western segment.

A source of water and a coal chute were enough to create a town, and new villages sprouted nearly as fast as tracks were laid. Many had more amenities than the average pioneer settlement, because the railroad could bring the world to their depots. In this area four railroad towns changed their names and three were named for brothers. McCarty's and Grants were both railroad construction camps, named for the contractors building the line. McCarty's was called Santa Maria de Acoma for a while. Grants Camp became known as Grant to the post office, Grants to the railroad, and Grantes to Hispanic residents, before the name officially changed in 1935 to Grants. Eighteen miles west was a section house and depot known as Baca. It was renamed (probably in the 1920s) for the traders Harold and Robert Prewitt. Harold became a wealthy rancher after he and lumberman George Breece started a sheep operation. Thoreau bloomed as the planned community of Mitchell in 1890, when Austin and William Mitchell chose the site as shipping point for their timber enterprise. The Mitchells didn't last long, but their town survived as Thoreau. Locals have argued about whether it was named for the famous philosopher, a logging company bookkeeper, an army paymaster, or a railroad official.

Of all the railroad boomtowns to grace the tracks, however, Coolidge was the most colorful and most named. It came to life in 1870 as Bacon Springs, home of Uncle Billy Crane, who had been a scout for Kit Carson. The government Star Route from Ft. Union to Prescott, Arizona, passed through here. Later the Santa Fe Trail followed this route. Crane ran a stage stop on the Santa Fe–Prescott line, cut timber for the Zuni Indian agent, sold hay and cattle to the army, and established an officers' club. This took no small amount of courage. In 1870 Lorenzo Sanchez Sr. was driving a mule team in the area and came upon another caravan, its three drivers riddled with arrows and the wagons plundered and burned. Teamsters typically grouped for protection and traveled with as many as twenty-five to thirty wagons together.

In 1880 Bacon Springs, 136 miles from Albuquerque, became the first division point for A&P construction crews. The village then became known as Crane's Station. The railroad regarded Uncle Billy so highly that it gave him a section of land and a lifetime rail pass. In 1882 the A&P renamed the place Coolidge, after T. Jefferson Coolidge, one of its directors.

Lumbering flourished there for a time. Two Canadian brothers, James and Gregory Page, started a mill and lumberyard at the settlement in 1881, and Henry Hart had mills there in 1889. The railroad's tourist business apparently started in 1882, when one entrepreneur began selling petrified wood at the Coolidge Harvey House. The place was also a popular shipping point and trade center for area cattlemen, and soldiers from Fort Wingate frequented Coolidge's saloons. By 1888 Coolidge had a livery stable, butcher shop, two general stores, a tailor shop, a rooming house, an eatery, and the best-stocked bar in western New Mexico. At its peak it had fourteen saloons. For a time Coolidge was the only town of one hundred between Albuquerque and Winslow, and its real estate was worth five times that of Gallup, about thirty miles farther down the track.

The place, a rendezvous for desperadoes, had its share of gunfights and one hanging. In 1882 the justice of the peace complained that there was none. He sent a telegraph to Fort Wingate, saying "Civil law is unable to cope with the gamblers here." It seems that thirsty rascals stole a wagonload of beer from the A&P, and the railroad threatened to recall its construction gang and level the entire town unless the beer was recovered.

In 1890 the railroad moved its division headquarters to Gallup, and a week later, all but two buildings burned. The post office renamed the waning settlement Cranes, but the railroad changed it in 1898 to Dewey. Two years later it became Guam. By then, it was little more than a depot. Guam became Coolidge again in 1926, this time when a trader wanted to honor the President.

Booms and Busts

Jesus Blea, a veteran of the Civil War Battle of Valverde, moved his family to the area in 1872 and acquired a ranch four miles north of San Rafael, just as the railroad cut through the malpais in January 1881. Blea called the place Los Alamitos, for the little cottonwoods at a spring bubbling from the malpais. In their shade he built his home, near a remnant of the adobe house of Jose Antonio Chavez, who had lived there in 1862. Los Alamitos, located halfway between Albuquerque and Gallup, with accessible timber and water, soon became a construction camp for the Canadian brothers Angus, John, and Lewis Grant, who contracted to build track from Isleta to Needles, California. Grant's Camp became a coaling station for the railroad, with a depot, section house, and coal chute; soon it had a telegraph station and a post office, with Blea as postmaster.

The year after the Grant brothers built their line through the area, Blea sold land to Simon Bibo for the first store, Bernalillo Mercantile Co. The brothers Simon, Nathan, and Solomon Bibo were economic pioneers, members of a wave of German Jewish immigrants who arrived in New Mexico in the last century. Simon came to New Mexico as a freighter in 1866, started a trading post at Cebolleta in 1869, and hauled corn for the military to Fort Apache, Arizona. Nathan, meanwhile, became a sutler at Fort Wingate. The brothers, from the 1880s until the 1920s, operated stores or trading posts at Cubero, San Rafael, Laguna, Moquino, and Bibo. Solomon opened the first trading post at Acoma Pueblo in 1882, married Juana del Valle, the daughter of a former Acoma gover-

Section house at Grants Station, 1881. Grants started as a railroad construction camp and then became a coaling station. (Photo by Ben Wittick, courtesy Museum of New Mexico, 15792.)

27

nor, and in 1885 became Acoma's first and only non-
Indian governor.

Not far behind the Jewish traders were Lebanese
merchants. Both groups fled religious persecution in
their homelands and in New Mexico found opportunity
where others saw a wasteland. They quickly learned to
speak Spanish and Indian languages and didn't share the
Anglo prejudices of their day. The Lebanese entered the
area as wagon traders. In 1888 Elias Francis started a
store in Cebolleta, expanded into farming and ranching,
and sent for his nephews Abdoo Fidel and Joseph
Hanosh. Merhage Michael, another wagon trader, also
opened a store. The names and family businesses live
on in the area.

Rail transportation meant access to bigger markets,
which spurred farming, ranching, and logging. At the
same time, ranchers and loggers could expand by buying land from the struggling A&P, which shed property
from 1883 to 1889 for from fifty to seventy-five cents an
acre. From San Rafael to El Morro and Acoma, sheep
raising flourished from 1880 to 1925, and sheep camps
could be seen all around the malpais. Cattle ranchers
also enjoyed good markets. New agricultural communities grew. Mormons founded settlements in El Morro
valley in 1876 and at Bluewater in 1889. Other homesteaders settled in the Zuni Mountains, which became a
prime farming area.

The railroad's need for crossties kicked off timbering
in the Zuni Mountains. Large-scale logging employed
hundreds in the area from 1890 until the 1940s. Companies had their own railroads into the mountains, and
dozens of rowdy logging camps sprouted. Early in the
century, Grants and Thoreau, thirty miles to the west,
were lively scenes of railroad workers, cowboys, sheep
ranchers, miners, and loggers. In the many watering
holes, fights, stabbings, and shootings were the order of
the day.

A second store, the Bond-Sargent Co. (later the Bond-
Gunderson Store), opened in Grants in 1915. The two
stores sold everything—Starr cars, International trucks,
hay, beans, wagons, wagon parts, Stetsons, ladies'
shoes, and Rawlins hosiery. Bond-Sargent even had caskets and would supply the hearse and driver, if needed.

In 1916 the Stock Raising Homestead Act, which
allowed a person to file on a section (640 acres) for a
thirty-four-dollar filing fee, started a new wave of settlement in the area. Homesteaders soon learned the land
wouldn't provide a living, but they could work as loggers, miners, or cowboys. (Mining started in 1916, with
a small copper mine at Diener, in the Zuni Mountains,
and lasted until the early 1930s.) Most homesteaders
starved out, and their abandoned cabins on the east side
of the malpais are testimony to hard times.

The killer Spanish influenza epidemic of 1917 and 1918 took its toll here, as it did around the country. For months "not a day went past that the church bell did not toll to announce the death of someone," Josephine Barela wrote. Sickness wiped out entire families, but the mining camps were especially hard hit. Nearly half of the 120 miners in one camp, mostly young, single immigrants, were buried in mass graves. In Grants caskets stacked up in front of the funeral parlor.

Grants by 1928 had two hotels—the Yucca Hotel and Mother Lucy Jane Whiteside's boarding house—and was home to six hundred people. The lumber boom pushed the slumbering village into the twentieth century. The Breece Co.'s railroad roundhouse and homes for workers, called Breecetown, ballooned the town's population to four thousand. In 1929 Grants got its first electric and water utilities, high school, and telephone exchange. Anybody without a place to sleep found a warm place around the town's planer mill, which burned sawdust 24 hours a day.

Bootleggers flourished, and the quality of the local hooch was said to be good. Even years later one rancher was finding stills near El Morro. After prohibition ended, bars proliferated until there were twenty-two, most with gambling. "The only honest feature connected with the operation," said longtime resident Marvel Prestridge, "was the accuracy of the large deposit made each day to the bank." Strong whiskey and marked cards all helped part the patrons from their money. The bar fights were legendary, but nobody could whip Copio Baca, the big deputy at San Rafael, and the dances he patroled were always orderly.

In the 1930s the Depression squeezed Grants, just as loggers were running out of trees and demand. "We used to sell hides whenever we could," recalled Max McBride, who homesteaded just east of town in the 1930s. "We had chickens and cows. Sold eggs and milk and made a little money that way and sold wood to the schools. There was no work to be had in town."

World War II created a demand for fluorspar, used to harden steel, and in 1940 three mines opened in the Zuni Mountains, employing 150 people. After ten years of shipping the greenish, glassy crystal in gondola cars, the mines closed in 1952, because of foreign competition. The mining camps were mostly Hispanic, said Dovie Bright, whose first husband managed a fluorspar mine. "Everybody got along. There were never any arguments or ill feelings in the mine camp." To lure teachers to the camps, the company would match the government's pay and build them a house.

The war also cut off pumice imports from Italy, and in 1938 the Barnsdall Tripoli Co. opened a pumice mine north of Grants. Now operated by U.S. Gypsum, it's the area's only surviving mine.

As the area economy headed downhill, two farmers at Bluewater found the area a fine place to grow vegetables. By the 1940s fields from Grants to Bluewater were green with feathery carrot tops. Most of the fieldhands were Navajos in traditional dress. Filipinos were the packers. Grants bragged of being carrot capital of the nation, with two thousand boxcars rolling out of the town in a season and a crop valued at $2.5 million. The produce kept four packing sheds and two wooden-crate manufacturers busy. With a population boom of 270 percent in the 1940s, Grants was the state's fastest-growing town. For two decades Grants carrots were the best on the market. By the late 1950s, however, Bluewater growers couldn't compete with California, and the cellophane bag eliminated the need for fine, leafy carrots. At the same time, the last of the timber operations was shutting down. Grants was heading toward another bust.

Route 66

If the railroad brought commerce to western New Mexico porches, the automobile would bring the world. The legacy of Route 66 in this area is still fresh in local memories.

By the 1890s, elected officials were aware of the need for better roads in the territory and even passed a law requiring men to work two days a year on the public highways. By 1915, merchants were pushing for good roads.

That year trader Nathan Bibo wrote the *Carbon City News* that if the state and county road boards didn't treat the people of western New Mexico as they should, the businessmen should organize and raise money because the improved road would draw traffic through the area. At that time, the worst road was at Horace Station, six miles east of Grants, "where the malpais is very bad." He figured $100 could fix it up and another $100 would provide a bridge at the same spot.

New Mexico had 4,250 cars and 92 dealers in 1915. McKinley County had 62 cars. Travel time from Gallup to Albuquerque took thirteen hours over a 174-mile road scarred by sand traps, arroyos, and ruts that mostly followed the railroad tracks.

In August 1915, when World War I was a year old, the *Gallup Independent* reported progress on a new road that would become a portion of a transcontinental highway system called the National Old Trails Highway.

By 1916 even roads in the Zuni Mountains had improved. The *Carbon City News* reported, "Automobiles and Fords are able to go somewhere but not get back." In May "autoists" reported they had made the trip from Gallup to Albuquerque in 12 hours, but there were a lot of side roads and no signs. In June, another party made the trip in a Hudson in a speedy nine hours.

Businessmen of the Southwest took a step beyond the Old Trails Highway in 1927 by forming the U.S. 66 Highway Association. Their goal was pushing for an "unbroken concrete slab from the Great Lakes to the Pacific" by 1928. Backers said that for military reasons alone, the road should be paved.

In those days, recalled Wally Gunn, it took days to get from Grants to Laguna. The first car at Laguna was a Buick, won when everyone in the community subscribed to the *Saturday Evening Post.*

The state made progress on Route 66 but, by 1929, New Mexico had just 105 miles of concrete highway out of 5,400 miles of roads. Five magnetic nail pickers removed 131,194 pounds of debris ranging from carpet tacks to horseshoes. The *Cleveland Press* gleefully reported that New Mexico had an official nail picker, which it hailed tongue in cheek as a creative way to employ political hacks.

Scene from U.S. 66 in Grants, 1956. (Photo courtesy Museum of New Mexico, 56395.)

In June 1934 impatient residents of Route 66 towns converged on Santa Fe to demand that the state highway commission complete early the "Main Street of America" in New Mexico. From Gallup, a special train of boosters traveled to the capital wearing badges demanding "Finish 66."

Clyde Tingley, elected as governor on a good-roads platform, harnessed Depression relief programs to provide jobs and improve the state's roads. By 1937, Route 66 was paved and straightened (removing Santa Fe from the route) through the state.

The road's now celebrated motel courts, diners, and

Burma Shave signs popped up from Cubero to Gallup. One favorite was Wallace and Mary Gunn's Villa de Cubero, the first motel built west of Albuquerque and a retreat of movie stars. Lucille Ball stayed here during her divorce from Desi Arnaz; J. Robert Oppenheimer and his associates came here to relax from the pressures of early Los Alamos; and Ernest Hemingway stayed here while writing *The Old Man and The Sea.*

But 1956 was the beginning of the end; Congress enacted legislation mandating an interstate highway system, which wasn't completed until the 1980s. In 1985, Route 66 signs were removed after the road was decommissioned. Pieces of the old road still exist in Santa Fe Avenue in Grants, Railroad Avenue in Gallup, and portions from Laguna Pueblo west.

Uranium Days

> *we live and die to mine*
> *to eat as we are eaten*
>
> *in the mine there is the music*
> *of the train*
> *and the whistle of a miner*
> *as he walks down the track*
>
> *deep in the stope there is a song*
> *whose verses are buried in the muck*
> *and the slusher keeps humming*
> *while the skips knock on the guiderails*
> *as they go up and down the shaft*
>
> *it's just a shallow mine*
> *this open grave*
> *wherein will rest a miner*
> *until nothing is left but bone*
> *white as the day moon*
> —Robert Gallegos, Grants
> uranium miner

In a broad valley eighteen miles northwest of Grants, four thousand prospectors milled nervously. Minutes away was each man's chance to strike it rich. At 10:00 A.M. on September 17, 1956, they surged forward, swarming over the brown hills. It was a scene reminiscent of land rush days, but this was a uranium rush. The Atomic Energy Commission had opened an 11,875-acre tract here. At the appointed hour, each prospector had to locate a claim, drive a stake at the site, and then file in the county courthouse. In two days 1,500 claims were filed, followed by years of lawsuits.

The "most spectacular operator," according to one account, was Richard Bokum, then thirty-eight. He was

one of four Princeton graduates who called themselves
the Green Hornets. They prospected near Ambrosia
Lake and then raised $100,000 to buy leases. Bokum
held grazing rights in the area and had already drilled. On
the day of the uranium rush, his two hundred men, hired
from Albuquerque and Santa Fe, already knew where to
drive stakes and plant flags. A Bokum plane circled overhead, and at the sight of each flag, the pilot relayed
word to the courthouse in Gallup, where Bokum's partner began filing claims. In the first 13 ½ minutes, Bokum
and his partner filed 117 claims. This scramble culminat-
ed six years of frantic searching for a formerly worthless
ore.

In 1950 Paddy Martinez, a Navajo, discovered uranium on Haystack Mountain. The usual version of the
story is that a simple Navajo sheepherder made the legendary find, but that does Martinez and his discovery an
injustice. As a boy Martinez was a sheepherder and
probably learned his first English playing with homesteaders' children in the Zuni Mountains. He worked for
the pioneer Román Baca at San Mateo and then bad-
gered a section foreman on the Zuni Mountain Railroad
into hiring him. For fifty cents a day, he carried water for
the Navajos building railroad tracks. Dressed in flour
sacks, Paddy "just ran with that bucket all day long,"
recalled one old timer. Impressed at how hard the boy
worked, the foreman bought Paddy his first workshirt
and blue jeans.

At twenty-one, while working for an Indian agent,
Martinez won a gun battle with a murderer he was sent
to bring in. He was also a cowboy remembered as "a
pretty good bronc rider." And he ran a store, was a section foreman on the Breece railroad, and worked in the
carrot fields. With his large family, he lived in a hogan
with a view of Mt. Taylor. His son Leo Martinez recalled
that his father had overheard two men in Grants talking
about uranium. Always curious, he talked to them about
the rocks they had. Riding his horse one day to get bak-
ing powder for his wife, he spotted similar rocks near
the road on land belonging to the Santa Fe Railroad.
Martinez told his skeptical wife, "I found some uranium.
We're going to have lots of money."

Martinez rode to Bluewater Village, caught the bus
and took the rocks to merchant Carrol Gunderson. Gunderson sent the sample to the Santa Fe Railroad, which
wasted no time sending out a surveying party. What
they found was a remnant of the area's volcanic up-
heavals. From cooling molten rock, gaseous and liquid
solutions of uranium had escaped into surrounding rocks
to form deposits. Other deposits were formed by surface waters 150 million years ago and remained in the
Morrison formation. The railroad retained Martinez as a
mining scout and paid him $250 a month until his death.

Overnight, it seemed, prospectors swarmed from Thoreau to Cubero, on foot, horseback, and Jeep with Geiger counters and witching rods, and from the air with scintillators. They were "cowboys, Indians, geologists, women, children, desperadoes, claim-jumpers, businessmen," wrote Gary Tietjen, "a continual stream of humanity flowing in on every road and trail." The *Grants Beacon* predicted, "Uranium Ore Is Here To Stay."

The focus of all this activity was Ambrosia Lake. Visitors have always chuckled at the name given the broad, brown valley spiked with uranium headframes. One imaginative tale has it that a settler named Ambrosio was found in a *playa* with an arrow in his back. The truth, as usual, is less interesting. Don Ambrosio Trujillo, of San Mateo, homesteaded here in 1867 and built himself a laguna by building a dike at one end of a clay bed. Trujillo's oasis lasted until the dust-bowl years, according to long-time resident Abe Peña.

One of the best-known uranium prospectors was Stella Dysart, whom the uranium industry would call the "First Lady of Ambrosia Lake." Stella was a self-made businesswoman from Los Angeles, who rose from dressmaker to oil speculator to uranium tycoon. Beginning in 1923 she educated herself in every aspect of the oil business and got a real estate license. An attorney who became her mentor had bought 5,000 acres at Ambrosia Lake from J. F. Branson, the same promoter who was hawking oil land near Thoreau. Soon the two owned oil rights on 150,000 acres, which they were selling in 10-acre blocks. After the attorney died in 1925, she divided and subdivided, selling plots as small as $\frac{1}{16}$ acre for eighteen to twenty dollars each during the Depression. Ultimately four thousand people, mostly Californians, bought her properties.

Stella had a smooth tongue, but she apparently believed the land held oil. Bringing equipment over a dirt track into Ambrosia Lake, she had three wildcat wells drilled—all dry holes. Stella could be seen, dressed in riding pants and high laced boots, driving into Grants to get her equipment repaired. Because the trail regularly became a mire in rainstorms, she spent more than one night marooned in her car but she said that's when she did her best thinking.

The weather was the least of her troubles, however. Her workers strayed regularly into the twenty-two bars of Grants or the whorehouses of Gallup (Grants residents insist their town never had a house of ill repute), and Stella herself had to fill in as tool dresser (drilling assistant). She also cooked for her workers.

By the 1940s Stella was broke, and because of a brush with the Securities and Exchange Commission, the government had restricted her land sales. When

Paddy Martinez found uranium, she figured her land would have uranium too. Getting her car stuck once again in a mudhole proved to be the first good fortune she'd had. Louis Lothman, a Houston geologist, pulled her car out and acquired drilling rights on her property. Drilling on weekends with borrowed equipment, in 1955 he found uranium 292 feet underground. The next year Rio de Oro Uranium Mines Inc., which developed her mine, was the first to bring uranium ore to the surface.

The Atomic Energy Commission announced that the area held 72 percent of the nation's uranium reserves. Carrot farmers sold their water rights to uranium companies, and the boom was on. The rush birthed the village of Milan in 1957. As Tietjen wrote, "every legitimate landowner in Ambrosia faced a long struggle with shysters of every description, determined to get some part of the gravy." The worst and most brazen of the vermin were claim jumpers. One night a rancher caught a claim jumper trying to drive his drilling rig through locked gates. They were also intercepted driving earth movers and trailers onto other people's claims.

Uranium mine trainees, Kerr-McGee, 1976.

A few ranchers organized the Rancher's Exploration & Development Co. to develop uranium on their lands. The company's first president was a young man named Maxie Anderson, later an internationally famous balloonist. Known to be fast with his fists, Anderson was said to start board meetings with the request, "Gentlemen, check your guns in the outer office." To fend off claim jumpers, the company hired Gus Raney, a local legend whose intense blue eyes over a black beard had a wild enough look to scatter interlopers even without the firepower he always carried. Guns and fistfights maintained some order, and when Gus caught a claim jumper, he was known to tie him to a tree for a few days to contemplate his ways and then turn him loose, minus boots. Lawmen, helpless to do anything because the law hadn't caught up with the times, looked the other way.

From 1959 to 1965, uranium created thirty-two hundred jobs, but miners' wives moving to the town cried. Grants didn't look like much—a town four miles long and a block wide that earned a mention in *Ripley's Believe It Or Not.* It lacked amenities like pavement or sidewalks, and outhouses faced the main drag. In time housing developments mushroomed, service clubs organized, and Grants grew more genteel. In the 1960s the government began to phase out its uranium purchases, and by the end of the decade they stopped. The town weathered another bust, until the Arab oil embargo in 1973 sparked another boom.

> *for twenty-five years*
> *you've sweated*
> *working for*
> *this mining company*
> *but now*
> *the price*
> *of ore*
> *has trickled*
> *from your forehead*
> *to the corner*
> *of your eye*
>
> *yesterday you could*
> *hold your own*
> *with the best*
> *and somewhere*
> *out there*
> *someone will remember*
> *how they needed*
> *arms like yours*
> *and a back like yours*
> *and a heart like yours*
> —Robert Gallegos

By 1979 seven thousand miners blasted and scooped ore around the clock from forty-five uranium mines, to feed five mills. The carrot capital had become the uranium capital. Then inflation, overseas competition, and political fallout from the Three Mile Island nuclear power plant incident combined to strangle the industry. Layoff after layoff followed, until every mine closed. Some still believe uranium will come back, but city officials have pursued other kinds of development. With the increasing number of visitors drawn to El Malpais, Grants is thinking of itself as a tourist town, with as much to offer as the better known meccas of Taos or Ruidoso.

the mine talks
she whispers
through the faults
those secrets
that a miner
wants to hear

she says

every old miner knows
that when he's gone
his spirit is made
to return
to an abandoned stope
where it continues mining
with only pick and shovel
until it has scratched
its way to the surface

it's the curse
of those who cheated death
when they were young
                                    Robert Gallegos

Hiking El Malpais

The author-adventurer Charles Lummis wrote of the malpais in the last century, "No one inexperienced can conceive of the cruel roughness of these flows. The strongest shoes are absolutely cut to pieces in a short walk; and then woe to the walker if he have not arrived at more merciful ground." Lummis told the story of how Charlie Ross and his band of horse thieves rode wildeyed into the malpais, figuring to lose the law hot on their heels. The rustlers missed the trail, but tried to cross a narrow part of the flow. "It was a cruel and indescribable passage. They got across and escaped—for the pursuers were not so foolhardy as to enter the lava—but on foot. Their horses, including a $400 thoroughbred, were no longer able to stand." The horses wore their hooves off on the jagged rock, so the thieves fled on foot, leaving a trail of blood from their own torn feet. Lawmen never caught Ross and his bunch, but they put the horses out of their misery.

"El Malpais will never be a high-use recreation area," concluded veteran travel writer Ruth Armstrong. "It is too brutal for that. . . ." The good news is that El Malpais is so wild and so rugged, it's rarely crowded. And the costs of trail building will confine development to small portions of the area, over time. The two federal agencies estimate it will take fifteen years to carry out all their plans. The bad news is that delicate or inexperienced hikers should stick to the trails developed so far. El Malpais is no place for the novice, and even experienced hikers can't afford to be cavalier. This isn't like any other place you've hiked. Caution and preparation will reward you with a rich experience. Carelessness will turn it into your worst outdoor nightmare.

Before You Venture into El Malpais, Read and Understand:

1. Wear sturdy shoes or boots with good ankle support, to protect your feet from jagged rock. This is no place for sneakers. You may also appreciate leather gloves, in case you lose your footing and need to catch yourself in a fall.

2. Because of loose lava rock, cracks, and crevices, footing here can be tricky. Here you need to keep your eyes on your feet. If you want to look around, stop.

3. This is an easy place to get lost. Don't just strike out across the malpais, and don't stray from the trail. Even on a marked trail, keep the trail markers in sight.

4. The McCartys Crater area was used as a bombing range during World War II, so hiking here is discouraged. It's still possible to find fuses and live bombs. If you find anything unusual, contact the Park Service or BLM.

5. Take plenty of water. There is no water in the malpais. A half gallon per person is not too much.

6. Wear a hat and use sunscreen.

7. There is cactus everywhere. You will probably be glad if you take tweezers along.

8. On many malpais trails, it's foolish and cruel to take a dog. On trails with small amounts of lava rock, Rover will probably be okay on a leash. But be sure you take enough water for the dog, and if Rover or Muffie has a pink nose, apply sunscreen often. Also watch out for cactus spines or thorns. And don't expect your dog to instinctively avoid collapses or cracks—watch out for them.

9. County road 42 and roads into the malpais are slicker than greased slime when wet. They also form big pools that lie in wait for unsuspecting motorists. Avoid driving them during wet weather. If a big rain starts while you're hiking, hustle back to your car.

10. Portions of the malpais are sacred to neighboring Indian people. If you encounter a group holding a ceremonial, show your respect by leaving quickly. Don't try to observe from a distance. If you come across a ceremonial site, show respect by not touching it.

11. Because Indian people have used the malpais for centuries, the place also draws pot hunters—thieves who illegally remove artifacts from the area. The pots and other items belong to Acoma and Zuni ancestors, but their plunder robs us all of our cultural heritage and hampers archeological research forever. If you surprise pot hunters, report them immediately to the State Police, the BLM, or the Park Service. Get a vehicle description and license number, if you can.

12. Scientists are still studying such things as bighorn sheep remains, ice in caves, and tree-ring samples. Please leave animal bones in place. If you find bighorn remains, report them to the agencies.

13. Allow ample time. Because there is no path to follow in some of these areas, and trail markers are hard to see even in daylight, finding your way out at night would be impossible.

14. New Mexico leads the nation for deaths and injuries caused by lightning. If you hear thunder, leave before the storm gets to your area. Severe thunderstorms can travel at speeds up to seventy miles an hour.

15. Malpais is a new recreation area. Both agencies will change existing routes and trails and develop new ones, so check directions before you hike. Also, western New Mexico has few developed trails, so the hikes in this book follow land features, logging roads, old railroad beds and even cattle trails. Always carry a topo map and use it and your common sense.

16. To pilots, cautions fellow flier Steve Havill, "Flying the malpais may be a little like flying the ocean—there's much to be gained and not a lot of room for error or inattention." Sharing the air space, he adds, are golden and bald eagles, who may be soaring at one thousand feet or more, while the smallest raptors hug the ground. Ravens, the "acrobats of the air . . . will use all the airspace, from consorting with eagles (and airplanes) to buzzing Winnebagos."

Access

You can reach El Malpais from I-40 via either NM 117 on the east or State Road 53 on the west; county road 42 is to the south and west. The trails in the following two sections are presented in the order you will encounter them, when driving south on the two highways from I-40. Here is what you will see:

Driving south on NM 117, you can see the upper McCarty's lava flow to the right—the newest, at about one thousand years old. The scenery changes dramatically to sheer sandstone cliffs. At 9 miles south of I-40 is the BLM ranger station. About one mile south of the ranger station is the Sandstone Bluffs Overlook, which offers a sweeping view of El Malpais and other area features. On the right, about 5 miles farther on is the eastern trailhead to the Zuni-Acoma Trail, once used by the tribes of that name and one of the region's oldest trails. Two miles south of that is the state's second-largest natural arch, La Ventana ("the window"), and in another

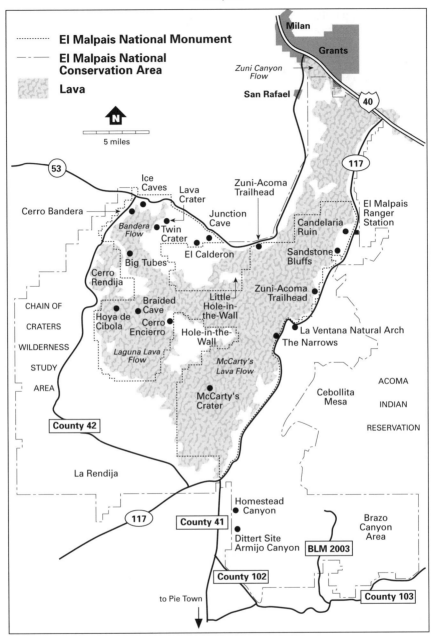

El Malpais National Monument
El Malpais National Conservation Area
Lava

N
5 miles

Milan
Grants
Zuni Canyon Flow
San Rafael
40

53
117

Ice Caves
Lava Crater
Zuni-Acoma Trailhead
Cerro Bandera
Junction Cave
Candelaria Ruin
El Malpais Ranger Station
Bandera Flow
Twin Crater
El Calderon
Sandstone Bluffs
Big Tubes
Cerro Rendija
Braided Cave
Little Hole-in-the-Wall
Zuni-Acoma Trailhead
CHAIN OF
Hoya de Cibola
Cerro Encierro
Hole-in-the-Wall
La Ventana Natural Arch
CRATERS
The Narrows
WILDERNESS
Laguna Lava Flow
STUDY
McCarty's Lava Flow
ACOMA
AREA
Cebollita Mesa
INDIAN
McCarty's Crater
County 42
RESERVATION
La Rendija
Homestead Canyon
Brazo Canyon Area
117
County 41
Dittert Site
Armijo Canyon
BLM 2003
County 102
County 103
to Pie Town

2 miles, The Narrows, where the lava flowed nearly to the foot of sandstone cliffs. The country ranges from grasslands and parklike valleys to rimrock to forest.

NM 53 is another world, with El Malpais on one side and the Zuni Mountains on the other. The road winds south and then west, through stands of tall ponderosa pines and junipers. About 3 miles south of I-40 is the old village of San Rafael, which is worth a detour. Other features are the Zuni-Acoma Trail, 14 miles from I-40; El Calderon area, a

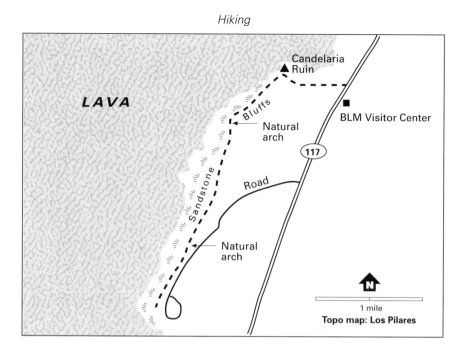

LAVA

Candelaria
▲ Ruin

Bluffs

Natural
arch

■ BLM Visitor Center

117

Sandstone

Road

Natural
arch

N

1 mile

Topo map: Los Pilares

volcano and other features, 18 miles south; and Bandera
Crater and Candelaria Ice Caves, 23 miles south.

County road 42, 26 miles down NM 53, leads to the
Big Tubes area, Hoya de Cibola, and Cerro Rendija, all
about 6 miles in. From NM 117, take county road 42 to
Hole-in-the-Wall, the biggest kipuka (island) in the lava.
And from either direction, the county road takes you to
the Chain of Craters.

Trails from NM 117

Sandstone Bluffs
*Getting there: From I-40, drive 10 miles south on NM
117. A short drive west from the sign takes you to an
overlook where you have one of the best views of area
sights.*

The Sandstone Bluffs are part of the sandstone and
rimrock country of Cebollita Mesa that border El Malpais
on the east. Here, wind and water shaped 500-foot sheer
cliffs, pillars, amphitheaters, columns and arches. Garden
of the Gods in Colorado has nothing on this place.

Before you stretches the black remains of the rivers
of fire. Dominating the horizon to the north-northeast is
Mt. Taylor, an old volcano whose eruptions ended about
2.5 million years ago. Straight across the malpais are the
Zuni Mountains, where the tallest peak is Mt. Sedgwick
at 9,256 feet. The most dominant Zuni mountain nearby
is Gallo ("rooster") Peak, at 8,664 feet. You can also see
volcanoes, including Cerro Bandera, Cerro Rendija, Cerro
Negro, Cerro Lobo, and Cerro Montoso to the west and
southwest. To the south and across the highway are

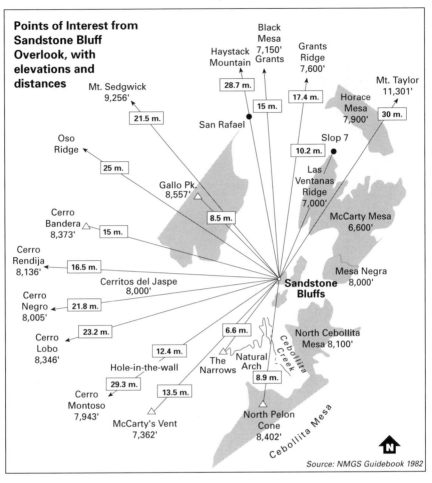

Points of Interest from Sandstone Bluff Overlook, with elevations and distances

Mt. Sedgwick 9,256'
21.5 m.

Oso Ridge
25 m.

Gallo Pk. 8,557'

Cerro Bandera 8,373'
15 m.

Cerro Rendija 8,136'
16.5 m.

Cerritos del Jaspe 8,000'

Cerro Negro 8,005'
21.8 m.

Cerro Lobo 8,346'
23.2 m.

12.4 m.

Hole-in-the-wall
29.3 m.

Cerro Montoso 7,943'

McCarty's Vent 7,362'
13.5 m.

Black Mesa 7,150' Grants

Haystack Mountain
28.7 m.

Grants Ridge 7,600'

San Rafael
15 m.

17.4 m.

Horace Mesa 7,900'

Mt. Taylor 11,301'
30 m.

Slop 7
10.2 m.

Las Ventanas Ridge 7,000'

McCarty Mesa 6,600'

8.5 m.

Mesa Negra 8,000'

Sandstone Bluffs

6.6 m.

North Cebollita Mesa 8,100'

Cebollita Creek

The Narrows Natural Arch
8.9 m.

North Pelon Cone 8,402'

Cebollita Mesa

Source: NMGS Guidebook 1982

One of three natural arches at Sandstone Bluffs.

cliffs of alternating sandstone and shale that front a slope tapering toward Cebollita Mesa on the east. The mesa, sandstone capped by lava, probably from Mt. Taylor, holds some 80 to 100 playas (lakes) ranging in size from a quarter of a mile long to a few hundred feet. Far to the south are the Sawtooth Mountains near Socorro.

People tend to think of Sandstone Bluffs as simply an overlook, but it's one of the more spectacular, if unheralded, places to hike. You have two choices. Hike north along the top of the bluffs and watch for three arches. Or climb down below for a walk along the malpais. (This isn't hard. We got my 70-year-old father down here.) Either way, the sandstone formations are stunning.

Distance: 1–2 miles.
Time: 1 hour to half-day.
Difficulty: Easy except for scramble up and down.
Topo Map: Los Pilares.

La Ventana, the state's second biggest natural arch.

Candelaria Ruin (See Malpais Archeology, p. 82)

La Ventana

Getting there: From I-40, take NM 117 17 miles south. A parking lot is off the road.

A short walk will take you to the arch that the Spanish called La Ventana ("the window") and La Puente ("the bridge"). People thought for years that this was the biggest natural arch in New Mexico, until a bigger arch came to light in the Farmington area. This is still the most accessible, and its dimensions—25 feet thick, 125 feet high, 165 feet across the base—give it a place among the world's great arches.

Unseen hands sculpted this sandstone work. Like similar arches in Utah, wind and water erosion wore at the soft Zuni Sandstone, which was a sand dune millions of years ago. Unlike the Utah formations, small springs started the process, as slow-moving water caused the soft rock to break or peel off in layers, a process called exfoliation. At the same time, alternate thawing and freezing worked at vertical cracks, bringing down bigger slabs. The process will continue through time, until the arch falls.

Narrows Rim Hike

Getting there: Take NM 117 19 miles south, or two miles past La Ventana arch. At the south end of The Narrows, a gravel road angles off. Park here.

Anglos call this place The Narrows, and Spaniards called it La Angostura ("the narrow place"). Here waves of black lava, tinted green by lichens, reach nearly to

the base of the five-hundred-foot escarpment. The hike begins with a short but steep scramble up to the top of the sandstone rim. You are now in Cebolla Wilderness, a 62,100-acre area. There is no trail, but it's an easy hike to simply follow the rim north for continuous and spectacular views of El Malpais, Mt. Taylor, and finally La Ventana. But don't be so taken with the views that you forget to mind the edge! Walk far enough, and you can see how the lava flowed around the sandhills and up against the prow of the Narrows. Behind lies the snow-capped pyramid of Mount Taylor and Gallo Peak, to the west.

The Narrows, where lava ebbed nearly to the base of cliffs.

Distance: 3 miles.
Time: 3–4 hours.
Difficulty: The climb up and back down are somewhat challenging; the walk along the top isn't difficult.
Topo Map: North Pasture.

McCartys Crater

Getting there: Take NM 117 about 25 miles south from I-40.

At a point where the lava nearly touches the road, you can see the small crater that coughed up the massive flow that reaches all the way to the interstate and beyond, to the village of McCartys. Eventually there may be a short spur road and parking area here, at the best viewpoint of McCartys Crater. This is a place to enjoy the view and not hike. In 1943 the government removed nine square miles of El Malpais for a bombing range, and McCartys Crater became its bull's-eye for

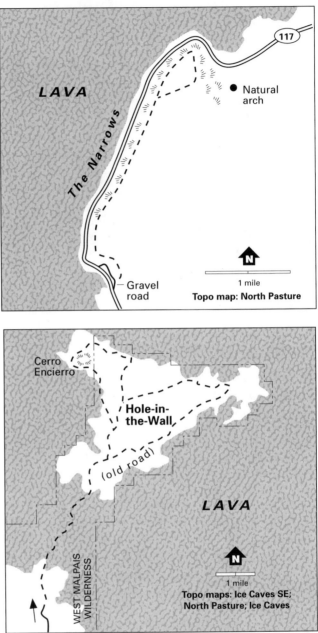

ten months. The military closed the range in 1944, because it's almost impossible to walk here, much less maintain a target. Steve Havill, pilot, teacher, and malpais expert, has written that from the air, McCarty's Crater "clearly shows the scars of World War II bombing practice. The craters look like they were blown out of the malpais yesterday."

The army tried to find unexploded bombs and in 1953 salvaged eighty tons of scrap metal, declaring the

area "safe and free of dangerous and/or explosive material." But in 1986 area rancher Sleet Raney found two
unexploded bombs in trees near the crater. An ordnance group detonated the bombs and warned that
other live bombs were probably still in the area. Other
ranchers have found bombs five and six miles away. As
recently as June 1990, an army ordnance team had to
be called in to dispose of a bomb, and seven bombs or
fuses had been found the year before.

Fuses the size of a tennis ball can have the force of a
hand grenade. Because hikers could stumble across one
of these things, El Malpais officials discourage hiking
here. If you find anything suspicious, notify the Park
Service or BLM.

Homestead Hikes (See Homestead Hikes, p. 93)

Dittert Site (See Malpais Archeology, p. 83)

Hole-in-the-Wall
*Getting there: From I-40, drive south on NM 117 34.5
miles to county road 42, on your right. After about 2
miles, the road will fork. Take the right fork to the wilderness boundary, about 4 more miles. Park and follow the
road in.*

Hole-in-the-Wall is the largest kipuka (island) in El
Malpais, a 6,000-acre parkland of ponderosa pine and
grass, surrounded by recent lava. Because it's part of the
40,100-acre West Malpais Wilderness Area, you can't
drive into it, so you're in for a long, dull hike into this
kipuka.

Locals have stories about outlaws and draft dodgers
holing up here, but this isn't the infamous Hole-in-the-
Wall of Butch Cassidy fame. "I was there once," said
one old-timer. "There are remains of an old log house
that's completely down and the logs rotted away, and
a stone house that's still standing. A deserter from
the army hid there for seven months during the war.
The old hitchin' rack is still standin' an' around it are
seven horses' skulls, each with a bullet hole between
the eyes. It would make a peach of a hideout, for
nearby is a cave formed by the lava which filled a
canyon level full, and then cooled on top, allowing the
rest to run out, roofing the gorge over for several
miles."

We spent a couple of days hiking around in here and
didn't see any of the colorful stuff described by the old-
timer. In fact despite its romance, there isn't a lot to see.
There is a Basque homesteader's house, now deserted,
and a stock tank. The land is flat to rolling, all of it bounded by lava, and is home to antelope.
*Distance: 3 miles just to get to Hole-in-the-Wall, and as
much hiking as you can stand after that.*

La Rendija, a crevice in the plains portion of the National Conservation Area.

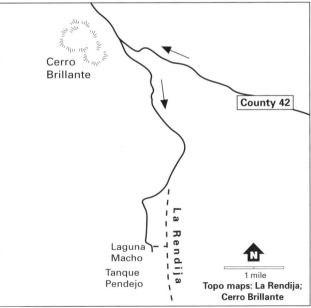

Time: Half-day to all day.
Difficulty: Easy.
Topo Maps: Ice Caves Southeast, North Pasture, Ice Caves.

Chain of Craters Loop (See Continental Divide, p. 222)

La Rendija Crevice
Getting there: From the I-40 exit to NM 117, drive 34.5 miles south and west and turn right on county road 42. About 10.5 miles down the road, take a left that's so sharp you will almost be headed back the way you came. In just over 1 mile, come to a fence and go in. In another 3.4 miles, stop at Laguna Macho, a stock tank.

This simple hike follows La Rendija Crevice (no relation to Cerro Rendija) as far as you care to go. Mountain lovers might find it dull, but it's an opportunity to experience the plains south of El Malpais. I really like the area, a rolling land with tufted mounds of lava under a great dome of sky. Curtains of clouds hang in the distance. Antelope like it too. A herd races away as we approach.

Distance: Up to 4 miles.
Time: 1 to 4 hours.
Difficulty: Easy.

Gus Raney
As you followed NM 117 south, the lava narrows to a tip the homesteaders called Point of Malpais. On your way to county road 42, you pass a tiny cabin surrounded by car skeletons. Tip your hat to Gus Raney, the malpais' most notorious resident. Raney was a local character who fed and fabricated stories of his exploits, but friends and detractors agree, he wasn't somebody to trifle with.

As a reporter I'd met Gus when he dropped in the newspaper office. In his slouch hat and flowing beard, he looked like a man in the wrong century, and I'd heard tales of his dead children and alleged murders. Like everybody else who knew him, I found his eyes the most frightening. I later thought better of Gus, after visiting his cabin with his nephew, Ray Rainey. (Gus, for unknown reasons, always spelled his name differently from the rest of the family.) Gus claimed he was born in 1882, but he was actually born in 1903. He said he'd been a gunman in Pancho Villa's revolutionary army and told friends he was twelve when he killed his first man. For years he maintained he was a lawman in three counties, but he was never more than a reserve deputy. He had zealously guarded uranium claims against claim jumpers and served on a couple of occasions as tracker and informer. Wayne Winters, the former publisher of the *Grants Beacon*, described him as "con man, murderer, liar, back shooter and thief."

Gus was born in Uvalde County, Texas. His family moved to Cliff, in southwestern New Mexico, when he was five. "He was mean from the time he was little," recalled a classmate from his country school. In the 1920s Gus married Myrtle Watkins, whom he called Sugarfoot, and they had four children—Hail, Orval, Sleet, and Ethel.

Gus is said to have killed a slew of men. He was convicted of two murders and accused of two more. In 1932 he got into a dispute with two men who had leased his 160-acre goat ranch near Cliff. He rode up to their shack, pulled a Colt .45 as he walked through the door, and shot both men. Then he loaded them in a wagon, hauled them close to town, and turned himself in. One man later died, the other recovered. During the trial Gus claimed the victim pulled a gun from under his pillow; the survivor said his friend was tying his shoes, when Gus shot him in the face.Gus did time in the state pen, leaving Sugarfoot and their children destitute. Shelter was a rock overhang with a tarp until 1936, when Governor Clyde Tingley issued him a pardon. Starting fresh Gus moved north and bought 1,280 acres of land at Point of Malpais for ranching. But death would visit again soon.

In 1939 Hail and Orval drowned in a stock tank near the ranch. Some locals believed Gus killed his boys, but Ray said the family story was that the boys were riding back and forth through the stock tank for fun, when their horse fell and pinned them in the water. State police found no evidence of foul play and figured one boy fell in the water and the other drowned trying to rescue his brother. Gus didn't have a photograph of the boys, so he took their bodies to an ice cave in the lava, where they froze sitting up, and had a photograph taken of himself with his fallen sons. This was a favorite yarn thereafter, but it wasn't as ghoulish as it seemed. In the last century, children who died were frequently propped up, eyes open, for a last photograph. Again it seemed Gus was out of his time.

Area homesteaders apparently didn't think ill of Gus. "I know him from when he was supposed to have killed his two sons out there," recalled Sue Savage, who homesteaded nearby. "They used to come to dances at the schoolhouse, he and his wife, and they could really dance."

After the drownings the family moved to Mogollon for a time, but then returned. They lived in a tent in Grants one winter when the weather was below zero, said Jim Savage. Gus was often in thin financial straits. That winter he was repairing cars to earn money, and Jim, who was working in a garage at the time, gave him parts on credit. "Gus and I were good friends," Jim said. "People used to ask me, 'Why do you have friends like that?' and

I used to say, 'It's a whole lot better to have them as friends than as enemies'."

Gus once told Jim he'd show him bars of gold in a cave. "I thought it might be a one-way trip for me," Jim said. "I might go in there and not come back out, so I never did go." It was a tale Gus told for years. The former *Beacon* publisher suspected it was a con to part the greedy and gullible from their money. But the story would have tragic consequences years later. In 1972 Gus, then sixty-nine, was hard up again and owed money to Max Atkinson. Atkinson agreed to settle for a beef, but when Atkinson began to skin the dead steer before Gus could brand it, Gus shot him twice in the stomach at close range and then put a bullet in Atkinson's head. Probably because of his age—Gus claimed to be ninety—he got four years' probation. Gus was still on probation when I met him in 1975. He couldn't carry a gun, which cramped his style considerably, as he generally carried four to six—several on him and a couple more in his vehicle. At that point, locals said, he had Sugarfoot carry the gun when they came into town for mail.

An outing I will always cherish was dinner at Gus and Sugarfoot's cabin in the malpais. Ray bought several sacks of groceries and we drove out. He knew the procedure when visiting Uncle Gus. He approached the outside gate slowly, shouted a greeting, and then kept his hands on top of the gate where Gus could see them. When Gus had ascertained who was there, he went out, tied up several vicious dogs, and invited us in. Their log cabin was a vintage homestead—one room, with the kitchen in a lean-to in back. Sugarfoot whipped up a fine meal, including home-made biscuits, on a cookstove, while we visited with Gus. I remember thinking the cabin should be preserved whole in a museum. As we talked Gus pulled out guns from everywhere to show us.

Despite his own run-ins with the law, Gus thought highly of lawmen and talked about helping them. He also mentioned seeing strange lights out in his isolated stretch of the malpais. He suspected smugglers and drug runners, a suspicion that proved accurate. And he also claimed *UFOs* had landed there. One comment would surprise people; Gus complained about the treasure hunters hounding him and trespassing on his land. "If I knew where buried treasure was," he said, gesturing to his simple home, "do you think I'd live like this?"

In 1983 Gus was in trouble with the law again and something of a celebrity. Deputies found two bullet-ridden bodies near the cabin and charged Gus with murdering a father and son who were known to be avid treasure hunters. Claiming to be 101 years old (he was 81), Gus got a lot of attention, including a big, public party on

his birthday in November. A month later he died of a heart attack and was buried at his cabin near the graves of his boys.

Trails from NM 53

San Rafael
The little valley of the Gallo presents a most singular appearance. Directly down the centre, and rising to a height of some 12 feet, a stream of lava has flowed and apparently ceased somewhere near our camp of yester-day . . . The whole valley is so completely filled with the solid lava as to leave only here and there a narrow belt of meadow.
   Lt. Edward F. Beale, 1857, near present-day San Rafael

Four miles south of Grants on NM 53 is San Rafael, a village of history and charm worth a detour on your way to El Malpais attractions or El Morro. Early explorers, including Coronado himself, marveled at the waters of Ojo del Gallo. The spring, named for wild game drawn to the deep, crystal pool and the lush grasses of the surrounding valley, became a stopping place for every traveler. In 1862 the army built Fort Wingate here, of adobes and timbers from the Zuni Mountains. When the army decided to move the fort to Gallup, it invited settlers to occupy the lands, and they wasted no time. Monico Mirabal and Jose Leon Tellez were first, followed by Pablo Salazar and Romulo Barela. Most of these men and other early settlers were Civil War veterans. Some had participated in campaigns against the Navajos and Apaches.

Crucifix at San Rafael

Settlers used the fort's own adobe bricks and timbers or cut *terrones* from the grassy meadow to build houses less than a mile away. The volcanic ash in San Rafael's adobe bricks dried to form a sturdy building block. For the ceilings and roofs, they set vigas on braces, topped them with boards, and then piled on more than a foot of dirt. Inner and outer walls were plastered with mud, and floors were packed hard. To whitewash inside walls, they used *yeso* (gypsum), a mineral they found in the area. They baked the gypsum in *hornos* (outdoor ovens), pounded it into powder, mixed it with water, and painted it on the walls with a piece of sheep pelt.

Within a year the new village of San Rafael had 678 residents and was bigger than the older settlements of Cubero and Cebolleta. The settlers grew beans, corn, and, it is claimed, sugar cane, but sheep ranching soon flourished, and sheep camps dotted the valley. Shepherds in the 1920s made about twenty dollars a month plus food, according to Manuel Padilla, a longtime resident.

Monico Mirabal's descendants became the biggest sheep ranchers and one of the state's most prominent

Mirabal house

families. From the highway you can see their elegant, white home. Mirabal had moved by oxcart from Cebolleta to Fort Wingate in 1864. He cut hay from the valley's rich *vegas* (meadows) with a hand scythe, tied it in bales with buckskin, and sold it to the army. When the financially troubled A&P railroad began selling its land in the valley, the Mirabals acquired thousands of acres. The Mirabals had five sons and five daughters; the oldest boy, Silvestre Mirabal, became one of the wealthiest men in the state. Silvestre had just six months of formal education. After his father died, he became head of the family and worked until he had saved enough to provide for the family for six months. Then he went to the Catholic school and said he wanted to learn everything he could in six months. The superintendent assigned a young nun to tutor the boy. Until the day he died, his daughter Venerada "Benny" Mirabal said, he wrote beautifully, as the nun had taught him.

A cowboy and freighter early in his life, Mirabal started a sheep and cattle business. He was known to be a shrewd businessman, a hard worker and so thrifty that his attire caused strangers to mistake him for a hired hand. He once said he only spent money for land. In a single transaction in 1919, Mirabal bought 170,000 acres in the Zuni Mountains from lumberman George Breece and then sold the timber back to him.

"Silvestre Mirabal was the richest man in the state—everybody knew that, property-wise," said longtime resident Red Prestridge. "He didn't spend it, but he had it." Neighbors estimated Mirabal owned 384,000 acres, and one journal claimed he was the biggest landowner in the

state. He also held a number of elected positions, including state representative and member of the Constitu-
tional Convention. He's memorialized in the Cowboy Hall
of Fame in Oklahoma City. He died in 1939.

For years, San Rafael was a prosperous place. Some
of the early homesteaders, like the Mirabals, lived well
and had servants. And the saints' days were festive.
During the annual fiesta in November, professional gamblers came from Albuquerque, along with the violinist
Joe Barnett, wrote Josephine Barela, "and no doubt
under the hypnotic spell of his music, many a local shark
lost his shirt." Belinda Mirabal said Barnett built the
Sunshine Building and several other buildings in Albuquerque with his winnings. "He took a fortune out of
this area because there was a lot of money here then,"
she said.

Another landmark is the church, built around 1881,
with money Fr. Juan Brun raised from the valley and
distant lumber camps. He left after his brother-in-law,
Dumas Provencher, was murdered. Provencher, a French-
Canadian, had settled near San Rafael after the Navajo
campaign and became a prominent rancher and lumber
dealer. During the election of 1888, as an election judge,
he overheard remarks that Republicans, who feared losing their stronghold in the county, planned to storm the
polling place and destroy the ballot boxes and registra-
tion books. Provencher rushed back to the polling place
and warned Deputy Martin Gonzales. Just then a bullet
fired through the window ended Provencher's life. At the
funeral his widow confronted two men, but the murder
was never officially solved.

After Fr. Brun left, the people were without a priest
for more than twenty years. Like many New Mexico villages, San Rafael relied on Los Hermanos, the Penitentes, to preserve the faith. They also held passion plays.
In 1910 the Franciscan Fathers sent Fr. Robert Kalt. He
had the church rebuilt after a fire in 1930. This church
boasts the most beautiful crucifix in the state. Across
the road Guadalupe Grotto, a shrine to Our Lady of Guadalupe, was made of sixty-five tons of lava in 1969.

San Rafael retained its character for so long that in
1947 the movie "Four Faces West," with Joel McCrea
and Frances Dee, was filmed here.

In 1950 years of agricultural and industrial water use
consumed the landmark spring, and the waters of Ojo
del Gallo flowed no more. But with the decline of mining in recent years, the spring has ebbed back to life.
Once again ducks and game are drawn to its sparkling
waters.

Zuni-Acoma Trail
They are burnt rivers, that ran as fire and remain as stone.
Charles Lummis

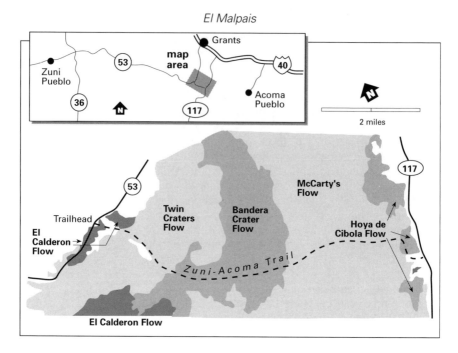

El Calderon Flow

Getting there: The western trailhead is 14 miles south of Grants, on NM 53. The eastern trailhead is 15.5 miles south of I-40 on NM 117. This trail takes you from one side of the malpais to the other. It's best to leave a car on one end and drive to the trailhead on the other side, a distance of 37.8 miles. Get a free backcountry permit from the NPS visitor's center. This trail description is from west to east.

Here is a hike through history on one of the oldest hiking trails in the state. The Zuni-Acoma Trail, known among park rangers as ZAT, is a portion of the centuries-old network of Indian trails connecting Acoma and Zuni pueblos. It's also one of the most unusual trails you'll ever hike. By trail I don't mean a path through the woods. You will be following rock cairns, four-by-four posts and some concrete posts marked "Escalante Trail," through a maze of lava and ponderosa pines. Some of the cairns are the original Indian markers; you can tell by the lichens growing on one side. Trail markers are frequently hard to spot and may be obscured by shade or new growth. Because the trail jags often to avoid a crevice, ridge, or collapse, don't leave one trail marker until you've spotted the next. It's slow going at first, and then it becomes a game. This is when it's good to have several watchers.

Within the first half-mile, the trail appears to follow a two-track road, but don't be seduced by it. A hard-to-see post to the right should pull you from the road and up a hill. You will be walking across scattered lava in a grassland-Ponderosa area, until you encounter the first flow, which is the oldest lava and underlies most of the other

flows. It originated from the cinder cone El Calderon, four miles west.

Scene from the Zuni-Acoma Trail, on the east side looking toward sandstone cliffs.

After two miles you will pass a sinkhole and cross the first of many lava bridges (rock piled into crevices) built by Indian people. When the terrain gets rougher and you're hiking solid lava, it means you're on a newer flow, this one from Twin Craters, seven miles northwest, near Bandera Crater. Here the jagged aa (pronounced AHah) lava, along with a profusion of small crevices make it necessary to watch your step. For the rest of the hike, you will also see the ropy, rumpled looking pahoehoe (paHOYhoy) lava. Watch for a limestone island called Encerrito ("little pen"). Soon you will cross still newer lava, the flow from nearby Bandera Crater. Elsewhere this flow holds the most extensive lava tubes in the malpais. You'll be hiking along many humpback ridges of lava rippled with pahoehoe.

Finally you reach the McCartys flow, the most recent at about three thousand years old—just yesterday, geologically speaking. This is a wonderfully wild-looking place, where stunted trees and wildflowers grow out of a solid, undulating plain of black rock. Here a profusion of grasses, bushes, and flowers find a bit of soil in a crack and survive against all logic. During a rest stop, as I was wondering what might live here, the biggest daddy longlegs I ever saw ambled across my pack.

Near the end of the trail is a bit of flow from the Hoya de Cibola volcano, 14 miles west. The lava will become more and more jumbled, until it abruptly ends at about 5.8 miles. Cairns will direct you over the remaining sandy trail.

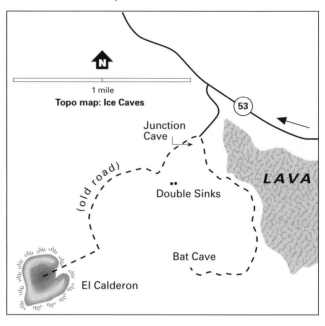

Distance: 7.5 to 8 miles.
Time: 6–8 hours.
Difficulty: This is challenging-to-difficult hiking, where footing is often tricky. It takes longer than you think. Allow plenty of time.

Junction Cave/Bat Cave (See Caves, p. 73)

El Calderon

Getting there: Turn left from NM 53, 19.6 miles south of I-40. After a quarter-mile you'll find a parking lot and trailheads.

To reach El Calderon ("the cauldron"), follow the two-track that angles off to the right from the parking lot. At the first fork, bear left. (The right fork leads to Cerritos de Jaspe.) Near this fork is a grove of aspens on piñon-juniper turf, one of the novelties of plant life in El Malpais. At just over a half-mile, you'll see a cone of red cinders, more obvious because it's been mined for cinders.

El Calderon is the oldest volcano in the monument; part of its flows, which traveled as far as I-40, have been dated at 188,000 years old. An easy and short walk up this hill of red cinders leads to the top. You can see where one lava flow exploded out the side. Flows from El Calderon are more weathered-looking and have a lot of vegetation where water has carried in soil. This flow spread quickly, judging by its many lava tubes.

For a more interesting hike back, look east toward a power line, which follows one lava tube and hike along that tube until you spot the parking lot, about 1.5 miles.

Distance: About 1 mile along the two-track, 2 miles as loop.
Time: 2 hours, round-trip.
Difficulty: Easy.
Topo Map: Ice Caves.

Bandera Crater/Candelaria Ice Cave

Getting there: Drive 24.7 miles south of I-40 on NM 53. The turnoff is marked by a sign.

Two of the most outstanding features of El Malpais are Bandera ("flag") Crater, the area's largest cinder cone and one of the youngest, and its neighboring ice cave. Privately owned for years, both may be acquired by the Park Service.

Bandera Crater, wrote Charles Lummis, "is a great, reddish-brown, truncated cone, rising about 500 feet above the plateau, and from three sides looks very regular and round . . . The whole cone is covered several feet deep with coarse, sharp volcanic ashes, or rather cinders . . ." Neil M. Clark is one of many to marvel at the ice caves: "Caves with perpetual ice in the middle of lava that was once a lake of fire constitutes one of the planet's odder negations of probability."

They're a short hike away on a broad, flat cinder path. The Bandera trail spirals gently around the south side of the crater, passing a spattercone, which was once a lava fountain. This is a surprisingly pretty walk, with benches along the way, the better to enjoy dazzling views in all directions. The late afternoon sun backlights Ponderosa needles, and in winter, the snow makes abstract black-and-white patterns. "The volcanic features seen along this trail cannot be surpassed anywhere in the United States," writes Roy Foster in *Scenic Trips to the Geologic Past*.

Following a deep canyon, the trail curls back toward the crater at a point where lava breached the cone and poured out, hardening into a sixteen-mile lava tube. As Lummis put it, "A terrific potful it must have been, and doubly fearful when that stupendous weight burst out the side of the pot and poured and roared down the valley a flood of fire. Think of a lake of lava so heavy that it simply tore out a mountain-side 800 feet high and 500 feet thick at the bottom!"

Repeated surges created this cone. At first lava ebbed quietly from Bandera, but then eruptions followed, becoming more violent until they fired cinders, gases, and bombs of hot volcanic rock into the air. The cinders formed a cone, and lava welled up in the center, finally breaching the sides in a torrent of fiery rock. The last flows may have been as recent as ten thousand years ago. The flow from this crater is riddled by lava caves called tubes—probably the most extensive series of tubes in one flow in the United States—and an unusually large number of ice caves with massive stores of ice.

The trail ends at the crater's breach, about midway up. Because of loose cinders and steep slope, there is no trail or access to the rim. "A strange, wild sight it is when we gain the edge of the crater," Lummis wrote. "A fairly terrific abyss yawns beneath us; an abyss of dizzy depth and savage grandeur . . ."

Bandera Crater is a half-mile across and 640 feet deep—about 200 feet deeper than the surrounding terrain. It rises at least 1,000 feet above the original land surface. A massive cinder slide into the crater has obscured a lava core in the throat of the volcano. Erosion will one day create a volcanic neck like Cabezon Peak and Shiprock. High up on the northwest side is a remnant of lava. Navajos once called this volcano *dibé bighan* ("sheep house"), because in cold weather the warmth of cinders on the southern exposures drew bighorn sheep, which the Navajos could trap by blocking the entrance. Zunis may also have trapped the hapless bighorns here and domesticated them for wool and meat.

The first Anglos called it Flagpole Crater, and a crude sign on top used to advise visitors, "About 75 years ago the United States Cavalry placed the American flag on top of this crater." That apparently referred to soldiers at nearby Ft. Wingate. In the late 1960s, there was a small ski area just east of the crater called Bandera Ski Run—about 1,500 feet down a cinder hill. It had a tow and ski shed and was open from December to March, depending on snow.

Ice Cave

The ice cave is a quick walk through the tortured aa lava. From the cave's platform, walk down seventy steps to the mouth of the cave. You can't enter, but a second platform gives you a good enough view of a small, green pond with a wall of layered green ice, which gets its color from algae that survives the cold. You can't see the eighty-foot dome ceiling, but it reportedly sparkles with ice crystals. This is a sacred place to Zuni Pueblo Indians. John Stewart MacClary wrote in 1936, "Imagine a bank of solid ice, mild aquamarine in color, from 12 to 14 feet in height and some 50 feet in width, calmly resting in a tunnel of what once was molten stone—the hottest manifestation of the earth's internal heat!" This is one of the few caves in the country where the cave temperature never rises above freezing, even when the summer sun heats up surrounding lava rock. El Malpais has at least six ice caves, probably more. This one has the largest volume of ice.

A local wag once joked that the ice caves are here because the lava flow covered a glacier. Actually the cave holds its ice because of the shape and direction of the opening, the direction of prevailing winds, a low average temperature outside, and the insulating proper-

Ice Cave (Photo courtesy U.S. Geological Survey)

ties of basalt. During the winter the south-facing entrance is warm, and air flows in from outside, forcing warm air out and replacing it with colder air, which is heavier and remains there. As water seeps in through lava rock above, it freezes and releases heat to the mouth of the cave, increasing the flow of warm air out. In the summer the overhanging cliff shields the cave interior, and lava on top insulates the cave from surface warmth. With little circulation, most of the ice remains. Only a portion of the ice wall sees sunlight, and then only for a few minutes a day, for ten days in December. The other ice caves in the United States share the same characteristics.

Pottery shards scattered inside indicate that Indians spent time in the ice caves. The first non-Indian to find the caves may have been Benito Baca, who homesteaded two miles away during the 1880s. In 1918 Bob Lewis tracked rustlers into the malpais, and when he found ice caves, used them as a water source. He did nab his rustlers and brought them in. Lewis returned to the area ten years later and reported that the ice had grown. In 1923 four Gallup men on a jaunt explored the "malpie" and were astounded to find in the hot July sun a chilly crevice. Descending into the opening, they found it colder and colder, until they could see their breath. "Suddenly a cave opened before them and in it there was enough ice to run this city for a considerable time. And in the middle of July, too!" the *Gallup Independent* reported.

After that visiting the Perpetual Ice Cave, as it came to be called, and Inscription Rock (El Morro) became a favorite weekend outing for area people. Homesteaders traveled to the caves in wagons, made ice cream, and had picnics. Seeing its tourism potential, the Ramah Commercial Club put up a sign and marked a trail with rock cairns and tree blazes. Homesteaders Cecil and Roy Moore in July 1929 opened a dance hall here, with dances every Saturday and Sunday that were probably popular with loggers and ranchers.

El Morro custodian Evon Z. Vogt warned the National Park Service that locals and homesteaders would cart off all the ice in the caves, unless something was done to protect them. He recommended that the caves be added to El Morro, but the agency considered the place too small and too inaccessible. As late as 1946, local ranchers were still getting their summer supply of ice here.

The intrepid tourist in those days could use a poorly marked trail, scramble over lava rocks, and step down rude ladders to see the cave. In 1938 three Kentucky school teachers lost their way and were rescued three days later, banged up and hungry, but alive. Not long after, Cecil Moore leased the caves from land baron Silvestre Mirabal, who had bought them from a logging company, and built a trail and a seventy-five-foot stairway. A year later Moore had four cabins, a restaurant, and a picnic ground; admission was twenty-five cents. Mirabal died in 1939, and family members operated the caves off and on during World War II.

In 1946 Mirabal's grandson David Candelaria and his wife Reddy took over the caves, added more cabins, and removed the campground. It wasn't just another roadside attraction with concrete tipis and caged rattlesnakes. The Candelarias took their stewardship of this wonderful place seriously, explaining it to visitors and, like park rangers, asking them to stay on the trail.

The National Park Service plans a visitor center here with a paved access road, a tour road, and two new trails—a half-mile nature trail along a lava-flow ecotone (mixed environment of piñon, juniper, and aspen trees) and a second along the top of Sandstone Ridge, where the visitor has spectacular views of area features and continuing into Spattercone Valley. From the tour road, there will also be a spur road leading to a trailhead for Dripping Lava Cave (see Caves below) and Lava Crater.

Distance: 1.2 miles (round-trip) to Bandera Crater, 0.4 miles to the ice cave.
Time: 2–3 hours for both.
Difficulty: Easy, unless you're not acclimated to the 8,000-foot altitude here.

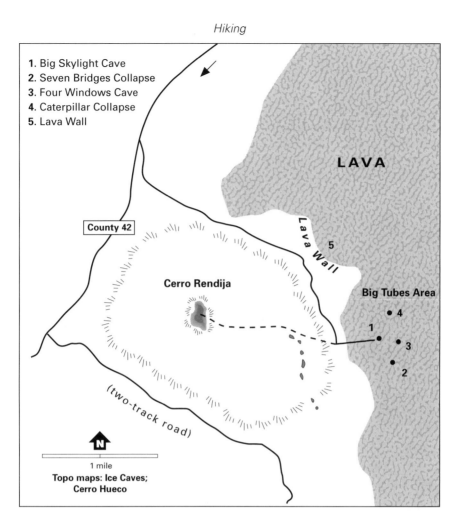

1. Big Skylight Cave
2. Seven Bridges Collapse
3. Four Windows Cave
4. Caterpillar Collapse
5. Lava Wall

LAVA

County 42

Cerro Rendija

Big Tubes Area

(two-track road)

N

1 mile

Topo maps: Ice Caves;
Cerro Hueco

Big Tubes Area, Braided Cave (See Caves, p. 75)

Cerro Rendija

*Getting there: Drive 26 miles south from I-40 on NM 53
and turn left on county road 42. Within four miles you'll
see a broad, low hill on the left; that's Cerro Rendija. (Up
ahead on your right is Cerro Americano.) On the north
side of Cerro Rendija is a two-track road marked "East
Rendija," 4.5 miles from the turnoff. Turn left here and
drive 2.7 miles on good road to the parking area and trailhead for Big Tubes area. On the way in, you'll pass a lava
wall, the highest in El Malpais. Cross the road and begin
hiking up the east side of Cerro Rendija.*

Cerro Rendija ("crevice hill") is one of the more dramatic shield volcanoes, created 110,000 and 200,000
years ago by a series of earth-rending blasts that
scooped out craters and blew the mountainside out.
Lava bled down the slope. Now peaceful, it's filled with
soil, grass, and trees. The western and northern slopes
of Cerro Rendija are closest to the county road, but the

climb is far easier from the east, where the slope is quite gentle. From the east side, you can't really see Cerro Rendija through the trees, but hike uphill, bearing somewhat left. This is an older part of the lava flow, and hiking here is an easy amble over scattered, worn lava, through ponderosa pines, juniper, and piñon. The slope is gentle, until you are near the top, when you scramble up a short, steep slope of cinders and clinkers.

(Pages 64–65) Cerro Rendija

There is no single cone here. The "top" is actually a series of craters about three-fourths of a mile from end to end that form the shield. Each one is filled with trees and ringed with jagged rock, bright red in places from the iron content. From here you can see features of El Malpais in all directions—the Chain of Craters to the west, Cerritos de Jaspe ("little hills of jasper") to the east, and Mt. Taylor to the northeast. After you've explored the rim, you can head out by following the rendija, or rip, to the south.

The Park Service plans road improvements that would provide a new trail to the top of nearby Cerro Bandera.

Distance: About 4.5 miles.
Time: 5 hours at a leisurely pace.
Difficulty: Moderately easy, except for the scramble to the top.
Topo Maps: Ice Caves, Cerro Hueco.

Hoya de Cibola

Getting there: Take NM 53 26 miles to county road 42 and turn left. Go 6.3 miles to a turnoff marked "Primitive Road" and turn left. About 2.1 miles farther, the road will fork. Turn right and continue 2.1 miles to a T. Go right just one-tenth of a mile to another fork and turn left at the two-track, which ends in just over a mile at a crater. High-clearance or four-wheel-drive vehicles only.

Hoya ("pit") de Cibola refers to the crater. Its neighboring shield volcano is Cerro Hoya. From the end of the track, you have a view into the crater, one of the most interesting in the malpais. You will see a road into the crater, the remains of an old cinder-excavating operation. Walk into the crater. It looks different from below—more of a canyon that winds and twists. There are the usual robust-looking trees found in malpais pits, the result of ample water and minerals trapped in the bottom. The floor of the pit is a multihued jumble of lava rock, with colors ranging from sulfur yellow to bright red to purplish black.

Walls are the layered rocks typical of malpais tubes on one side and on the other side an unusual sandstone with the texture of alligator hide. In another place a blackened wall ends high up in a crack sheltered by an overhang. A waterfall of bird droppings and pile of sticks below tell us we've found the raptor Hilton.

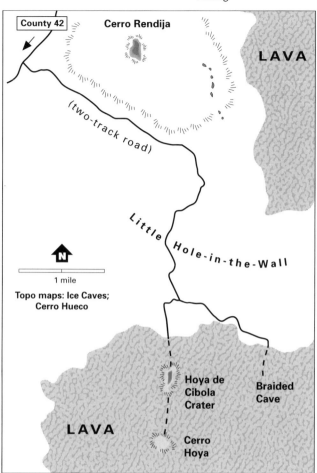

This big subsidence pit produced some local magma but isn't the source of the 110,000-year-old Hoya de Cibola flow. The source is Hoya de Cibola volcano, about a mile away, and its flow is one of the oldest in the malpais. The Hoya De Cibola tube systems are some of the biggest and most beautiful in the monument, with sections of stacked and parallel tubes, skylight windows, domed ceilings, and intense reds. The most spectacular of this system is Braided Cave. Despite its short distance from the pit, the volcano isn't easy to find, because of rugged terrain with jumbled mounds of lava and a healthy stand of ponderosas. Don't try this without a topo map and compass. There is, however, a broad trail that's actually an old forest fire line. To find it, turn from your view of the crater where the road ends on top, face the opposite direction and walk downhill.

You should run across the fire line within a few minutes. Follow it into the woods as it curves around the crater to the south. In about 0.7 miles, you should be able to see the cone to your left. Leave the trail, which

(Left) Hedgehog cactus on Cerro Hoya. (Right) Wall detail, Hoya de Cibola crater.

angles off to a road, and start climbing this short cone. After a quarter-mile scramble up loose lava rock tufted with grass, you'll reach the top. The view from here is one of the best in the malpais. Rising among a blanket of trees are volcanoes that seem to ring the shield volcano you're on. Directly to the north, you can see the rim of the crater you just left; just behind and to the right, the nearest feature is Cerro Rendija. To its left the biggest cone you can see is Cerro Americano. Just over the right shoulder of Rendija is Cerro Bandera, and Bandera Crater, the flatter mound, is to the right (east) of that.

Between Bandera Crater and Twin Craters, farther to the east, is Lost Woman, whose flows are intertwined with those from two other neighboring cones. Across the malpais the creamy cliffs of the Narrows form a bright contrast. On a clear day you can see the Sawtooth and Datil mountains, to the southeast. Walk around the top of Hoya De Cibola and on the south face you'll find a colony of hedgehog cactus that look so happy they probably talk and dance when people aren't around. In one place the rock turns abruptly from black to red—a burst of iron. Before you head out, look once again for the pit and get your directions straight, in case you miss the fire line.

Distance: 2.5 miles, including walk into pit.
Time: 1–2 hours.
Difficulty: Some scrambling over lava, but not a difficult hike.
Topo Maps: Ice Caves, Cerro Hueco.

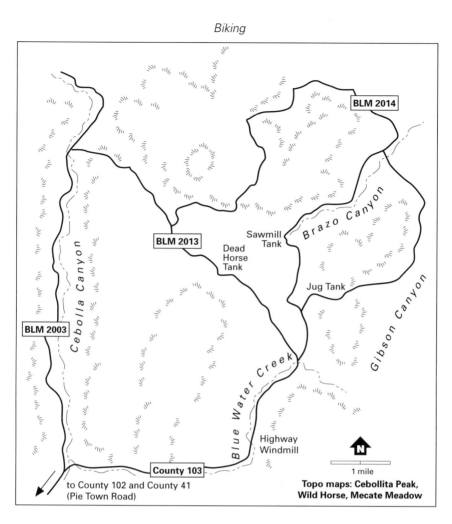

Biking

Bikers might expect to find just tire-slicing lava in El Malpais, but there are some good trails.

■ Cerritos de Jaspe off NM 53, has a network of old ranching roads suitable for biking.
■ Chain of Craters (see hike description under Continental Divide)
■ County road 42, 26 miles down NM 53, is so terrible most of the year that there's little traffic on it. It leads to the Big Tubes area, Hoya de Cibola, Cerro Rendija, Hole-in-the-Wall, and the Chain of Craters.
■ Brazo Canyon. From NM 117, take the Pie Town Road (County 41) about 10.5 miles and turn on County 103. After about 14 miles, turn left on BLM 2013 or 2014 for a loop tour of canyons and historic homesteads. Some roads in the area may be closed to bicycles because of wilderness designation.

Caves

No matter how hot it is outside, the lava tubes are oh so cool underground. It is high adventure, as you can get well below the surface of the earth and at times it seems like mountain climbing underground."
"Where to go camping in the Zuni Mountain District,"
Zuni Chapter, Boy Scouts

Cavers, novice and experienced, will find a new world of caving in the tubes of El Malpais. And even people who don't particularly like the idea of a cave will enjoy lava tubes. Here cooling lava crusted to form a stone tunnel around the river of molten lava moving through it. El Malpais has at least eight such tube systems. One sixteen-mile tube is the longest in North America, possibly the world. Others are more than fifty feet in diameter and several miles long.

The Park Service has decided to make a few of the best caves available to the public with developed trails and interpretation. Others will be harder to find, with simple cairn trails through the lava, but even if they're less than two miles from a road, it might take a half-day of difficult hiking to find them. Still others will be left in their wild state for people to discover on their own. Much is left to explore, and the Park Service in fact is counting on cavers to help locate wild caves.

The most popular and accessible caves are Bat Cave and nearby Junction Cave, in El Calderon area. The biggest and most impressive caves are in the Big Tubes area, where a cairn trail leads to Big Skylight Cave and Four Window Cave. Also spectacular is Braided Cave, named for its network of interlocking tunnels more than a half-mile long, near Hoya de Cibola Crater. This one is a three-thousand-foot segment of dark cave, unusual for lava tubes, which are usually short. It will remain a backcountry cave with a simple cairn trail. Candelaria Ice Cave, next to Bandera Crater, is already developed, but you can't go inside. (See Trails From NM 53, p. 60). In the future the Park Service plans a trail to Dripping Lava Cave, with a catwalk down to the entrance and a trail the length of the chamber. This is a spectacular cave, two thousand feet long with a ceiling seventy-five feet high. It has an ice pond and colorful "lavacicles" that formed from droplets of lava.

The tube systems (a system is a main tube and its side branches) take a lot of different forms. Collapsed tubes, for example, look like canyons filled with rubble; some are up to a hundred feet deep and extend for miles. Or what appears to be a natural bridge is actually a narrow band of tube in a collapse. Many collapses lead to intact caves that may extend for a few hundred feet or for miles, with many branches. And ice caves are found in lava tubes that have collapsed and sealed at

one end; they may contain delicate ice-crystal ceilings and ice stalagmites. The Bandera flow has more tube systems than any other flow in the country; it's "one of the great lava tube systems of the world in terms of length and complexity," according to the Park Service. The main system is sixteen miles long; individual tubes up to seven thousand feet long have numerous branches. Less than 20 percent of the system takes the form of open caves, but the underground passages and open

(Above) One of the skylights in Four-Window Cave. (Below) Collapsed tube.

collapse structures offer a greater variety of surprises to the explorer.

Archaeologists know from ash deposits that Indian people used the caves and probably relied on the ice caves for water. In the last century, bears lived in malpais caves, along with coyotes, wildcats, and mountain lions. And locals have found bighorn skulls in them. More recently scientists have been drawn to the tubes. In 1926 a member of the U.S. Geological Survey speculated, "The banding of the ice in the cave suggests a

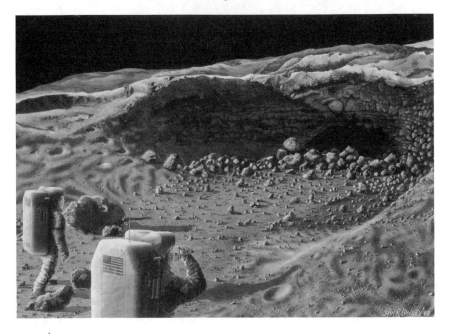

Artist's conception of lava tubes on the moon. (Artwork by Mark Dowman, courtesy NASA.)

possibility of working out a chronology. The mass is made up of layers of ice. Each layer may represent a year's accumulation or may represent a climatic cycle." Scientists in 1990 studied the ice to learn about climatic changes and rainfall cycles and concluded that the ice is three thousand years old.

NASA scientists have studied El Malpais off and on since the 1960s, when NASA got its first good photographs of the moon, and a scientist flying over El Malpais was struck by the similarity. Astronomers can see lava channels and tubes on the moon and believe there are thirty intact lava tubes. In the late 1980s, NASA investigators explored El Malpais lava tubes because lunar lava tubes might someday harbor a base. Scientists have compared geographical features on the moon, such as the Marius Hills, with the Bandera tube in the malpais and Hadley Rille wall with the layers in a collapsed lava tube.

On the moon, the temperature ranges from 230° to −270° every fourteen days, but astronomers believe that, like their earthly counterparts, the temperatures inside lava tubes might be more constant. The tubes would also afford protection from radiation and meteorites. From El Malpais the scientists learned two things: that tube openings on the moon might be difficult to find and to enter, because of rubble from ceiling collapse, and that moon tubes with jagged basalt could be treacherous to astronauts in cumbersome space suits. They were encouraged to find malpais tubes with smooth floors. Because moon tubes are probably ten times as large, a vehicle could be driven inside an uncluttered tube.

Caving Tips

1. Listen to the Boy Scouts: "The area is primitive, trails are scarce and the terrain is quite confusing, especially if it snows . . . Be aware after visiting these caves the boys will be 'high.' Watch for fatigue and limit their cave exploring if you think they've had enough. Fatigue causes most tube accidents . . . Sneakers can be cut to ribbons on this unforgiving surface. If your Scouts are unprepared, do not let them go on this [Big Skylight] trail."

2. Stay together.

3. Carry three reliable light sources and enough water. Wear gloves, knee and elbow pads, and sturdy boots. If you like the present shape of your head, wear a hard hat or a miner's or caver's helmet.

4. If you find anything in the caves—bones or artifacts—leave them in place and advise the Park Service. And take care to keep from breaking delicate formations, such as lava stalagmites.

5. Sensitive plants, such as mosses, ferns, and liverworts at cave entrances and under windows, won't stand much foot traffic. Watch out for the Hammond's flycatcher, which nests only at the entrance of cold caves.

6. It's easy to get lost here. The basic rule is to follow the same tube system in and out. Wandering away from the system can invite problems, because in many places you can't see landmarks.

7. Even though the iron content of the malpais may throw off a compass in some places, don't attempt to explore without one.

8. Get a caving permit from the Park Service.

Junction Cave/Bat Cave
(See map of El Calderon, p. 58)

Getting there: Turn left from NM 53 19.6 miles south of I–40. In a quarter-mile you'll find a parking lot and trailheads.

A short walk from the parking lot takes you to Junction Cave, which is probably the most accessible lava tube in El Malpais. This three-thousand-foot cave is part of an extensive tube system created by a channel moving to the southwest from La Tetra, a vent about three miles to the northwest. In the back is an unusual deposit of silt and sand. Its flow borders El Calderon flow. You can explore Junction Cave with a flashlight, but like other tubes, it requires climbing over a lot of rock dropped from the ceiling.

Near Junction Cave are the Double Sinks, which are collapse structures. One is thirty feet across, the other about ninety feet, and both are sixty feet deep, connected by a lava bridge. These two are surprise features that appear suddenly. The two bowls hold a profusion of ferns and mosses.

From Junction Cave the trail continues on to Bat Cave. This is a pretty trail, past swaths of blooming lavender verbena in the late summer. Here you can watch the bat flights at dusk from June through October. Out of consideration for your health and their need to be left alone, stay out of their cave. The smell alone should be enough to keep you out. To watch the bat flight, sit on the eastern edge of the tube, so that you can see the bats against the fading light of the west. Bats won't fly into your hair and will avoid you, but if you have lingering doubts, wear a hat. The inhabitants of this cave are Mexican free-tailed bats, so called because their tail extends slightly beyond their membrane. They have a muzzle like a mouse and big ears. The males are slightly smaller and darker than the females. Bats segregate themselves into bachelor, maternal, and nursery colonies, and this is a bachelor colony. At Braided Cave is a maternal colony of pregnant females. They mate in the fall and hibernate in Central Mexico.

The estimated population of eight thousand is a fraction of the forty thousand counted in the 1950s, probably because of pesticides. In the winter a smaller population of Townsend's big-eared bats lives here. Gardeners have always loved the bat's rich guano, and this cave was once a guano mine.

After sunset, when the sky changes from burnt orange to lavender, the bats begin their show. A few scouts first check the weather, and if it's not raining, nature's only true flying mammals will pour from the cave, circling several times before fluttering off to the south, in search of moths. This departure will take about twenty minutes. A hungry bat will enfold supper in its wings and then eat, and its appetite for bugs each night is equal to its weight. The range of these particular bats is up to a hundred miles. At the end of the night, they'll jet home—returning bats have been clocked at 80 miles an hour—fold their wings and dive at the cave, then open their wings and fly in.

Distance: 0.9 mile to Bat Cave.
Time: 1 hour, round-trip.
Difficulty: Easy.
Topo Map: Ice Caves.

One of many cave entrances in the Big Tubes area.

Big Tubes (East Rendija) Area
(See map of Cerro Rendija, p. 63)

Getting there: Drive 26 miles south on NM 53 to county road 42 and turn left. In 4.5 miles turn left to a road marked "East Rendija" that circles Cerro Rendija, a shield volcano you may also want to explore. Drive 2.7 miles on good road to the parking area and trailhead. On the way in, you'll pass a lava wall, the highest in El Malpais at 100 feet in places. The Park Service plans to realign and improve route 42 and build a new access road into the area.

On the way in you will pass a wall of lava more than one hundred feet high in some places, the highest such wall in El Malpais. Because the wall holds moisture in some of its pockets, plants that might not live here otherwise take hold and grow. From the trailhead follow rock cairns for a short (less than a half-mile) but rugged hike to Big Skylight Cave, Four Windows Cave, and Caterpillar Collapse. You will cross loose lava rock and a turbulent flow before coming to a sign indicating that Big Skylight is to the left, Four Windows to the right. From the sign cairns lead to Big Skylight Cave just beyond the sign and, farther in the same direction, Caterpillar Collapse. From a point between the two, rock cairns lead to Four Windows Cave.

We found the cairns difficult to follow and did a substantial amount of wandering around, at one point resorting to compass and map before we found everything. If you're totally confused, you need to understand that this is a braided, or branched, tube system here. Follow the branches and you should eventually see everything. Allow plenty of time to explore.

Big Skylight Cave is the first feature you're likely to find. It gets its name from the round opening in the roof that illuminates a carpet of bright-green moss in this six-hundred-foot-long cave. The opening of the cave is fifty feet high and sixty feet wide, and the ceiling is sixty-five to a hundred feet high. The horizontal layering you see on walls is the result of fluctuations in the lava flow as it moved through the tube. You can explore a portion of this cave with lights, climbing over big chunks of lava that dropped from the ceiling as the lava cooled.

Caterpillar Collapse was created when the roof of a tube fell in, and it looks like a boulder-filled canyon. Named for the twisting shape of the tube, this collapse is filled in places with aa lava.

Four Windows Cave also has skylights—four of various sizes. The entrance here is about fifty feet by fifty feet, and the cave is nine hundred feet long. Should you choose to explore the interior, cavers report that Four Windows' features change as you go through it. The ceiling rubble in your way at the entrance yields to a smooth floor of original ropy lava in the Cauliflower Passage and changes again to small rubble in the One-Foot-in-the-Gutters Gallery. Finally, in the back are crawlways and rubble near the fourth exit. The Cauliflower Passage has a smaller side passage for the daring. Walk far enough back for a dramatic view of the windows' illumination of the caves.

To reach any of these features requires a scramble into the tube and over boulders. Amazingly, small pincushion cacti grow defiantly right out of the boulders, so watch your handholds.

Distance: 1 mile to features, round-trip; 2–3 miles total for exploring.
Time: 5 hours (allow more for cave exploration).
Difficulty: Short but rough hiking over difficult terrain; rock scrambling.
Topo Map: Ice Caves, Cerro Hueco.

Lava Roll Cave
Getting there: Drive 26 miles south on NM 53 to county road 42 and turn left. In 4.5 miles turn left to a road marked "East Rendija" that circles the shield volcano Cerro Rendija. Drive 2.7 miles on good road to the Big Tubes parking area and trailhead. I didn't explore this cave myself but relied on a veteran caver's description.

Lava Roll Cave takes its name from a late lava flow

that passed through the tube, leaving a layer of lava along the wall that later curled away. It's near the back door of Four Windows Cave (allow time to find the entrance; there are no more precise directions), but the two are apparently not connected. According to caver Duke McMullan, getting in means tying a rope to a big rock at the entrance and dropping about 25 feet. Much of the interior is also a technical climb and "definitely not a free climb," McMullan wrote, unless you're "closely related to a spider." Near the entrance, a smooth lip "just about says keep out!"

McMullan and his party landed on a breakdown (rubble) pile that appeared untouched by other cavers. He describes the cave as "one large passage of roughly the same height and width as the entrance area to Four Windows" and estimates its length as between 150 and 250 feet. The cave bends to the left about halfway through, but entrance light is visible until near the back. Like other lava caves, the floor is littered with collapsed rock from the roof, but the floor is relatively clear along the right side of the passage.

Braided Cave
(See map of Hoya de Cibola, p. 67)

Getting there: Drive 26 miles south on NM 53 to county road 42 and turn left. After 6.3 miles, turn left through a gate to a rough two-track marked "Primitive Road." (High-clearance vehicles required). About 2.1 miles from the gate, the road will fork. Take the right fork and continue 2.1 miles to a T marked by a sign and go left. At two more forks, bear right and, about a mile from the T intersection, park.

Veterans of spectacular limestone caves may not be as dazzled with Braided Cave as I was, but I found its interwoven passages a page from every kid adventure book I ever read. In moments away from the group I was with, I could allow myself a bit of wonder and discovery. A sign at the trailhead advises that Braided Cave is a half-mile. Cairns mark a short hike (0.4 miles) over rock and through scattered ponderosa pine forest to the edge of a tube from the Hoya de Cibola system. Eco-vigilantes who want to keep people out of the area have been known to tear down the cairns; if this is the case, take a 120-degree compass bearing from the mailbox at the trailhead.

At the edge a cairn marks a natural stairstep descent into the tube. Bear left, or east, for a pleasant hike through a series of short tubes and skylights. Rubble on the floor is ceiling collapse. You can see, from deposits along the walls and in patterns on the floor, the flow path of the molten lava. The entrance to Braided Cave is unmistakable; you face two distinct tunnels, which join and part several times, each with branching tunnels. Because

they all eventually come together again, it's difficult to get lost in here. But to be on the safe side, bear right going in and again coming out. That way you see nearly everything.

Most of Braided Cave is an easy walk, with smooth floors and high, broad ceilings. We startled a few bats in the nursery colony here and hurried on to avoid bothering them. In places the Park Service has tried to protect animal bones, including the bighorn sheep, likely dragged in here by a predator. Take care to not disturb them. Toward the back the ceiling drops, and to see any more, you have to duck walk. This is when you'll be thankful for a hard hat. To see the very back means a belly crawl. Here are tiny, red-and-white lava ceiling drips that resemble soda-straw formations. In a recess are snowy crystalline deposits like cotton candy.

Distance: 2 miles round-trip; the cave itself is about a mile long.
Time: 3 hours at a leisurely pace.
Difficulty: Some rock scrambling, but otherwise not difficult.
Topo Maps: Ice Caves, Cerro Hueco.

Entrance of Braided Cave.

Archeology

The first people in the area were Paleo-Indians, who camped here from about 10,000 to 5,500 B.C. Using *atlatls* to propel spears, they hunted mammoth and a kind of bison that's now extinct. As the big animals died out and the climate became warmer and drier, people cooperated in hunting and gathering. This was the Archaic period, from 5,500 B.C. to about A.D. 400. People planted corn for winter supplies and used grinding tools to process seeds and nuts.

Beginning around A.D. 400 or 500, in the Basketmaker period, the people called Anasazi were living in northwestern and northern New Mexico. In this area they made their homes east of the lava flows, where a series of canyons cleave the western face of Cebolleta Mesa. They had become more dependent on agriculture and grew corn, beans, and squash to support their bigger and more complex villages. At this time plainware pottery and the bow and arrow first appeared.

Initially, the Anasazi lived in pit houses dug from the earth and roofed, but by A.D. 700, in the early Pueblo I period, villages had both pit houses and above-ground houses with stone foundations and walls of *jacal,* a series of vertical poles that were interwoven with branches and covered with adobe. Villages were usually located on the slopes of a drainage, but toward A.D. 950, they were built on benches at the sides of canyons or on low knolls and, later, on the valley floors. The large number of sites from this period indicate a population in-

Walls remaining at Dittert Site.

crease, possibly of Mogollon immigrants from the Mimbres Valley. This area apparently straddled a cultural border between Chaco to the north and the Mogollon civilization to the south.

From 950 to 1175, the Pueblo II period, the Chaco civilization was taking shape in the San Juan Basin. Houses of mud or stone and adobe were clustered around community centers of many stories, with great kivas and plazas. Public works included dams, roads, and buildings. In these years the area climate was ideal for growing corn, and the population increased. An elaborate network of roads like the spokes of a wheel linked outlying communities to the Chacoan centers. The typical outlier had a public building with large rooms of Chacoan masonry and a kiva built into the room block. The people lived nearby in small houses. These villages were built near good farming plots at the mouths of canyons, the edge of plains, or in wide canyons. On the edge of the malpais, the Candelaria Ruin and the Dittert site are such outliers. Because of pothunting, erosion, and even homesteaders reusing the shaped stone in their own dwellings, few are intact.

From 900 to 1350, the people valiantly adapted to changes in climate. They first planted at low elevations, because of cool weather. "Atchin" fields at arroyo mouths caught water and took advantage of the fan's soil buildup. As the weather warmed up, from 1040 to 1130, they also planted fields at higher elevations. From 1130 to 1150, a drought afflicted the entire region; after this, precipitation was light. At the same time, the population had increased dramatically, so that demand would have outstripped the thinning food supplies. In the Chaco center, construction halted after 1140.

The year 1175, which begins the Pueblo III period, marks a time of change and upheaval for the people, as they abandoned their small settlements and gathered in big fortified communities on mesa tops along both sides of the malpais. Maybe it was a time of political turmoil or warfare in the area, or unrest in response to an altered climate. The villages took an L or U shape, and great houses were two or three stories high, with ladders. Buildings became larger and were clustered together. Construction of public buildings ceased, while massive compound walls appeared. Other constructions, which could have been lookouts, appeared on mesa tops. Kivas grew larger but went unroofed. By the mid-1300s the Cebolleta Mesa area was abandoned, and the new centers were big villages at Acoma and Zuni pueblos. With the collapse of Chaco, villages grew still larger, reaching a thousand rooms in some places.

Acoma people say they have inhabited their citadel on a 367-foot rock since at least A.D. 600, and archaeologists can confirm their occupation from 1150. By the 1650s Acomas were farming in Cebolla and Cebolleta canyons, on the eastern edge of the malpais, and irrigating lands near the San Jose River and at Ojo del Gallo, near present-day San Rafael.

Long before the Spanish arrived in 1540, Zuni people lived in seven large and well-fortified pueblos along the Zuni River. When Coronado arrived in 1540 to claim the fabled Seven Cities of Cibola for Spain, he found pueblos of massive, terraced room blocks with streets and plazas. Around the pueblos were irrigated fields of corn, beans, and squash. The people had an extensive trade system and sophisticated pottery.

The Zuni-Cibola Trail connected pueblos along the Rio Grande with Acoma and Zuni. A branch of this trail and one of the oldest passages in the region was the Zuni-Acoma Trail, across the malpais between the two pueblos. The other fork of the Zuni-Cibola trail, called the Navajo Trail, passed down Zuni Canyon, through the Zuni Mountains, and ended at Zuni Pueblo.

Laguna Pueblo is generally believed to consist of tribes collected from other pueblos, but Lagunas claim roots in Mesa Verde. Origin stories tell of people migrating south to settle at a lake on the Rio San Jose, and archeological work confirms villages here in the 1300s and 1400s. Modern Laguna took shape in 1699, when the people built a mission church under the direction of their first padre, Fr. Antonio Miranda. There was, in fact, a *laguna* ("lake") here, where lava and beavers trapped water. When people arrived the beavers left, but Laguna people maintained the dam until the 1800s, when it fell into disrepair and the lake evaporated.

Navajos entered the area after 1300. They learned to plant corn from Pueblo people but continued to hunt for game. Their communities of Ramah and Cañoncito formed after they returned from Bosque Redondo.

Candelaria Ruin
(See map of Sandstone Bluffs, p. 41)

Getting there: From I-40, drive 9 miles south on NM 117 to the BLM Ranger Station. Hike directly west of the ranger station toward a rocky knoll, with Gallo Peak looming behind. (You will have to climb a right-of-way fence.) There is no trail. In less than a half-mile, you will see a kiva depression. Rubble of the ruin dots the knoll.

Early people in this region left behind one of the richest archeological areas in New Mexico, with hundreds of prehistoric ruins and sites. They range from outposts to pueblos of many rooms. Candelaria Ruin (formerly Las Ventanas) was one of more than one hundred Chacoan outliers and an important regional center. Occupied between A.D. 1050 and 1200, it had about sixty rooms on the ground floor and another thirty on upper stories, all made of shaped basalt and sandstone. It also had a great kiva and tower kiva. Adolph Bandelier described these ruins and noted "an immense dark malpais on the west."

Charles Lummis called Candelaria Ruin "one of the handsomest" of the prehistoric ruins. In the last century, he described it as "a large stone pueblo surrounded by a noble stone wall." Nearby, he wrote, was an ancient house in a valley with "a frozen black tide" of lava lying across the floor. Lummis was apparently repeating a local legend; nobody has ever found the house in the lava.

I wish I had seen Candelaria Ruin in Lummis's time. The tower kiva was backfilled in 1981 after partial excavation, to protect its walls. At present there isn't much to see. However, if you hike south from Candelaria Ruin along the rim toward Sandstone Bluffs Overlook, the views are spectacular. In about 1.5 miles of zig-zagging, you should come to a small but wonderful arch in a dramatic wall of yellow sandstone. Just behind is a spire. There are two more arches here. I kept company with ships, faces, and animals sculpted from white, yellow, pink, and deep purple stone. Here and there were dead trees, twisted as a barber pole. Stick to the rim or high ground. Otherwise you could find the climb out a challenge.

The Park Service is planning a half-mile spur road and 1.3mile trail that would lead to Candelaria Ruin as well as the arch, some overlooks, and a prehistoric road.

Distance: Less than a mile round-trip to Candelaria Ruin; loop to Sandstone Bluffs is about 4.5 miles.
Time: 1 hour for Candelaria Ruin; 3 hours for loop.
Difficulty: Easy walk to ruin; some climbing with loop, but not hard.

Dittert Site
(See map of Armijo Canyon, p. 94)

Getting there: From I-40, go south on NM 117 to the Pie Town turnoff, just shy of 32 miles, and turn left. Look to the right here to see the remaining walls of an old stage-coach stop and corral. After 3.8 miles, turn left opposite King Ranch headquarters, follow a good two-track road for 1.3 miles to the Cebolla Wilderness boundary.

As you face the boundary sign, begin walking at about 10 o'clock from the sign and cross an arroyo. You

Dittert Site.

should see the wall of the ruin ahead. Behind you is the jagged outline of the Sawtooth Mountains, to the south. The land here is high-plains country, with a big sky and endless horizon. In less than a half-mile, you should come to the ruin; from here you can walk up and explore the mesa. My frequent hiking companion, Kathleen Havill, identifies wild oregano, mustard, gummyweed, gaillardia, and blue gilia and marvels at the birds—chick-adee, tufted titmouse, western tanager.

Dr. Alfred E. Dittert studied Cebollita Mesa and named the phases of human occupation here. Between 1947 and 1952, Dittert and fellow archeologist Reynold J. Ruppe reported some three hundred archeological sites and opened about one hundred. The Dittert site is noteworthy for its thirty rooms and kiva, with a great kiva nearby. Like other sites in the area, this village was associated with the Chaco culture, to the northwest, and other cultures south and west. It's a good place to see traces of Chacoan roads.

People lived on the site from the eleventh to the thir-teenth centuries; roof beams from the kiva date to A.D. 1233, while room dates range from A.D. 1236 to 1267. It was built on an earlier mound, using at least two differ-ent masonry styles. This site was abandoned in good shape, with furniture still in place, apparently because its occupants intended to return. The BLM acquired the site in 1958 and stabilized it in 1976.

Distance: 1 mile round-trip.
Time: 1 hour.
Difficulty: Easy.
Topo Map: Sand Canyon.

Homesteaders

They came in family groups, in any sort of conveyance that would roll, their household furnishings piled high and the overflow—washtubs, baby buggies, chicken coops— wired to any anchorage that would hold.

In trucks, in automobiles, dragging heavy trailers, the rare exception in horse-drawn wagons, they came, and with them, a new order.

Agnes Morley Cleveland

Lewis Bright with his second dugout house.

Lewis Bright sat on the corner of an old daybed in the dugout that was his home in the 1930s. His cigarette smoke wafted around the narrow, curled brim of his sweat-stained cowboy hat toward the ceiling planks. "As you can see, it needs some work," he said. "Sure as the devil, when you're not around, [the wear and tear] will cause you to think about doing some work." Years and hunters have taken their toll on the house. But even so, it's a page from history.

In 1932 Lewis spent a week touring the malpais area with horse and bedroll. Then twenty-four and just out of the army, he decided to homestead, because "there was something romantic about it." He learned it wasn't too romantic. He camped out and with poles and logs built a dugout, which he "put up fast and hard." Its floor and roof were dirt. "That seemed to be pretty popular at that day and time." Coal-oil lamps were the lights, and a cookstove provided plenty of heat, even on a cold winter night.

Lewis married Lorene and later built two more dug-outs. The last one had two rooms, a fireplace, windows, walls of rock that had to be hauled in, and a plank floor. "Lorene had it fixed up pretty dang nice," he said. "We used to have a bed over here, and we'd start a fire over here and watch it burn."

Pioneering didn't end in the last century. From about 1918 to 1940, this area was still a frontier that beck-oned two waves of homesteaders—probably the last in the continental United States. The big difference was the automobile. Although a few traveled across the eastern New Mexico plains in covered wagons, most arrived in a jalopy. Once here the vehicle became a kind of buffalo, with no part wasted. Its doors and windows might reappear in a cabin; the tailgate became a table. The front seat was furniture, and the chassis worked as a wagon. Smaller metal parts became rude hinges or implements.

Local Hispanic families had homesteaded here since passage of the first homesteading law in 1862. Then Congress realized that in the harsh West, people needed more than 160 acres to survive. The 1916 Stock Raising Act brought the first wave of outsiders, by expanding the claim to a section of land (640 acres). The new home-

stead law passed just as wool and meat prices soared with wartime demand. In 1918 homesteaders began settling along both sides of the malpais, down into El Morro valley and beyond, at Fence Lake. Often members of a family would file on adjoining sections. They wrote relatives and friends about their new homes, and the letters brought another wave. In hard times homesteading offered the prospect of land and a living. In the early 1930s, people poured into the area. If the good land was taken, they bought relinquishments from homesteaders who wanted out. They also leased school land from the state or rented from a landowner. Many simply squatted.

The General Land Office in Santa Fe was a busy place in those days. Would-be homesteaders, mostly from Texas and Oklahoma, must have thought they were in another country, as they made their way through the town's winding streets past burros carrying firewood. At the land office, they learned what tracts were available. Then they ventured out to the hills and valleys, looking for old section markers to locate their place. If they liked it, they returned to Santa Fe and filed, scraping up a fil-

Car used up part by part by homesteaders.

ing fee of thirty-four dollars "and that was about it," said Lewis Bright. "Everybody was broke." They had to live on the land for at least seven months of the year for three years, build a home, and make eight hundred dollars in improvements. Then for another thirty-four dollars, they could "prove up" and get title to the land.

Malpais homesteaders didn't have much, but they weren't the Joads. It was not until 1934 that drought and high winds combined to create the Dust Bowl. The two waves of homesteaders in western New Mexico largely settled before the Grapes of Wrath migration to California. Most of them had a little money, livestock, or equipment. Many were laborers, tenant farmers, or the extra sons of big farm families. Single women who were teachers were also among the homesteaders. Because most homesteaders' children were getting no schooling, families or communities offered teachers whatever they could manage. To all of them, this latter-day homesteading was an opportunity.

A Roof over Your Head

A homesteader's house went up quickly. Mostly they built log cabins, poled houses, or dugouts, but a few built rock houses, using the squared stones from Anasazi ruins. Later on they learned how to make adobes from their Hispanic neighbors. "We set stakes by the north star at night to be sure the front was square with the world," wrote Roy Boyette, who homesteaded between Atarque and Fence Lake. For a log cabin, the men of the family cut down trees and then trimmed and notched the logs, which could be a foot in diameter. To get the logs up, some jury-rigged a pulley, using a log ramp and ropes attached to mules. When the walls were up, it was time to "chink and daub," or fill cracks with small pieces of wood and mud.

The remains of log houses built by the Savage and Bursom families are tucked into the rincons of Cebolla Canyon. One house of ax-cut and sawn logs and adobe chinking was luxurious by homesteader standards, with two large rooms and two smaller rooms. Pickets and chicken wire framed its front yard. The entrance to another house is through an old car door. A wagon body was cannibalized to make another dwelling, which was part log and part dugout. The "stellar attraction," said an archeologist's report, is a "beautiful root cellar with walls of split cedar . . . inside are some shelves and bed springs."

Sue Savage and her children arrived here in 1932, after her husband died and a crop failure took everything they had. With her in-laws, the Bursoms, they traveled from eastern New Mexico in a train of seven wagons and settled near Point of Malpais, the name homesteaders gave the flows' narrow southern end. She filed on 180 acres. "I could have gotten quite a bit more, but I didn't have the money," she said. Sue Savage's sons— the oldest was seventeen-year-old Henry—built their house. "We had what you call a living room. It had a home-made stove, but it was more comfortable [than a fireplace]. I had a cellar that was lined with cedar, and it's still so nice. We used it for a bedroom too for the boys sometimes."

Those who didn't have easy access to tall ponderosa

trees built a pole house, also called a picket house, from piñon trees. It had walls of vertical poles, with mud daubed in the cracks. Byron Aldridge's father put up an L-shaped pole house with one big room and a kitchen. "We stuck up a post in four corners and run a longer pole across the top and then stood up shorter piñon posts underneath this with windows cut out occasionally," he said. The floor and the roof were dirt. The Aldridges moved here from Texas in 1931, after reading about the area in a farm newspaper. His father traded

(Left) Window of cabin in Homestead Canyon. (Right) Homestead near Chain of Craters.

their 1928 Chevy truck for two horses, a harness, a wagon, and some plows. Their homestead was two miles north of Point of Malpais. After his father died, his mother proved up.

The dugout was a house built partially underground and favored by homesteaders for its warmth. Lewis Bright said he used a team and slip to scoop out the dirt and straightened the walls by hand. The above-ground portion was a log cabin, chinked with narrow pieces of wood held in by nails and daubed with concrete. The fancier dwelling might have a lumber-and-tarpaper roof, but most had dirt roofs. Roy Boyette wrote that he split smaller poles for roofing slabs. "Then I threw on a six-inch layer of chips, then a layer of sagebrush, then more chips and after that a foot of dirt. I had the dirt higher in the middle of the roof for drainage." Floors were dirt. Kept damp and packed, they were hard enough to sweep. The floorplan might be one big room, or a bedroom or kitchen might be separated by a log wall or curtain.

Esther Brown's family left Texas in 1922, when her father traded his truck for a half-section relinquishment at El Morro. They had a one-room cabin, built with logs skidded from the Zuni Mountains. It had a dirt roof with flowers growing in it, she recalled, and a dirt floor, which her mother swept with a rabbit-brush broom. "Abraham Lincoln didn't have a thing on me," she said.

Inside, most homestead cabins were probably like the one John L. Sinclair described at Moriarty: "The house had one big room—where they all slept and sat around—

and a lean-to where Faybelle cooked the vittles. Along the front was a porch. Faybelle pasted newspapers on the inside walls for insulation three layers thick—and she saved all the picture papers for the outside layer and made sure to get them right side up so the folks could look at them . . ."

Homesteaders built corrals of piñon or juniper poles to hold a milk cow and a team of horses. Later they added a root cellar, a chicken house, a barn, and other outbuildings. In these dwellings they withstood weather everyone agrees was worse. "We had all kinds of weather out here," recalled Byron Aldridge. "The first winter we came was the winter of the big snow."

Many homesteaders remember "The Big Snow" on November 21, 1931. It was thirty inches, the deepest on record, followed three days later by a second storm. They looked out their cabin doors at five feet of snow, which stayed all winter, and survived on gravy and home-made bread, along with jackrabbits, porcupines, and piñon nuts. Some Navajos starved or froze to death. Livestock loss was substantial. "I guess the following spring after that, they picked up stock clear down half-way between here and Albuquerque that came out of the mountains to get out of that snow," Lewis Bright said.

The Dry Country

Except for the lucky few with a spring, everybody used wagons or other vehicles to haul their water in fifty-five-gallon barrels from a neighbor's well or springs—Cebollita Springs on the east side of the malpais, Paxton Springs on the west side, or Agua Fria Springs in the Zuni Mountains. In July 1934, while homesteader Chet Lowrey was making the two-day trip to Paxton Springs for water, a fire at his place consumed livestock, outbuildings, corrals, and feed. When he got home, only his house was still standing.

Most homesteaders changed clothes about once a week and did laundry on a rub-board with their own home-made soap. For the weekly bath, they heated water in a fifty-five-gallon drum. The few who could afford to drill their own wells usually paid a water witch ten dollars to find water. The water witch would walk the property with a forked stick pointing to the sky; when the stick dipped toward the earth, it meant that water lay below. "We were always short of water," said Byron Aldridge. "We never did get a well." For that reason homesteaders didn't have much luck with farming. "If you could get corn, that was pretty good," he said, "and in those days, a good rain was an emotional event."

Lewis Bright cleared lava rock out of a field to grow

corn and beans. The beans were "better than the irrigated ones we get now." Work was done with horses. "There were no tractors a homesteader could afford," he said. "I had a pretty good team and another old horse I could throw in on a three-horse deal to plant and plow." He also caught a mustang that had come down to San Rafael to drink from the spring and broke it to pull a wagon. He borrowed a drill early on and then got a one-row planter for beans and corn.

Esther Brown's family cut trees down and cleared brush with a grubbing hoe. Her father used a walking plow to break ground. They worked hard all summer raising corn and beans, along with some pumpkins and potatoes. "Back in those days," she said, "the rattlesnakes were so thick that you just couldn't go anyplace without walking on one or killing one."

One homesteader didn't waste his time struggling with corn and beans. The *Gallup Herald* reported in 1918 that Otto Cavaggia's homestead near Gallup was occupied by the red light district.

The Daily Bread

Homesteaders could count on potatoes, radishes, carrots, and beets from their gardens, if they could foil the gophers. Deer browsed on corn and greens, but those same deer often became dinner. Fencing was a luxury. At $2.50 for a roll of wire, it was "a terrible burden on anybody in those days, just to get that much wire," said Lewis Bright. Many had a milk cow and a flock of hens, and learned that their chickens could support a family. In the Depression, when eggs were selling for a dime a dozen in other places, they fetched ninety cents here, because they were scarce. An old grocery receipt shows that the Brights got credit of $2.25 for a crate of eggs and then bought corn flakes for fifteen cents and bacon for twenty-five cents. "About the only thing a fella had to make money on was a milk cow or team that you plowed them ol' fields up," Lewis said. To get groceries and mail, he rode horseback or took a team and wagon to San Rafael—a day's trip both ways. Merchants and traders commonly extended credit, and farmers and ranchers settled up once or twice a year.

Most homestead wives canned or dried fruit and vegetables and stored cabbage, pumpkins, beets, turnips, and potatoes in a root cellar, a trench, or a small cave. Before refrigerators they kept food in a screened box outside the window. A resourceful family could get by with just an occasional trip to the store to buy sugar, coffee, flour, and meal or luxuries like raisins.

Game was abundant. Wild turkeys were everywhere in El Morro valley, and deer browsed in the pastures. "This was a paradise in those days," Esther Brown said. "You could get your feet wet in the stirrups from dragging in the grass, it grew so high." Once she watched in fascination as Navajos hunted jackrabbits. Fifty people on horseback spread out and drove the rabbits toward the center of a circle, where they killed them with clubs.

Homesteaders quickly took up the Navajo practice of gathering piñon nuts. One person could harvest thirty-five pounds in a day—more by robbing packrat nests. They were not only good eating, they became currency, because the trader would buy them. One community paid its teacher partly in piñon nuts. Homesteaders said peanut-fed pork, a southern delicacy, couldn't hold a candle to pigs allowed to run in the piñons and fatten on the fallen nuts.

Daily fare tended to be game or bacon, fried potatoes, pinto beans, dried fruit, and rice pudding. And visitors were welcome at the table. "A lot of times your neighbors come by when you was gone," Lewis said. "They'd come in and eat, which was customary and they expected the same thing out of you." Nobody had locks on their doors. "You couldn't even afford a lock."

It Was a Living

No matter how frugal and resourceful they were, the malpais homesteaders never became self-sufficient and always had to work somewhere else. Some left the area periodically to take short-term jobs; others became cowboys, loggers, or miners—"just about anything we could do to make a dime. Anything!" Byron Aldridge said. "Sometimes we had to take our pay in hay, beans, oats or something like that, which was very welcome even so." When people came into town to get groceries, Lewis Bright said, they usually carried a load of wood. "Practically anybody out on a doggone homestead cut a little wood and brung it in." A big load, cut, split, and delivered, brought $2.50. Pointing out a corral down from his house, he said, "When you have to, you'll do a lot of things. When I didn't have anything else to do, I used to break horses in here for people around the country. I was a pretty good rider then." Besides cowboying he worked at a small sawmill that cut logs into "four slabs and a tie" and sold ties to the railroad. He also helped build state road 53 as far as the ice caves.

After Sue Savage arrived, her five sons found work where they could, logging or cowboying, but their mother had the only prospect for regular pay. Sue was a teacher. A neighbor told them, "You're the third group of people who've tried to live here. You won't stay."

"Which we didn't, you know," she said. Son Jim added, "They all starved out. The whole situation was hand-to-mouth as far as money was concerned."

Sue began teaching homesteaders' children on the other side of the mesa, at the Armijo Ranch. She was first paid in groceries. Later she earned about fifty-eight dollars a month and then seventy-five dollars. "I took my meals with Mrs. Armijo. I'd go over on Sunday evening [and stay] Monday, Tuesday, Wednesday, Thursday and I'd eat breakfast on Friday, and then I'd come home over the weekend. The boys stayed at home. My oldest son Henry, he cooked and took care of the children." The Savages later built a school on their place, which is still in good repair. "It was made of big logs, but it was floored, and we had blackboards and windows," she said. "I taught all the way from the eighth grade to the first."

In 1936 the WPA built a small school at the settlement of ranchers and homesteaders in Tank Canyon near Cebollita Mesa, and Sue taught there. She also taught at El Morro and Bluewater. By the time she retired, Sue figured she had taught at twenty-two schools. Because Sue was either teaching or attending summer school to get her degree in education, the Savage children—five boys and a girl—were mostly on their own. Everyone learned to cook, sew, and sole their own shoes.

In 1933 the federal Work Progress Administration initiated a program to build and repair roads, which provided jobs throughout the area. Men made $2.50 a day; those with a team of horses could make $5. Others built stock tanks, terraces, dams, and schools under other New Deal programs. Jim Savage recalls a WPA camp near the Narrows with a big dining tent. Invited to eat, he sat down at the counter for a meal of pinto beans, tortillas, and coffee. "I kept noticing red meat and little bones," he said. "It was porcupine."

Esther Brown's father opened a trading post and traded piñons with the Navajos for groceries. She would take care of babies in cradleboards while their parents shopped, and she taught Navajo girls to play softball.

In the early 1940s, the war effort needed fluorspar, and mines opened in the Zuni Mountains, employing many of the homesteaders. Byron Aldridge worked in the mines for forty cents an hour. Lewis went to work driving a truck at one of the mines, and the Brights moved into one of many little cabins nearby. When his boss and his wife, a young woman named Dovie, left the area, Lewis bought their house for his ranch headquarters. In 1982, after both were widowed, Lewis and Dovie married, and for the second time Dovie moved into the same house as a new bride.

Getting Around

For transportation homesteaders usually had cars or trucks—"some kind of old clunker," Jim Savage said. But driving was chancy. In the winter blocks would freeze and crack. Sometimes the arroyos ran too high to cross. And wet clay became an impassable muck. "In those days, there were model Ts everywhere, and people would walk off and leave 'em," Jim said. "I remember one time my mother and I were going along in a Model T [a 1926, his first car] on that old road, and that was clay, just slippery as all get-out when it rained." They got stuck by Swede Turner's house. The stout Swede was known to eat a dozen flapjacks, a dozen eggs, and a pound of bacon at a sitting. "He came out and just reached down and picked up the bumper and just set the front wheels down and said, 'Now see will she go.'"

A Fiddle and a Guitar

What did they do for fun? "There was a dance once in a while or a shot of moonshine," Lewis said. "That's about the size of it." Dovie Bright said many people played musical instruments and got together to make music and have dances, usually at the school. And they rode to the ice caves and took home a sack of ice to make ice cream. For others the arrival of a few newspapers was occasion to invite in the neighbors for a reading party.

In El Morro valley, said Esther Brown, people looked forward to July 24, Mormon Pioneer Days at Ramah. "People would come from all over by covered wagon and on horseback and you would just have to push your way down the streets of Ramah."

At Point of Malpais, the homesteaders had baseball teams. One time the local team was going to play against a group of Indian workers building fence, and they didn't have enough players. The Indian men said, "Pick out whatever you need from among us," Byron Aldridge recalled. "We picked out four men. They were the best they had, and we still lost."

The End of an Era

Through the 1930s most homesteaders starved out or found better jobs during World War II. A few managed to hang on to their places, buy out their neighbors, and become successful ranchers. Lewis Bright never returned to his homestead, but he did keep it and make improvements over the years. The place was just too inaccessible and "damn lonesome," he said. It never made him sad to visit the homestead. "It does bring back a lot of memories."

Lewis C. Bright died in November 1990. He was eighty.

Homestead Hikes

Two easy hikes will take you to a few of these homesteads. Remember, take only pictures!

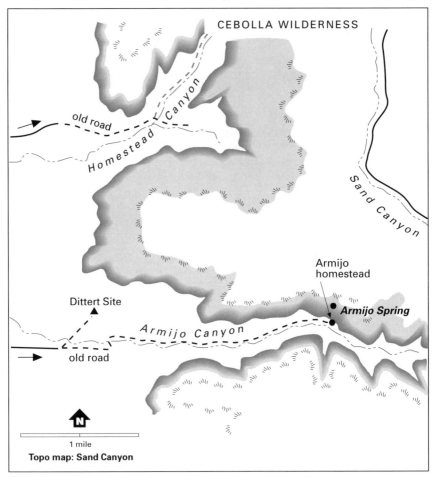

Topo map: Sand Canyon

Armijo Canyon

Getting there: Take NM 117 south about 33 miles to the Pie Town road and turn left. After 3.8 miles, opposite the King Brothers ranch turnoff, turn left again and drive about 1.3 miles to the wilderness boundary.

Hike up the road into Armijo Canyon, an easy saunter of about two miles to the Diego Armijo homestead. One of the best preserved of the 1930s homesteads, this one is a sampler of construction styles: jacal on one wall, adobe on another, chinked logs on a third, and all insulated with cardboard. The fireplace is stone and adobe. Uphill are outbuildings and water tanks. Author Charles Lummis described jacal this way: "The jacal is made by setting a palisade around the space desired to be housed, roofing it with poles, straw and dirt, and chinking the cracks between the upright logs with adobe mud."

While other homesteaders had to haul water from springs and wells, the Armijos were blessed with a spring up the hill. In the spring's grotto, the family gave thanks for this blessing at a small altar they carved out of the sandstone and outlined in turquoise paint. Next to the altar is etched "E.S.D.U.S. RCC UCTAG P.M." Nobody knows what that means. The santo has long since been removed. The family also went to pains to build a road up to the spring and a stone wall to divert runoff.

BLM archeologists and volunteers have restored the homestead, replacing vigas and reroofing both house and springhouse. They dug buckets of mud out of the house to reveal a stone floor covered with handpainted linoleum.

After summer rains, the unseen hand creates wild-flower gardens here: snakeweed in big yellow bouquets, purple asters, blue gilia, gummy weed, perky sue, waisthigh beeweed, sand verbena, gentian, wild zinnia.

For a half-day hike, turn back here. A more ambitious hiker can continue on the road up the canyon, cross the mesa to the north, and hike back down Homestead Canyon, for a view of more homesteads.

Distance: 4.3 miles.
Time: 3 hours.
Difficulty: Easy walk except for the short but steep hike to the spring. This is probably a hot, dry walk in the summer and is better in spring or fall.
Topo Map: Sand Canyon.

(Left) Armijo homestead before restoration. (Right) Log cabin in Homestead Canyon.

Homestead Canyon
(See map of Armijo Canyon, p. 94)

Getting there: Take NM 117 south about 33 miles to the Pie Town road and turn left. From this turnoff, go 3.3 miles until you see a two-track road to the left (east) and take this road to the wilderness boundary.

This canyon to the north of Armijo Canyon holds one of the area's best homesteads, but it requires some hunting to find it. Begin by hiking up the road about 0.6 miles, and at a faint track, head right (south). Sandstone cliffs surround an open area, and you'll come across old fences and unused irrigation ditches that hint of human activity. On a low hill in the middle of the flat is the long, log cabin with three south-facing doors with door handles formed from heavy wire. The logs at its base are as big around as a stout man. Although the ceiling has collapsed, you can still see the wood-and-mud chinking and cardboard used as insulation. Adjacent outbuildings include a root cellar, a bunkhouse, and a collapsed outhouse (two-seater). Because of trees on the north side of the hill, the cabin is visible only from the south side.

Return north to the road, which winds pleasantly through piñon, juniper, and rabbit brush and up over a ridge. The road disappears at one arroyo, where a flash flood wiped it out a few years ago. Watch for tracks up the other side. The road will reach the top of a ridge and then angle down to another road cherry-stemmed into the wilderness area. On that road is another homestead.

Distance: About 9 miles, round-trip, including detour to find the homestead.
Time: 5 hours.
Difficulty: Easy hike over level to rolling terrain; some gentle hills. Good winter or cold-weather hike.
Topo Map: Sand Canyon.

Treasure Stories
I've heard that the definition of a miner is a damn liar with a hole in the ground. And a prospector is a damn liar without anything but a dang good imagination. You can talk to most of 'em, and dang near ever' one of 'em tells you about some rich prospect they struck. But they're always broke and beggin' a grubstake. If their mines was half as rich as their imaginations, they could take a handpick and a gold pan and make more money in a month than most bank presidents could by wearin' out a half a dozen fountain pens.

Bob Lewis, prospector, cowboy and peace officer

The malpais's tortured surface and hidey holes have provided refuge to villains and fodder for tall tales of hidden treasure. In more than a century of intense searching, nobody has found a dime's worth of gold in the malpais, but that doesn't dim the stories. In fact they've been grist for countless con artists, who found their treasure in the wallets of the gullible and greedy.

The Lost Adams Diggings
The best-known tale of all, that of "The Lost Adams Diggings," begins in 1864. A freighter named J. J. Adams joined a party of miners to follow a Mexican man called Gotch Ear, who said he knew where there was gold. Gotch Ear had been captured by Apaches as a child. He would lead the group, he said, for a small payment. Because Adams was the only one who had horses, he became leader of the party. Traveling northeast from Gila

Bend, Arizona, the twenty-one men crossed country where they encountered no white men and didn't see a landmark any knew by name. Days out they crossed a trail Gotch Ear said would lead to a fort in the malpais, probably Fort Wingate, then located near present-day San Rafael. "Adams, as he subsequently demonstrated over and over, had almost no sense of direction and was very poor at retaining in memory any picture of any route he went over," wrote J. Frank Dobie in *Apache Gold and Yaqui Silver.*

Through a narrow canyon over timbered ground covered with lava rock, they followed Gotch Ear, who pointed out two cone-shaped mountains to the northeast. Finally they entered a Z-shaped canyon, where a boulder concealed the entrance. The rough trail along the canyon bottom stopped near running water, just below a low waterfall. Wasting no time they set to panning and found gold instantly—in one story "as big as wild turkey eggs." They paid Gotch Ear, and he left in the dark.

The next day the gold diggers got visitors: Chief Nana and thirty other Apaches, who didn't seem to mind the miners. The Indians did warn the men to stay below the waterfall, because they were camped above. Those with equipment continued panning, while others cut logs and built a cabin. After ten days of activity, the party was low on supplies. Six men, led by a man named John Brewer, left to buy supplies at Fort Wingate. Meanwhile a few greedy sorts crept above the falls for some surreptitious panning and found even bigger nuggets.

When the supply party failed to return after eight days, Adams and another man set out to find them. At the canyon's entrance, they found all but Brewer dead, and hid the bodies in a crevice for burial later. Hurrying back they were confronted with a more terrifying sight; the cabin was in flames, surrounded by hundreds of noisy Apaches waving mutilated body parts. Waiting until dark Adams and Davidson crept toward the cabin, where they had been hiding their gold, but they couldn't budge the collapsed rafters, and the stones were too hot to touch. Adams did snatch one nugget he had stashed near a tree. Then they turned their horses loose and quietly fled on foot.

After wandering for thirteen days and nearly starving, they encountered soldiers who took them to Fort Apache, Arizona. There a jumpy Adams saw an Apache riding what he insisted was one of his horses. He killed the man and was jailed. Escaping two nights later, he fled to California. Adams spent the rest of his life talking about his diggings, trying to find backers and organizing expeditions. Each one ended with Adams professing confusion, and a couple of times members of his party, who thought they'd been conned, nearly killed him. One member of an 1875 expedition, D. P. Carr of Georgetown, denounced Adams and his diggings as a fraud in 1890. Adams died in 1886 in a final, futile search for his diggings.

There were indications that Adams was telling the truth. The trader at Fort Wingate remembered six men buying supplies, paying in gold, and returning in the direction of the malpais. Another man found human skeletons in a rock crevice. In 1888 the missing Brewer told a tale of a Mexican guide, a canyon full of gold, and an ambush by Apaches. He had escaped on foot to the east and had been a trapper in northern Colorado, unaware of the widely circulated "Lost Adams Diggings" stories. Brewer likewise could never relocate the diggings. Davidson died soon after he escaped but left a map and diary that claimed the gold was on Zuni land. The men who obtained his map were also unsuccessful.

In the years since, hundreds have tried to find the Lost Adams Diggings—by foot, by horseback, by jeep, and from the air. Old-timers in the Grants area remember an old prospector named Malpais Joe, who claimed he'd found gold in the area and was always looking for somebody to stake him.

People have argued for years about where the diggings might be. While persistent accounts of Adams's recollections place the canyon four days' ride south of Ft. Wingate, some have insisted that the twin peaks were likely Bell Butte and D-Cross Peak in Socorro County and that the Indians were Alamo Navajos, not Apaches. (Alamo Navajos were known to intermarry with Apaches.) The grandson of Cochise said the diggings were in the Sierra Madres of Mexico. One Grants-area rancher said in the 1930s that Adams and a partner had mined in the Zuni Mountains. A story published in the *El Paso Herald* in the 1930s described the expedition as traveling between Magdalena and San Raphael. Others have said the place was in the Carrizo Mountains or near Silver City, Magdalena, Reserve, or Ft. Apache. The *Encyclopedia of Buried Treasure* reported that a party of trappers found the gold in the Black Range of eastern Arizona. A booklet published in El Paso in 1935 concluded that the diggings were near Datil.

Still other accounts show that Adams's credibility had worn thin much earlier. The *Grant County Herald* in 1881 called the diggings "a mere chimera" and advised fortune hunters to turn their attention to the real wealth of the Mogollon Mountains. One of the diggings seekers, the paper said, had actually struck gold near Silver City but left it behind to continue his quest; others later claimed his strike. In 1890 the *Albuquerque Daily Citizen* insisted, "The whole business is a lie." A man who knew Adams in California told the newspaper, "Adams is a counterfeit. The truth is not in him, sir, and never was. May the Lord have mercy on such men."

A Magdalena old-timer named Bob Lewis, who knew Adams, speculated that Adams had actually ambushed a caravan carrying a fortune in placer gold from California. "I know from Adams' personal character that he was not above ambushing such a caravan," he told a WPA writer in 1938. "I later saw a handful of this gold that Adams had saved when he buried the rest and it was a quality entirely foreign to that part of New Mexico and identical to some I had seen from California diggin's." Lewis said he set out in 1918 to find the bodies of the massacred Adams party and found five bodies about thirty miles northwest of Magdalena. An acquaintance, he said, found about twenty thousand dollars buried a few miles away.

In 1916 an advertisement in the *Gallup Independent* advised that Captain John Samuel Jones, who had spent a lot of money searching for the diggings over a ten-year period, had obtained new information from a nephew of one of the original Adams party. He offered to lead an expedition for expenses plus half the find. "[Neither] penniless schemers nor soldiers of fortune need apply," the ad stated. "This is a business proposition." The same newspaper reported five years later that Old Man Johnson "finally got discouraged in his 40 years' hunt for the Adams lost diggings and blew out his brains . . . He evidently lost faith in the policy of perseverance. Hundreds of other prospectors have sought out the familiar Adams diggings with no more success than the old man who spent so many years in the hunt for gold."

"In the malpais or out of the malpais, why can't the gold be found?" Dobie asked. "There is in the South-west no such thing as a canyon that a man with a pick and a burro has not picked into or walked over. Indeed, there is hardly a canyon in New Mexico or Eastern Arizona that some version of the Lost Adams Diggings has not led directly to." Dobie began his own quest in 1925—a search for the diggings' searchers. They came in two varieties—the true believers and casual searchers. The former, usually mountain rats and prospectors who devoted their lives to the search, usually believed in ghosts and signs "and all in luck—a luck pronounced impossible by geology." Most were "queer, eccentric, cranky." Dobie did find several who claimed they had found the diggings but were chased off by Indians, who knew that white men's lust for gold would bring more white men and ultimately the loss of their land.

In May 1890 a Kingston newspaper reported that Thomas Fitzpatrick, a mine superintendent, claimed to have found the "original and only Adams diggings, and they are 300 feet under the ground. Ore is a little higher grade than the old man Adams ever gave the public to understand." *The Shaft* described the ore as "silver glance ore."

Two who knew the diggings tales best, Dobie and *Albuquerque Tribune* columnist Howard Bryan, never desired to look for the Adams Diggings.

Frank Childers, an old-timer who had poked around the malpais, said, "There's a lot of windies told about them malpies. I've known a half-dozen people that died lookin' here for the Adams Diggings, and they never did find it."

But let's give the last word to one of the seekers, mountain man and trapper Nat Straw. "I know 10,000 places where the Lost Adams Diggings ain't," he said as an old man. "The Adams Diggins is a shadowy naught that lies in the valley of fanciful thought."

The Great Train Robbery

The Atlantic & Pacific Railroad's number 2 eastbound rumbled into Grants at 8:00 P.M. on October 8, 1897, and the shooting began. The express clerk fastened the doors of the express car and fled. The engineer dove under a loading platform. The train's twenty-one-year-old fireman, Henry Abel, started to run, but a bullet through his hat brim convinced him to stick around. Two men with six-shooters ordered him to get in the cab and pull the train farther east, after they had uncoupled the passenger cars.

At the stockyards on the east side of Grants, the rest of the gang waited. Two men held the horses, and six others stood guard. They blew open the door of the baggage car and then its safe and loaded a hundred thousand dollars in gold and currency into sugar sacks. They handed Abel a bottle of whiskey for the engineer and gave him fifteen dollars, "to have some fun." Then they rode into the malpais. Accounts differ about who robbed the train, whether they were brought to justice, and what became of the loot.

One old-timer said that the gang rode south of San Rafael and circled back on an old road used by herds of wild horses, where their tracks wouldn't show, finally arriving at what would later be homesteader Cecil Moore's place. The law brought famed Navajo scout Jeff King from Ft. Wingate to help track the gang, and they caught up with them near Fence Lake. In the gunfight that ensued, several robbers died and two—Bill "Kid" Johnson and Bronco Bill—were captured. Bronco Bill had a shattered arm and died in the Santa Fe penitentiary. Red Pitkin, Two Finger Jack, and Doug Perry escaped. Red and Two Finger Jack, were later captured, and Perry's partner shot him for the reward money.

"The law pressed the fugitives so closely that they cached the gold somewhere in the malpais, where it remains to this day," Gary Tietjen wrote in his history.

According to a WPA writer's account, a sheriff aided by Indian trackers found the robbers—Bronco Bill, Red

Pitkin and Billy Johnson—and ran off their horses. But the robbers shot and killed the sheriff and chased off the trackers and deputies. They buried the gold and walked to the Block Bar Ranch, where they bought horses. Lawman George Scarboro overtook the outlaws, shot Billy Johnson off his horse, and wounded Pitkin and Bronco Bill.

Dan "Red" Pitkin cropped up in Gallup in 1918, where he was arrested for shooting a marshal. The *Gallup Independent* described Pitkin as a former undersheriff, an ex-con and a leading Republican of the town, who was once implicated in a Santa Fe Railroad robbery. According to a more reliable account, Bronco Bill served his time in the Santa Fe penitentiary, was pardoned in 1917, and died later in a fall from a ranch windmill. Another popular account holds that the robbers were Black Jack Christian's gang, while another says the perpetrator was actually Black Jack's brother Bob, riding with George Musgrave and Theodore James. And because of the confusion in names, others believe Black Jack Ketchum, another notorious train robber, did the deed. Whoever did it, the gold was never recovered, fueling rumors that it's still hidden in the malpais.

In 1947 George Congden of Gallup wrote *New Mexico Magazine* that twelve years earlier, he had accompanied a writer into the malpais who wanted to resolve the question of hidden train-robbery loot. The writer had met a man named Twadell, who had prospected the malpais in 1897, hoping to find the Lost Adams Diggings or some other riches. Twadell had stayed in an old log cabin in the malpais. Returning after a week's travels, he heard voices in his cabin and decided to stay out of sight. He overheard three men talking about a lot of money and jewelry and learned that they intended to head south to Mexico after they got supplies from San Rafael the next day.

With two of the men gone, Twadell rode up to the cabin, but the remaining man began shooting, so Twadell returned fire and killed the stranger. Twadell removed part of the floor, buried the money he found, and left the corpse behind. He turned the man's horse out about fifteen miles south. Inquiring in San Rafael, he learned that the other two men had never shown up.

Twadell intended to accompany the writer to the cabin site, but he got sick and instead provided a map and clear directions. Congden had no trouble locating the cabin site, which by 1939 was a pile of burned rubble. He figured from the evidence remaining that the cabin was inhabited until about 1915 and had burned around 1920. Congden and the writer sifted through the ash carefully, until they found a disturbed area in the earth underneath and dug three feet down. "We at last concluded that someone else had discovered the hiding place and taken the money previously," he wrote.

The two men drove down the west side of the malpais to a roadside store, where they met an old man who had lived in the area for forty years. The old man said that in 1900, a horse had wandered into his feed lot with scraps of a saddle still clinging to it—probably the horse Twadell had turned loose.

Frank Childers had another story of Twadell, whom he described as an old man, partly paralyzed. Twadell poked around the malpais for a year or so by himself, and then his wife ran out on him. In 1932 he asked Childers for help. He told Childers that he and another man "had done something down Mexico way 40 years before. They thought officers were after them," Childers said. The partner said he knew of a place to hide and headed for the malpais.

They rode up to the cabin, where a light was on. Hungry and cold, they hollered greetings, and three men came out shooting. Everyone was killed but Twadell, who entered the cabin and found fifty thousand dollars in gold spread our on a table, apparently in the process of being divided. He figured it was from a train robbery. "Twadell said he already had about a thousand dollars on him, so he didn't take any of the money, but he dug a hole in the corner of the cabin and buried the whole $50,000. He headed across country and didn't come back for 30-odd years."

Childers said that he and Twadell found the cabin and that a local man remembered that years before someone had found four men shot in a gunfight. They went over every inch of the cabin and didn't find a single gold piece.

Hazel Fallon Rogers, of Thoreau, once said her father knew an old man at Ramah who had changed his name and always slept with a gun under his head. Her father heard that the man and his gang had robbed a train and hidden the money in the lava.

Cubero Gold

Charles Lummis heard a story on his cross-country trek about gold buried in a hillside near Cubero.

A Spanish expedition was returning from California, and hundreds of burros plodded under the weight of gold. Apaches attacked, and the Spaniards dug into a nearby hillside, timbered the tunnel, and hid their gold dust and nuggets (quite an accomplishment under siege!).

The few survivors reached Chihuahua and attempted unsuccessfully to return.

One survivor tried to raise money in Europe for an expedition and died in the attempt, but not before confiding to the German man who cared for him. The German then arrived in Cubero with a map and instructions, hired a few trustworthy men, and began digging in a hill near McCartys. But the German became sick and died, and the workers gave up on the search. Others followed—local Hispanics, ranchers, railroaders—until one group of locals reached loose earth and a timbered tunnel. "But no sooner did they strike the cavity than appalling noises rushed forth, and believing the place haunted, they ran away never to return," Lummis wrote.

There is a similar story about The Narrows. Here, legend has it, Spaniards hurriedly secreted in the lava fifteen burro loads of silver bullion. They were subsequently killed by Indians, but a snake symbol carved in the sandstone marks the spot.

The White House

In 1933 H. W. Stowell, exploring the malpais with a friend, encountered a campsite and waited for its occupant to arrive. It was "a typical old-timer," who invited them to share his camp. Stowell was sure the old-timer was there treasure hunting. "I've knocked around quite a bit, and pried into some queer places, but this is the roughest country in the whole U.S.A.," the old-timer said. "There's a yarn about the mysterious white house of the malpais, a cliff dwelling which several have seen from a distance, but which no one has been able to reach. From one of the big craters I saw it once in the last rays of the setting sun. It might have been a piece of lava turned up and stained white, but it sure looked like a house to me. There was a guy flying around over this lava bed with an aeroplane on and off for a year, but he couldn't locate it."

Gary Tietjen tells of three local men running cattle on the edge of the malpais, and one, a Navajo man named Baltazar Coho, spotted a large white house or church, but he was never able to find the place again.

In yet another version, a white pueblo supposedly lies out in the malpais near The Narrows, but those who see it are never able to find it again. In a treasure-hunters' magazine article, one writer recounts a tale told to him by an old Acoma man that peaceful people once inhabited small pueblos in the area. Harried by a more warlike tribe, the small pueblos decided to band together and build a city in the malpais. Then they torched their villages, destroying grain and tools, and moved to the new pueblo. Medicine men cursed with violent death any outsider who might find the village. (We've learned that Indian people have been known to tell tall tales to anthropologists and anyone else they consider a pest and then chuckle at the white man's gullibility.)

To his credit, however, the writer flew and hiked the malpais and concluded that the white pueblo was probably the ruin called Candelaria Ruin, on the eastern edge of the lava flow. Others have speculated that the white pueblo might be concealed in a lava tube, but he dismissed that theory, because prospectors searching for uranium in the 1950s walked and flew every inch of the Grants area without finding it. Those claiming to have found the pueblo, he wrote, "were stretching the truth a bit." A Grants local confirmed his impression, saying, "Sure, there's a White Pueblo ruin out in the malpais. Only thing is that it's enchanted. If you believe hard enough, someday you'll find it."

Other Tales

Another popular and persistent tale holds that during the Pueblo Revolt in 1680, Zunis hid a golden church bell in the malpais. In another story, there are two silver church bells hidden in a cave. A third story tells of Spanish colonists who built a settlement in the midst of lava beds and later, fleeing Indian attacks, hid their wealth in the malpais.

In one legend a traveler heard the sound of a church bell while traveling through the malpais near Acomita. Looking up he beheld a vision of a church with a golden bell. But he could never find the place again.

Still other legends describe old Spanish mines in malpais caves. Stowell's codger said a Mexican guide once showed him an ice cave "and frozen solid in the clear glass wall, I'll be damned if there wasn't an old man with red whiskers. A bit further on we came on nine human skeletons scattered promiscuous like under a tree. Thar's more curious things than that in these parts."

Modern Seekers

These wild tales circulate today, proving that P.T. Barnum wasn't wrong. In 1991 the FBI, Acoma police, and the county sheriff nabbed three men who had illegally tunneled 55 feet into Acoma land looking for buried treasure. Despite a lot of brave talk, nobody found anything. And in 1992 law enforcement officials raided a treasure hunters' camp of twenty men who had paid five thousand dollars to a fast-talker promising to lead them to gold.

Treasure hunters routinely vandalize ruins and destroy natural features and then claim federal agents are conspiring to keep the goodies for themselves. Probably the only thing ever hidden in the malpais was an occasional bandit or deserter. The only real malpais treasure, besides its scenery, is its trove of tall tales.

2

Mt. Taylor

Mt. Taylor

Most sacred is the bulk of Tsotsil, blue as a summer rainstorm, where it watches, from its high and level plateau, the black caterpillar trains of the Santa Fe crawl across the cindery plain between the Rio Grande and the Rio Puerco . . . Like the teocalli of the Aztecs, it rises from the mesa platform, a pyramidal, solitary mass of broken cones . . . For a whole day's travel, east and west, it dominates the landscape to the north of the railway, a semicircular volcanic mass, having a secondary cone within, one clear creek, and a giant's tongue of black lava protruded down the shallow red sandstone cañon where the railway follows the old trail past Acoma to Zuni. Tsotsil, it is called by the Navajo, in reference to the lava tongue, and, ceremonially, Blue Turquoise Mountain, sacred world altar of the South.

Mary Austin, 1924

(Pages 106–7)
Mt. Taylor, elevation 11,301 feet.

We like [Albuquerque] because our front yard stretches as far as you can see and because old Mt. Taylor, 65 miles away, is like a framed picture in our front window.

Ernie Pyle, 1942

Not every mountain has had a whiskey named after it. In April 1934 Anchor Grocery & Liquor Co. of Albuquerque began selling a three-year-old bourbon named Mt. Taylor. By June the firm reported heavy demand for its new brand. Today hikers, campers, and participants in the Mt. Taylor Quadrathlon know a different kind of high; from the top at 11,301 feet, you can see nearly a third of New Mexico.

Taylor is actually a smallish mountain perched on a vast, 8,200-foot pedestal of mesas, which are about 2,000 feet above the surrounding area. In 1933 one writer described the "Mt. Taylor wilderness" as a "sparsely settled area of about 800 square miles, extending northeast toward the Rio Puerco, as desolate, but weirdly beautiful a series of bad lands as one will ever see. The lava-capped mesa from which Mt. Taylor rises is 47 miles long from northeast to southwest and 23 miles broad." The mountain has been important to all the people who have lived here and has names in at least nine languages, including English, Spanish, Navajo, Acoma, Zuni, Tewa, Tiwa, Towa, Keresan, and Apache.

To Navajos it's Tsoodził, the Blue Bead Mountain, and one of their four Great Sacred Peaks. The Navajo creation story tells how First Man and First Woman climbed from four worlds below into this world, which had no form. They made the four sacred peaks in the cardinal directions: Sisnaajiní (Blanca Peak) in the east, Tsoodził

(Mt. Taylor) in the south, Dook'o'oosłííd (San Francisco Peak) in the west, and Dibé Ntsaa (Hesperus Peak) in the north. After creating Mt. Taylor, they fastened it to the sky with a great stone knife and decorated it with turquoise, dark mist, and animals. On the south slope, they placed two bluebird eggs and covered them with a sacred buckskin to make them hatch. That's why there are a lot of bluebirds on Mt. Taylor to this day.

These four mountains and the land bounded by them are the source of strength and health of Navajo people. Each is the home of supernatural beings who help heal the sick, send rain for farming, and protect people from harm. And each mountain has an inner, holy being that communicates with other holy beings, with those on the earth's surface, and with the wind. In every ceremony Navajos call on the mountains and their beings for aid, protection, peace, and prosperity. In addition on top of each peak is a sky pillar that holds the sky and the sun at a safe distance. Traditional Navajos carry prayer bundles with soil from each of the sacred mountains. They also believe the sacred mountains should not be climbed unless it's done respectfully, with prayer and song.

Acomas call the mountain Kaweshtima, where the Rainmaker of the North lives. Zunis once made an annual summer pilgrimage here, but now come only during a drought to visit a hole on the peak called Shiwanna Gacheti (lightning home). Closure of the hole can cause drought, so members of certain religious orders open the hole and pray. All of the tribes collect herbs here, and they once came here for obsidian.

The mountain's spiritual quality wasn't lost on Spanish settlers, either. They honored it with the name of a saint, San Mateo. Americans, however, named it for a president. In 1849 Lt. James H. Simpson of the U.S. Army's topographical engineers rode through the Zuni Mountains. In the distance, he wrote, "we caught sight, for the first time, of one of the finest mountain peaks I have seen in this country." He named it Mount Taylor, in honor of President Zachary Taylor. "Erecting itself high above the plain below, an object of vision at a remote distance, standing within the domain which has been so recently the theater of his sagacity and prowess, it exists, not inappropriately, the ever-enduring monument to his patriotism and integrity."

The name didn't immediately stick. In his diary of a trip to Navajo country in 1855, W. W. H. Davis, U.S. attorney for the Territory of New Mexico, refers to "old Mount Mateo." Over time Mt. Taylor and its range came to be called the San Mateo Mountains, leading to years of confusion because of another San Mateo range in Socorro County.

Mt. Taylor has provided minerals and timber, but its possibilities for recreation were also recognized early.

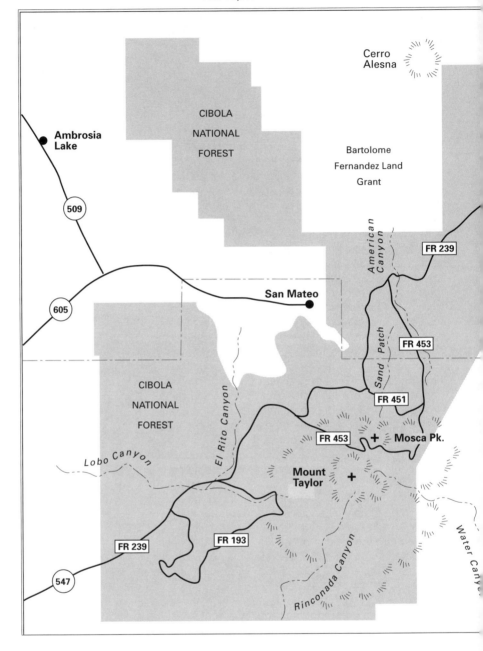

The U.S. Forest Service had a trail up the peak as early as 1933. And since the 1960s, promoters have studied it off and on for a ski area.

Geology

The Mt. Taylor volcanic field consists of the mountain itself, along with its platform of lava-covered, eight-thousand-foot mesas: Mesa Chivato, La Jara Mesa, San Fidel Mesa, and Horace Mesa. Mt. Taylor is the oldest volcano in the

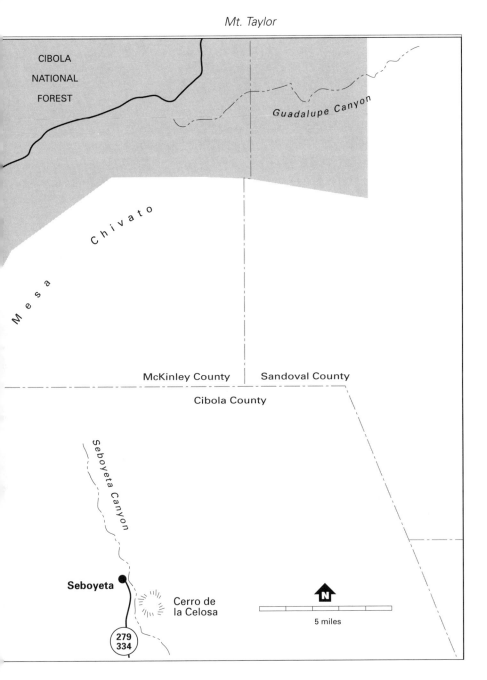

area and was most active between 3.3 million and 2.5 million years ago. Its horseshoe-shaped crater was once thought to be the bowl left by an earth-rending explosion, a la Mt. St. Helens, but in recent years, geologists have concluded that the cause is less dramatic— volcanic activity followed by the quiet hand of erosion.

The first eruptions here created Grants Ridge (north of Grants) and not Mt. Taylor. About 3.3 million years ago, in late Pliocene times, rhyolite magmas moved up

White deposits on Grants Ridge are perlite.

through fractures in the crust. They didn't flow but rather oozed out and piled up. Gases trapped in the lava as bubbles exploded at the same time, forming pumice, a kind of foamy volcanic glass, which has been mined here as perlite since the 1940s. Successive eruptions coated the region over the next million years with layers of ash and pumice. Near the vent falling rock, ash, and pumice collected as rhyolite tuff.

Soon after eruptions ceased at Grants Ridge, about 3 million years ago, they began in the area of My. Taylor's present crater. The cone largely began with eruptions of rhyolite lavas and tuffs, but quartz latite eruptions between 3 million and 2.6 million years ago built most of the volcano. Finally, over a 200,000 to 300,000-year period beginning about 2.6 million years ago, there was an eruption of latite from a summit above the present crater, and those flows formed cliffs and capped the flanks of the cone. All through the time of the Grants Ridge and Mt. Taylor eruptions, flows from basalt cinder cones around the base coated the sur-

rounding land with a protective cap that allowed it to erode into mesas. They now account for about 80 percent of the Mt. Taylor volcanic field.

Taylor wasn't as angry as its siblings in the Jemez. At its most active, it produced about one-tenth the volume of lava over the same period of time. And there were probably no earth-shattering blasts that blew the mountaintop away. Instead the slow and quiet process of erosion, which began even as the volcano was most active, wore away the crater to its present size and shape, ultimately reducing the volume of the cone by 15 percent and leaving behind lava masses and dikes. The highest point on the crater's rim, Mt. Taylor, and La Mosca ("mosquito") Peak, are all that remain. With sister peaks they form a ridge that partially encircles the five-mile-square crater, which is now the western end of Water Canyon.

Visitors and even New Mexicans often assume that Mt. Taylor's eruptions created El Malpais. In 1879 Captain Clarence E. Dutton, of the U.S. Geological Survey, was the first to observe that Mt. Taylor was obviously older than the flows of the malpais. Dutton wrote that "the rather imposing pile of Mount Taylor . . . stands upon a very large mesa of Cretaceous strata everywhere heavily capped with ancient lavas, some of which came from the great central pile and some from the parasitic cones which surround it.

"The scenery is strong and somewhat impressive, for the component masses of the landscape are all large . . . Mount Taylor, however, is exceptional, for this is a great mountain, with a roughly conical peak, with long sharp tumbling spurs, deeply incised ravines and intervening buttresses."

One unheralded but spectacular feature of the mountain is its ring of some fifty volcanic necks, most of them in the Rio Puerco valley (see Cabezon, p. 143). These necks formed when lava cooled and solidified in the throats of volcanos and erosion wore away the cinder cones. The biggest, Cabezon ("big head"), at 7,785 feet, is bigger than Devil's Tower in Wyoming.

Flora and Fauna
Describing blooms, bugs, and bunnies on Mt. Taylor is imprecise because information is either scant or dated. The U.S. Forest Service has never done a baseline survey of the mountain, and academic studies are more than twenty years old. But from what is available, along with reports and observations, we have an idea. Mt. Taylor has three of six transcontinental life zones occurring in New Mexico. The lower mesas and lower slopes, from 5,000 to 7,000 feet, are Upper Sonoran, the major zone with piñon and juniper trees and some ponderosa pine and cottonwoods along streams. Grasslands encircle the base. In the Transition zone, from 7,000 to 8,500 feet on northeast slopes and 8,000 to 9,500 feet on southwest slopes, ponderosa pine and Gambel oak dominate. There are Douglas fir and aspen on north-facing slopes and piñon on lower slopes. This zone also has small meadows of iris and a variety of grasses. Above 9,500 feet, mostly on peaks and high ridges, is the Canadian zone, with dense forests of Engelmann spruce, Douglas fir, and aspen. In the south and west, the face you see from I-40, are high meadows of forbs, grass, and lupine. One of the mountain's mysteries is this bald face, where logic would have trees. Biologists figure the exposure to sun and wind here, the high elevation, and the rocky soil have discouraged the forest.

The climate is mild and the weather generally dry, except for daily rains in July and August and heavy snows in winter. Rainfall ranges from ten inches on the west to twenty-five inches on top of the mountain, mostly from summer thunder showers. The only permanent sources of water are in upper Lobo Canyon and Water Canyon.

Birds are reportedly diverse and include wild turkeys and a few Mexican spotted owls. A 1906 Forest Service inventory of the area reported green-winged teal, sandpipers, killdeer, grouse, doves, eagles, hawks, and burrowing owls. Forest Service inventories in the 1930s reported that the collared peccary, or javelina, was found in the San Mateo mountains, as were wild turkeys, and scaled quail.

In 1960 University of New Mexico researcher Eugene Schroeder identified thirty-six species of mammals on Mt. Taylor. They included the wandering shrew; desert and eastern cottontails; blacktailed jackrabbit; cliff and Colorado chipmunks; rock, Abert's, and red squirrels; valley and northern pocket gophers; western harvest, deer, and brush mice; Mexican wood rat; long-tailed and Mexican voles; porcupine; gray fox; black bear; long-tailed weasel; skunk; elk; and mule deer.

The humble deer mouse was the most common inhabitant. Mule deer lived in all areas, and the Colorado chipmunk was found in all habitats except forb-grass meadows. Abert's squirrels preferred the west slope. Red squirrels and northern pocket gophers favored high elevations, while the brush mouse was fond of low elevation, rocky slopes and canyon walls. Schroeder didn't find coyotes, but believed they lived here. And he found a bobcat skull on a mesa fifteen miles north of Mt. Taylor.

He mentioned just one environmental impact: "Mexican voles in this area have had their habitat seriously limited by cattle grazing." But human impact hasn't fazed the porcupines. They were holding out in great numbers everywhere on the mountain, despite the num-

Mt. Taylor's bald face is probably the result of exposure to sun and wind, along with high elevation and rocky soil.

bers killed by ranchers, Forest Service employees, and others.

Schroeder described six species of bats: long-eared, long-legged, fringe-tailed, silver-haired, hoary, Brazilian free-tailed, and big brown. The latter was the most common.

Three introduced species are thriving here. Beaver have built some spectacular dams in Water Canyon and Lobo Canyon. Elk are now so numerous that in some places they threaten the deer. And the Barbary sheep's numbers are large enough to permit hunting.

Wolves, grizzlies, and mountain lions don't live here anymore. In 1916 a hunter bagged the last grizzly, twelve miles east of San Mateo. They were common here before 1900. A few mountain lions roamed the area around 1905 but had disappeared by the 1940s. In 1916 trappers took five wolves and a few years later found a den twelve miles northeast of Mt. Taylor with four wolf pups. A pup from this den probably became the mascot of the University of New Mexico. According to UNM history, a government trapper named Jim Young caught a wolf cub near Mt. Taylor in 1921 and gave it to the university. The sports teams, then called the "university boys," became the Lobos. UNM cheerleaders brought their wolf to every game. It grew tame but bit a child who teased it. Officials destroyed what was likely the state's last wolf, "for fear other illbred brats might become tempted to play with the wolf and bring on a damage suit."

History

Cebolleta

Navajos lived on and around Mt. Taylor from at least the sixteenth century. In 1730 Bishop Benito Crespo was taken with the prospect of making converts at "the place of the pagans, called Cebolletas," near Laguna. Spaniards then called the mountain and the bench it sat on Cebolleta ("tender onion") and in 1746 gave the same name to a mission they established for Navajos on the mountain's eastern flank. Within a year the Navajos left; the first colonists arrived about two decades later.

In 1767 King Carlos III issued a land grant west of Mt. Taylor to Bartólome Fernández. The following year Ignacio Chávez received a grant for land just north of Cebolleta, and Santiago Durán y Chaves petitioned for a land grant called Los Ojos de San Mateo, near San Mateo Springs on Mt. Taylor. Others moved to the northeast, in the Rio Puerco valley. Typically grantees were directed to take possession of land, provided "it does not displace Apache/Navajos or interfere with their cornfields." For a brief time, colonists and Navajos knew peace, but the Navajos came to resent these intruders and, with the Apaches, began raiding ranchos and settlements.

Bartólome Fernández was one of the officers who intercepted the explorer Zebulon Pike after he strayed into Spanish territory. Fernández had stocked his ranch with churro sheep and long-legged Mexican cattle, both hardy animals that could withstand drought and rough terrain, but he spent the rest of his days trying to protect his stock, herders, and property from Navajo raids.

In 1800 thirty families from Atrisco, near Albuquerque, settled at the abandoned mission of Cebolleta, promising the Spanish governor they would form a community and not abandon it. They confirmed their commitment by throwing stones in the air, pulling weeds, and shouting "God save the king" three times. They quickly began building a walled compound. Houses faced the plaza with only portholes in back. The tenfoot-high wall had two entrances of two-foot thick ponderosa pine with *torreones* (lookout towers). One torreon lasted into the early part of this century, and portions of the walls still stand. In 1820 they completed a church, Nuestra Señora de Los Dolores (Our Lady of Sorrows), which still survives.

The Cebolletaños spent decades fighting Navajos. As colonists gained in strength and numbers, the attacks and counterattacks grew increasingly vicious, and both sides took slaves. The Cebolletaños apparently became so proficient that Rio Grande settlers routinely commissioned them to capture Navajo children for slaves.

The most storied warrior was Manuel Antonio Chaves, whose skills as an Indian fighter earned him the name "El Leoncito" ("the little lion") among his peers. Chaves, who was nine when his family arrived in Cebolleta in 1827, came from a long and distinguished line of military and public officials, who could trace their lineage to twelfth-century Spain. His ancestors had fought the Moors, served under Don Juan de Oñate, and returned to New Mexico after the Pueblo Revolt with General Diego de Vargas.

In those days firepower was limited to clumsy flintlock muskets, and so Manuel became proficient with the bow and arrow. He fought the first of more than a hundred Indian battles at age sixteen. At eighteen, he started trading with the Navajos. During one trip, around 1834, the young Chaves set out with fourteen other young men to trade and possibly to take slaves. They came upon hundreds of Navajos gathered for a ceremonial. In a short but brutal fight, the Navajos killed everyone in the party but Manuel, who was left for dead with seven wounds, and an Indian boy servant, who was also wounded.

The two boys left the bloody scene and struggled homeward—two hundred miles without horses, water, or provisions and weakened by loss of blood. On the second day they reached Bear Springs, near the Zuni Mountains, and there the Indian boy died. Pushing himself on, Manuel came to a valley northwest of San Mateo Mountain. At a stream shaded by handsome oak trees, Manuel prayed that if he lived, he would return to the place and build a chapel. Days later, delirious, he encountered shepherds from his village, and they carried him home.

From that time forward, Manuel fought in a succession of Indian campaigns, against Navajos, Utes, and Apaches. Because Spanish, Mexican, and American governments could never spare enough soldiers to protect their settlements, especially an isolated place like Cebolleta, embattled colonists raised volunteer regiments. As his reputation grew, Chaves was called time after time to lead.

Manuel Antonio Chaves (Courtesy Museum of New Mexico, 9833.)

Chaves and his fellow warriors were never Indian haters, however. The historian Marc Simmons gives some perspective to this bloody period: "The Spanish people fought the Indians when they felt the occasion demanded it, but in times of peace they were quick to forget past grievances . . . (T)heir struggles with the Indians were tempered by the realization that they fought against a worthy foe, their long view tinged with no prejudice against race."

Chaves also helped put down the rebellion at Taos Pueblo, serving with Ceran St. Vrain, who became a good friend. When the Civil War erupted, he declined a commission in the Confederate Army and instead became a lieutenant colonel in the New Mexico Volunteers, under Kit Carson. In the Battle of Glorietta Pass in 1862, one of the bloodiest encounters of the Civil War, Chaves led four hundred men up a steep and difficult pass, where they destroyed the enemy's mules, wagons, and supplies, effectively ending the Confederate campaign in New Mexico.

With the end of the Civil War and the Indian campaigns, Chaves returned to ranching, but his accumulation of wounds gave him no peace. Those who knew Chaves said he sustained a wound for every battle and that his body was a network of scars. He died at home in 1889 at seventy-one. In this century, when his remains were moved to a cemetery, the casket contained two large musket balls, which he had carried to the grave.

San Mateo

Like its sister village on the opposite side of the mountain, little San Mateo has a long and bloody history. Cebolletaños as early as 1851 were exploring a grassy valley that hugged the northwestern flank of San Mateo Mountain. That year a party of Cebolleteños, led by Manuel's brother Pedro Chaves, a slave trader, camped in San Miguel Canyon, near present-day San Mateo. Stories differ; they were either exploring, returning from a military campaign against the Navajos, or fulfilling a contract for slave labor.

Tired and overconfident, they built a fire and played games and cards, scoffing at warnings from an Indian servant that they were being surrounded. "It was the hour when the devil gives advice and the evil take it," wrote local historian C. C. Marino. As they slept the Navajos struck with arrows and clubs "so that they awoke in the Eternity which Divine Providence had reserved for them . . ." The head of Pedro Chaves was found on top of Mt. Taylor. Only Chato Aragon survived. He dragged himself into a small cave. Each day for eleven days, he crawled to the stream to bathe his wounds and scratch a "raya" on the wall of an overhanging rock. Navajos returned to San Miguel Canyon, recalled an old Navajo warrior, to see if any Cebolletaños had come to look for their dead. They were horrified by the sight of Chato Aragon, writhing in pain, with an arrow protruding from his body. He was sobbing, muttering, and trying to get up. "Some of us said he was alive and it was necessary to kill him off to end his pain," the old Navajo said. "Others said it was his spirit calling to the spirits of the other dead men, and the chief ordered that none should touch him . . ."

The Indian servant had escaped and walked thirty miles to get help from Cebolleta, but the rescue party arrived minutes after Aragon died. For years Aragon's family made an annual pilgrimage to San Miguel Canyon to say the rosary. And in this century his marks still testified to his lonely death.

Stories also differ on who finally settled San Mateo. According to one account, when the Civil War ended, Manuel Chaves, remembering how his brother Pedro and others had died, declared it was time to take back land on the other side of Mt. Taylor from the Navajos. He organized a troop of forty men. They found fifteen hundred Navajos holding a *yeibichei* dance on the western side of the mountain and slaughtered every man, woman, and child. As Navajos were making their Long Walk to Bosque Redondo, Chaves brought his family to the place to live, founding the village of San Mateo. On the site of his desperate journey as a youth, he kept his promise to build a chapel and also erected a massive house of twenty-three rooms with thirty-inch-thick walls, surrounding a patio.

According to Marc Simmons, Chaves's half-brother, Román Baca, was the original founder. Baca, born in Cebolleta in 1833, was also a renowned Indian fighter who served under Kit Carson and a veteran of the Civil War. During Carson's 1863 campaign against the Navajos, Baca scouted the valley west of Mt. Taylor with a ranch in mind. He also knew well that this was the place of his brother's promise. After Baca and a group

Adobe ruin at San Mateo.

of Cebolletaños settled in the valley, founding San Mateo, he reserved the oak grove for Manuel, who moved there in 1876 and built his house and the chapel. Baca called his own forty-room house "La Providencia." He planted an orchard from seedlings brought from Mexico by priests and ran as many as forty thousand head of sheep, freighting the wool to St. Louis by oxteam, which returned with supplies and equipment. Over the years the brothers expanded their lands by acquiring land grants, including the massive Fernández Grant. Baca also claimed the San Mateo Springs grant and gained title in 1898. He served as a legislator and speaker of the house and held numerous county positions.

Indian raids continued for a time, even with many in confinement, but eventually residents enjoyed some peace. When they could devote themselves to farming, San Mateo settlers were the first to plant alfalfa, the result of an early village law requiring residents to reserve the craw of each wild goose and plant the seeds it held. They ate the new alfalfa as greens and gained a variety of wheat suited to the climate. For a time the Santa Fe–Prescott's six stagecoaches a week connected the village to the outside world, until the railroad put it out of business. Around Mt. Taylor there were stops at Puertocito, San Mateo, El Dado, Isawachie, and Cabezon.

Author-adventurer Charles Lummis, a friend of Román Baca's and a frequent guest, wrote that San Mateo was the only Spanish village in the territory whose Penitente procession included a crucifixion. Los Hermanos Penitentes, a religious society, was formed in the 1800s when settlements like San Mateo lacked priests. The Penitente brothers were known to have Holy Week ceremonies and processions that included self-flagellation in penance; some were so severe that it wasn't unusual for members to die. The processions, once open, went underground with the arrival of Americans. A 1924 newspaper account describes a Penitente procession in San Mateo. The *morada,* or chapter house of the brotherhood, had a chapel, altar, and rooms for members to live in during their retreat. From there a procession of masked brothers filed through the canyon and village led by someone playing on a *pito,* a homemade flute. Some followed dragging heavy crosses, while others beat themselves over one shoulder and then another with whips of braided yucca fiber, as women, children, and brothers chanted Spanish hymns.

They proceeded up a hill called El Calvario with one cross. When they returned, blood ran down their backs and soaked their trousers. Next they prayed at the graveyard and returned to the morada. According to the account, there were also Penitentes at Cebolleta, Cubero, and San Rafael. In the 1970s Penitentes were known to be active, but their practices were less severe.

Recent History

Mt. Taylor dealt commercial aviation its first setback. In the summer of 1929, Transcontinental Air Transport, Inc., an ancestor of TWA, combined plane and train to hurtle passengers across the country in the dizzying time of forty-eight hours. At a steep $350 one way, a traveler could fly by day and transfer to railroad Pullman cars by night. Charles Lindberg himself trained the pilots and mapped the route. When Albuquerque and Gallup were chosen as stops on the route, it was cause for excitement. In those days two planes landing in a week merited a newspaper story.

One early TAT passenger wrote of the western New Mexico scenery below, "The world below again strikes the note of scenic grandeur—stupendous bluffs of flaming red, hills of yellow, pink and black, the great lava flow that covers hundreds of square miles and still shows from the air the ripples where it heaved and twisted when hot. Oddly enough, the trees seem to grow best here . . ."

On September 3 the *City of San Francisco* took off from Albuquerque. Even though the company's weather service "was without equal in the world," according to accounts at that time, nobody anticipated a fierce thunderstorm on Mt. Taylor. The plane passed over Grants around 11:00 A.M. but then veered north to avoid an electrical storm. On September 4 the plane was reported missing with five passengers and three crew members. One passenger was local lumber tycoon A. B. McGaffey. The greatest airplane search in Southwest flying history began. Spurred by a five-thousand-dollar reward, local people on foot and horseback and in cars fanned out south and west of Gallup, where the plane was believed to be, but they were hindered by thunderstorms. Searchers found the charred plane two days later on the south side of Mt. Taylor. No one survived. Four local men were first to reach the crash site and did what they could before building a fire. They dragged up some steel boxes and sat down to wait for searchers. They later learned the boxes held fifty thousand dollars that was being transported from the Denver mint to the San Francisco mint.

San Mateo is best known today as home of one of New Mexico's oldest and biggest surviving cattle companies. The Fernandez Sheep Co. by 1916 had grown from the original land grant to be a sprawling cattle and sheep operation with three owners: A. B. McMillen, J. A. Jestro, and Manuel Chaves's son Amado. The younger Chaves then was a junior shareholder and apparently sold out to repay a bank debt. McMillen took over the operations and hired Floyd W. D. Lee as a cowboy. Lee worked up to ranch manager and in 1938 bought the ranch. His home and sheep-ranch headquarters were the former home of Manuel Chaves; he set up his cattle-ranch headquarters fifteen miles north, at El Dado ("the die"), a one-time stagecoach stop named for the loaded dice kept by the barkeep. Lee later bought checkerboard land (private sections of land alternating with government sections) from the Santa Fe Pacific Railroad. At one time the ranch's size was known to be three hundred thousand acres.

"Before the passage of the Taylor Grazing Act, those checkerboards caused much trouble," Lee wrote. "Homesteaders would come in and want to homestead a section so they could graze all of our land, use our water and our bulls. The method we used to overcome this would be to bring out about 10,000 head of sheep and just graze around and around the homesteader's section until there wasn't a bit of grass left . . . This may sound rather tough, but actually, we were doing the homesteader a favor. He couldn't possibly make a living off a section of land. He and his family would starve." The Fernandez Co., still owned by the Lee family, flourishes today and includes a surface coal mine.

As cattlemen were building the Fernandez empire, another kind of land consolidation was taking place on the mountain. The federal government established the Mount Taylor Forest Reserve on October 5, 1906, by proclamation of President Teddy Roosevelt. In 1908 the Mt. Taylor Reserve was combined with the Manzano Forest Reserve to form Manzano National Forest; the

*La Mosca Peak
fire lookout.*

Zuni reserve was added on September 10, 1914. Cibola National Forest was created in 1931 from portions of the former Datil, Zuni, Mt. Taylor, Magdalena, and Manzano forests.

In 1934 government works-project laborers finished work on a road to Malpais Springs in the Zuni Mountains and moved into Lobo Canyon. That summer twenty workers and seven teamsters began building a road up Mt. Taylor. Unskilled workers got a princely forty cents an hour, the teamsters seventy cents. Working six days a week, they could earn $19.20. An article in the *Grant Review* the same summer refers to a trail from Cañon Lobo ranger station to Mt. Taylor.

Logging on Mt. Taylor wasn't as intense or as destructive as it was in the Zuni Mountains. A Forest Service brochure dated 1934 shows Big Chief Lumber Co. as one of three timber operations in the area. That year Big Chief opened a planing mill in Grants, to make finished lumber, and operated logging camps on the mountain. Bernalillo Mercantile Co. also logged Mt. Taylor. In 1946 Bill and Red Prestridge contracted with New Mexico Timber Co., which had acquired even-numbered sections for $2.50 an acre from the railroad. The only road was rough, but "a model A Ford could kind of walk up on the rocks," Red Prestridge said. They built a log bridge and an oiled road. They lasted four years. Theirs was the last large-scale logging on Mt. Taylor.

The mountain has seen surprisingly little mining. WPA accounts describe locals scraping out coal for their own use. In 1938 the Barnsdall Tripoli Co. was operating a pumice mine eight miles north of Grants and milling it in town for use in cleansers, dentifrices, erasers, and acoustical instruments. U.S. Gypsum Co. later bought the operation and mines perlite to this day. The white scar from perlite mining can be seen for miles.

Today Mt. Taylor, for all its dominance of the horizon, is lightly used, and even on a weekend remains uncrowded compared to the platoons of picnickers, skiers, hikers, and bikers to be found in nearby Sandia and Jemez mountains. In its many quiet and beautiful spots, visitors can still sense that they keep company with the spirits of long-departed Navajos and Spanish settlers.

Hikes and Drives

Mt. Taylor has something for everyone: short, pleasant walks; pretty, secluded camping spots; challenging terrain for hikers and mountain bikers; jeep trails; and cross-country ski trails. And it's now home to one of winter sports' most demanding events, the Mt. Taylor Winter Quadrathlon. Alas it has just two developed hiking trails and one developed skiing trail. However, land features and old logging roads make other hikes and ski outings possible.

Mt. Taylor by Car

This is such a broad mountain with such a variety of possibilities, you might want to acquaint yourself with its network of roads. From Grants the Lobo Canyon Road, or NM 547, turns into Forest Road 239, which is a major arterial into Mt. Taylor. This road is maintained in the winter and leads to a lot of popular spots for tubing, snowmobiling, and cross-country skiing.

Tour #1: The Peaks

Four-wheel-drive or high-clearance vehicles are recommended; you can also drive within a mile or so of the top and walk the rest of the way. Six miles beyond the campground at El Rito Canyon, turn from FR 239 to FR 453, which takes you five miles to La Mosca, one of Taylor's peaks. The road passes the fire lookout on La Mosca and trails to Mt. Taylor and Water Canyon. It then tops a saddle between La Mosca and Taylor and drops down the back side of Mt. Taylor. The road balances atop slopes that appear to plunge endlessly before dissolving in deep woods. In American Canyon are broad, grassy meadows with an occasional cluster of oaks or aspens. We kept expecting to see Heidi or Julie Andrews skipping down the slope. Here, you can park and walk in any direction on these lava-strewn meadows that seem to float in the sky; from their edge you can see as far as Albuquerque. The stony point to the north is a volcanic plug called Cerro Alesna ("awl").

You can form a loop by continuing on FR 453 and reversing Tour #2.

Tour #2: San Mateo Springs–Spud Patch–American Canyon

Stay on FR 239 to a sign indicating San Mateo Springs. This is a miniwetland within a mixed-conifer forest. With its water source and varied vegetation, this place is heaven for birds and bird watchers. You can make the short walk up to the spring head or simply sit here and enjoy the scene. The place is musical with bird songs, chirping, peeping, chattering and warbling, punctuated by outbursts from a red squirrel. In minutes Kathleen and Steve pick out a Clark's nutcracker, chickadee, nuthatch, Steller's jay, and woodpecker.

Plant life here includes the Rocky Mountain maple, big aspens, fir trees, gooseberries, box elders, strawberries, columbines, yarrow, ferns, and other water lovers.

To reach the Spud Patch, continue on FR 239 about 0.4 miles and turn right onto FR 451. In less than 2 miles you come to the Spud Patch, a big grassy meadow surrounded by tree-covered hills and, on one side, sandstone chimneys. This is a favorite camping and picnic spot and a fine place to spend an afternoon walking and exploring. A couple of miles from the Spud Patch is American Canyon, another good place to camp or walk. From FR 451, turn onto FR 453 to La Mosca Peak.

Mt. Taylor Hikes

Gooseberry Springs

Getting there: The trailhead is off FR 193, a loop connecting to FR 239 at both ends. It's quicker to take the upper loop 5.2 miles to the trailhead. From the lower end, it's 12.2 miles. There is no trailhead marker but rather two small arrows and a small sign indicating Trail #77.

This is *the* trail to the top of Mt. Taylor (more delicate hikers, see Mt. Taylor Trail). The Forest Service has done a lot of work up here. Where the trail and an eroded jeep road once headed straight up a small canyon, the jeep road is now blocked and a new trail, built by prison inmates, snakes through the trees. In the fall aspen leaves are like rose petals scattered across the black dirt of the new trail. Two signs will give you conflicting mileages to the top of Mt. Taylor, and neither is right. In just over a mile, you'll come to an aspen gate, and if you look into the valley, the less-than-quaint steel tank you see is Gooseberry Springs.

After another half mile, the trees begin to thin out, and you'll be hiking up and then traversing the broad back of the great mountain. Late afternoon sun bronzes the tall grasses and polishes the pine needles. Several

*Gooseberry
Springs trail.*

times you will think you've reached the head of the giant, only to discover you're on its shoulder or its nose. At the top you can peer into the small throat of one volcano, but the views demand most of your attention. The notes hikers leave behind give you an idea of how people feel about the mountain:

■ "It sure is great to rediscover what life is really about again! A great hike and a great view. What a great sense of peace!"
■ "If I ever attempt this again, I'll have to quit smoking."
■ "A blessing being to the mountain top—my dream come true. Today will be four years sober."
■ "The YCC [Youth Conservation Corps] crew was here. We almost died, but we made it."

Distance: 6.2 miles round-trip.
Time: 5 hours.
Difficulty: Challenging.
Topo Map: Mt. Taylor.

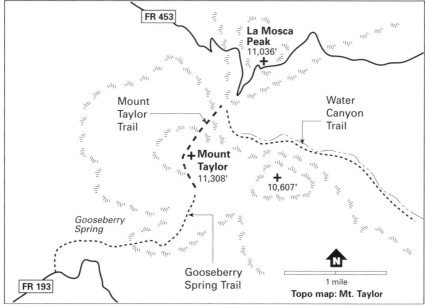

FR 453

La Mosca
Peak
11,036'
+

Mount
Taylor
Trail

Water
Canyon
Trail

+ Mount
Taylor
11,308'

+
10,607'

Gooseberry
Spring

Gooseberry
Spring Trail

N

1 mile

Topo map: Mt. Taylor

FR 193

Mt. Taylor Trail
(See Gooseberry Springs map, p. 127)

Getting there: Take FR 239 to FR 453, following signs for La Mosca Peak. At 4.6 miles from the turnoff, in the saddle between La Mosca and Mt. Taylor, the road forks. The left fork leads to the fire lookout on La Mosca, and the right leads to Mt. Taylor and Water Canyon. Take the right fork and park. A short walk up a two-track brings you to another fork. The road to Water Canyon continues down the hill; the road up Mt. Taylor is to the right. In between and unmarked except for a cairn is the short trail up Mt. Taylor.

Saddle between Mt. Taylor and La Mosca Peak, looking toward Water Canyon.

This is a short if breathless hike, to the top of the mountain from the back side. There is a switchback across a grassy slope before the trail dives into dark, cool woods, which are loaded with mushrooms during the summer rainy season.

Distance: 1.9 miles (round-trip) from fork.
Time: 1 hour, 20 minutes.
Difficulty: Altitude makes it hard to catch your breath, but I hiked this one with an elderly group.
Topo Map: Mt. Taylor.

Water Canyon
(See Gooseberry Springs map, p. 127)

Getting there: See Mt. Taylor Trail, above.

This is one of my favorites. The road is broad and flat for a way and takes you through unreclaimed timbered areas. Have faith; it gets better. Water Canyon, in fact, is one of the prettiest hikes in the Taylor area, with carpets of vegetation along springs and creeks. Water Canyon is the western end of a five-mile-square crater formed by Mt. Taylor, La Mosca Peak, and sister peaks. They are the remains of a bigger mountain, reduced over millions of years of volcanic explosions and erosion.

At about ¾ mile, the road forks again. Take the left, more-traveled fork. The road peters out at 2.3 miles and turns into a crude logging road. Continue on and find a trail through deep, shady woods—ponderosa pines and spruce. Shortly you will come to the little creek that gives the canyon its name—some of the only running water in the area. The greenery changes from grasses to water-loving ferns, yarrow, strawberries, mosses. I've seen bear scat here on two occasions, and we found a stump clawed open by a bear looking for grubs.

Get ready for a giant surprise after three miles. The downed trees look like more logging waste, and they are, but the loggers are four-footed. Keep walking and marvel at the Hoover of beaver dams—a big, complex of dams completed by Ward and June Beaver and the little

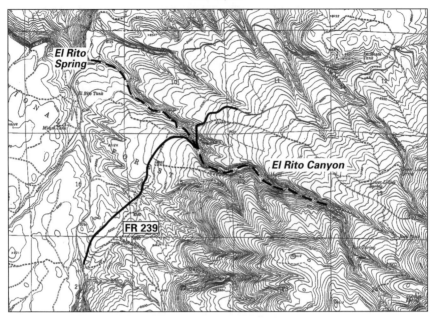

cleavers, who must have been Egyptian monument builders in an earlier life. In the fall yellow aspen leaves float in the water like little rafts. The beavers are long gone, but their complex lives on.

The trail ends at private property, just as the canyon opens up and the water disappears.

Distance: 3.8 miles (one way).
Time: 5–6 hours.
Difficulty: All downhill and then all uphill; moderately challenging.
Topo Map: Mt. Taylor.

El Rito Canyon
Getting there: Take FR 239 1.8 miles from the end of the pavement. A sign marks El Rito Canyon.

This is actually two hikes, and either one could be called the Walk of Many Vistas. From the road you can follow the streambed southeast, which is uphill toward Mt. Taylor, or northwest, which is downhill toward San Mateo Mesa.

The upper hike is the more rugged, but the canyon here is prettier. There is no developed trail, but you have a choice of routes. The easiest walk is along an old logging road up the right (south) side of the canyon. This one would also be a good cross-country ski trail. It veers off to the south about a mile up. You can also walk along the rim of the north side. Or for the best look at the canyon's rock outcrops, scramble along the stream bottom. This bed has running water part of the year. A portion of the area has been logged fairly recently, but this

is still a pretty place, with views of Mt. Taylor hovering above the trees and, to its left, La Mosca Peak and its thorny crown of towers. In the other direction, you can see Hosta and Haystack buttes to the west, El Malpais and Gallo Peak to the south.

View from El Rito Canyon toward San Mateo.

The lower hike is a bland but pleasant shuffle through ponderosa pines and scrub oak, but the abrupt finish makes up for any boredom along the way. Follow the streambed through the trees. In about a half-mile, you'll pick up a two-track that follows the stream. Hiking this one in the fall, we followed bobcat tracks incised perfectly in the snow. When the track and streambed cross a road, continue following the bed a short distance. Here is your reward. You will soon come to what looks like the edge of the world, as the stream (if the water is running) plunges over a horseshoe-shaped, sheer drop into the valley below.

San Mateo village isn't visible from here, but you can see the valley. Look farther into the distance, and you can make out the somber outlines of uranium-mine headframes in the nearly deserted Ambrosia Lake area. To your left is La Jara Mesa.

Distance: Upper El Rito is about 2 miles long. The lower canyon walk is about 1.8 miles.
Time: 4 hours, upper canyon; 2–3 hours, lower canyon.
Difficulty: Scrambling and bushwhacking make the upper canyon fairly difficult; the lower canyon is a reasonably easy hike.
Topo Map: San Mateo.

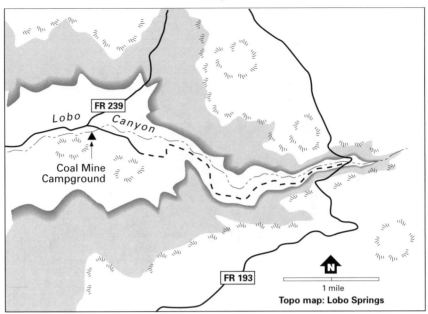

1 mile
Topo map: Lobo Springs

Lobo Canyon

Getting there: Take FR 239 past the lower loop of FR 193 to the upper loop of FR 193 and turn right. Continue on 193 about 2.5 miles. (If you reach the Gooseberry Springs trailhead, you've gone too far.) You're in the right place if you see a rock mound topped by a small, white cross.

This is an old road, which the Forest Service has closed with a series of berms. It's ugly at first, but keep walking. The road crosses the tiny stream fed by Lobo Springs and follows it down a tree-filled and, in places, very beautiful canyon. At one point you have a great view of Grants Ridge and beyond. (The white mound in the distance is a uranium tailings pile, due to be covered.) Beavers here have created a series of ponds, and you see signs of their logging everywhere.

This canyon ends eventually at Coal Mine Campground, about 3.5 miles from the trail's beginning.

Distance: About a mile to the first beaver dams; somewhat longer to the best views.
Time: 2 hours.
Difficulty: Moderate.
Topo Map: Lobo Springs.

Guadalupe Canyon

Getting there: There are several routes. Take FR 239 across the breadth of the Mt. Taylor area and out to Mesa Chivato, stretching to the east. About 25 miles from the end of the pavement, you enter a checkerboard of alternating public and private land. Continue 4 miles

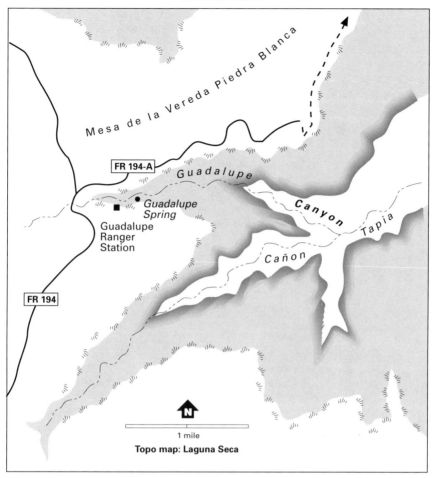

N

1 mile

Topo map: Laguna Seca

and turn right on FR 550. After 4.5 miles, turn left on FR 194. In 2.3 miles, turn right on FR 194A, just past a sign that announces Guadalupe Canyon. Park along here. You can also get here from San Mateo, on the west side of Mt. Taylor, using FR 456 to 239. A third choice is to take NM 44 from Bernalillo and turn left 18.7 miles from the San Ysidro intersection at county road 279 and continue on to FR 239A and then to 239, 194, and 194A, about 34.6 miles. For any of these routes, a four-wheel-drive or high-clearance vehicle is advised.

The dazzling Guadalupe Canyon and its neighboring Tapia Canyon are a recreation frontier. Remote and difficult to reach, the eastern flank of Mt. Taylor is an undiscovered area of great beauty. Forest Service planners intend to build a rim trail here. Hikers can choose the canyon bottom or a rim hike. From the Guadalupe Canyon sign, this drainage drops quickly into a steep, walled canyon. Birds are plentiful and noisy, and we scared two great horned owls from their roosts. Numerous rocky drops are no doubt waterfalls during the wet season here, and some pools remain. A mile in we encounter a deep pool, dense willows, and steep slopes and decide in favor of a rim hike.

In the scramble out is a little geology lesson. Crusty old Mt. Taylor poured lava onto the mesa tops surrounding it. Our friend John Roney, an archeologist with a good eye, spots a layer of baked red clay in the deepening canyon, just underneath the basalt canyon walls.

Because piñon and juniper trees, along with an occasional ponderosa pine and Douglas fir, grow right to the canyon's edge, the rim hike is a zigzag. Breathtaking views make it worth the trouble to stay close to the edge. The deep gash of Guadalupe Canyon yawns into a chasm and joins Tapia Canyon, which you can see as a sharp cleft snaking toward the Rio Puerco. The Sandia Mountains are blue and hazy in the distance. The rim hike ends at the tip of Mesa de la Vereda Piedra Blanca ("mesa of the white rock trail"), and as you make your way around the tip, you're staring into the great green bowl of Cañón Salado ("salty canyon"). From here you can walk back on 194A.

Distance: Canyon hike, 1 mile; rim hike, about 10 to 12 miles round-trip.
Time: Several hours to one day.
Difficulty: The steepness and loose rock make the canyon hike difficult; the rim hike is fairly easy.
Topo Map: Laguna Seca.

Rinconada Canyon

Getting there: From I-40, take exit 96 about 11 miles east of the easternmost Grants exit and drive down old Route 66 toward San Fidel (road is north of I-40). In about 1.4 miles, turn left (north) on FR 400 (also county road 15), which is a good gravel road. Proceed 4.7 miles to a fork in the road just before a concrete ramp over the arroyo. You will pass the ruins of a stone homesteader house on the left. Take the left fork, unmarked and unnumbered, which ends just beyond the fork, and park. (The right fork, FR 400 continues up the side of the mesa toward microwave towers.)

To me this area is a great environmental laboratory and a place of contradictions. From the trash/artifacts we found in one campsite and the scarcity of any sizable ponderosas, the area was apparently logged in the 1920s or 1930s. Where the Zuni Mountain logging regions have been replanted, coddled, and worried over by feds, Mother Nature here has been on her own to heal. My conclusion: She does better with some government welfare.

Cross a barbed-wire gate and follow an old logging road up the canyon. In some places it's broad and inviting, carpeted with leaves and pine needles; in other places, the road has lost its grip on the mountain and

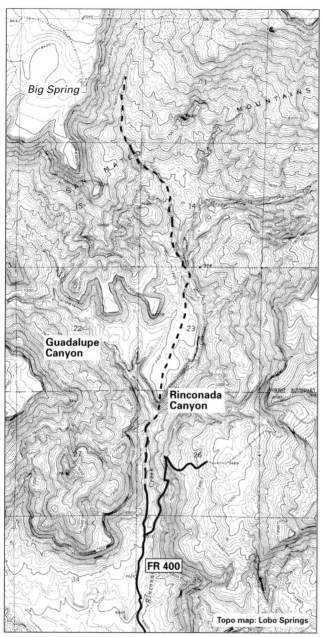

Topo map: Lobo Springs

slipped into the creek or turned into an ugly arroyo
gouged in the canyon side and deepening every year. In
still other places, if you find a trail you have cattle and
wildlife to thank for it. When in doubt simply follow the
creek bed. After you cross the barbed wire, you'll go
through three quarter-sections of private, BLM, then private land and past another stone homesteader ruin
before coming to the Forest Service boundary.

Growth in the creek bottom is lavish—box elders,

alders, oaks draped with grapevines, willows—but the dry mesa tops tell another story. The regal ponderosas are gone, succeeded by scrub oak and juniper, the poor cousins of the tree world. Other than jays, there are few birds here. Kathleen pats a baby ponderosa on the head and urges it, "Grow! Grow!" Enjoying the greenery of the creek bed, we encounter the road again in another half-mile, to the left on a sidehill. At 1.2 miles is the barbed-wire boundary and cattle guard marking private land. In this mostly waterless place, the lilt of a running creek is a luxury. Rinconada Creek is apparently a live stream (although water here is never a sure thing).

Rinconada Canyon.

At 1.5 miles is the Forest Service boundary. In another quarter-mile, watch for a sandstone promontory with a fine view up the canyon toward a distant butte. The vivid greens in the distance mark Big Springs.

The road curves broadly to the right around a low mesa at about 2 miles, and in this area you can see Guadalupe Canyon to the left. We leave the road and walk over the mesa, keeping the creek to our left. At the bottom a pile of slash marks an old sawmill site. Just beyond the road forks, with the right fork proceeding up Rinconada Canyon. This looks like a good hike too, but we bear left, following the water, up an unnamed canyon and find the trail again on a sidehill left of the creek bed. (Should you continue up Rinconada Canyon, you would be close enough to the Gooseberry Springs Trail to connect the two.)

The greenery is varied—monkey flower, yarrow, scarlet gilia, columbine, poison ivy. Rabbit brush is neighbors with wild rose.

At 4 miles, the road becomes an arroyo, and in another half-mile, we encounter aspens. Here a hummingbird works the scarlet gilia. The debris from an old campsite includes a rusted beer can, sardine tins, bits of lantern glass, milk cans, and purple glass. Because ponderosas grow quickly here, the big trees could be sixty years old.

We turn back for the biggest hiking thrill ever. Down the canyon at the sound of crashing brush, we look at the opposite canyon wall, expecting to see a deer. Instead a brown bear scrambles from the oaks, runs along the wall and then sits on a rock, sniffing the air. We study each other for a few minutes. I debate whether to change lenses for a photograph, but we decide not to linger. There could be a cub in the area, and while the bear makes no move toward us, she's less thrilled with our presence than we are with hers.

Distance: 9.6 miles.
Time: 7 hours.
Difficulty: Steady but not difficult climb, some scrambling and bushwhacking to find the road or trail. Map is most helpful here.
Topo Map: Lobo Springs.

Snowfields on Mt. Taylor.

Biking and Skiing

A few mountain bikers and cross-country skiers, trying to get away from the crowds, have discovered Mt. Taylor and the Zuni Mountains. Thrill seekers will enjoy the ups and downs of Mt. Taylor, while those out for a nice ride or glide will like the level-to-rolling Zunis. Both have a profusion of little-used forest roads and old logging roads, which are ideal for biking and cross-country skiing.

I'm a cross-country skier but not a mountain biker. Recommendations on bike trails come from federal agency people and biking friends.

Biking

■ FR 193 loop. From the Lobo Canyon Road, which becomes FR 239, turn right on FR 193, which climbs over Horace Mesa and returns to FR 239.

■ Peaks tour on FR 453 (see Tour #1 in Mt. Taylor Hikes).

■ FR 239. This road runs nearly the length of Mt. Taylor and its mesas. Bikers are fond of the Antelope Flats area, on the north side of the mountain.

■ Gooseberry Springs. The cover photo of *The New Mexico Mountain Bike Guide*, by Brant Hayenga and Chris Shaw, shows a stout-hearted and strong-limbed biker threading his way up the Gooseberry Springs Trail, which they call "certainly the most beautiful ride in the entire state." The Forest Service is concerned about damage to the trail from bike traffic, so keep that in mind.

■ NM 547. On any weekend you'll find numbers of bikers throwing themselves at the mountain here in preparation for the quadrathlon.

Skiing

■ Quad Ski Trail (see p. 140)

■ The Forest Service maintains FR 239 to snow play areas in the winter, which means that cross-country skiers can ski up the unmaintained portion of FR 239 to any other inviting Forest Road they find. One favorite, if ambitious, tour is to take FR 239 to FR 453 and ski to La Mosca and Mt. Taylor. Another small road will take you to the top of Mt. Taylor.

Volunteers grab bicycles from soloists in the Mt. Taylor Quadra-thlon at the bike-run transition point.

Mt. Taylor Quadrathlon

In recent years Mt. Taylor has taken on a whole new image, as the scene of one of winter sports' most rigor-ous events, the Mt. Taylor Winter Quadrathlon, held every February. Imagine bicycling, running, skiing, and snow-shoeing forty-four miles from Grants to the top of the mountain and back—in less than four hours! *Triathlete* magazine calls this one of the best such races; the rest of us might call it one of the craziest. Occasionally athletes are treated to good weather, but most years the mountain has thrown its worst at them: snow, high winds, blizzards, whiteouts. Said one winner, "You battle the elements and the elevation and yourself."

The Quad starts at 6,420 feet, in Grants. Entrants bike thirteen miles through Lobo Canyon to the base of the mountain, at 8,213 feet. Then they run five miles to 9,461 feet, as temperatures dive and the air thins. In the third leg, they cross-country ski up a steep two miles that end at 10,700 feet on Heartbreak Hill, so-called because the steepest portion comes last. They finish with a mile of snowshoeing to the top. "You can step on your own snowshoes," said one entrant. "There are lots of rocks, and in the two years I did it, I saw a lot of people fall. You can really hurt yourself."

Then they race back down. The downhill isn't necessarily easier. Most crash frequently on the steep skiing portion, and many also suffer during bicycling, as they fight exhaustion.

The Quad began in 1984 with eighty-seven contestants, as a way to promote the area. Nobody then knew how long the event would take, so when the athletes took off, so did Quad volunteers. A few hours later, a motorist happened to see the first bikers speeding toward Grants, and frantic phone calls got race officials to the finish line just in time. The event has grown to hundreds of entrants, many from other countries, and the organizers' sophistication has grown accordingly. Planning and preparation go on nearly all year, involving hundreds of people, and entrants have high praise for volunteers and local support.

The Quad isn't just for hardened athletes pitting themselves against the mountain. Lots of weekend warriors form teams or pairs—in one case a father and daughter—and compete for the heck of it. If you can't talk your friends into it, you can submit your name, and the quad organizers will team you up with others.

Contest divisions are male and female, and teams have a mixed division. Age brackets are under 18, 18 to 29, 30 to 39, 40 to 49, and over 50. My biggest surprise as a volunteer at the bike-run transition was grabbing the bike of a 72-year-old, one-armed soloist.

Event volunteers help athletes and offer snacks and water at each transition point, but the entrants themselves must pack clothing, gear, and food for six changes in activity. One winner said, "I start eating and drinking after the first run. Your body runs out. If you don't replace what you lose, you'll know it." He advises wearing a bottle of water on your belt and alternating between water and sports drinks.

Training tips: Focus on your weakness. For most, that's cross-country skiing. One winner trained by running eighty miles a week, biking two hundred miles and cross-country skiing several times a week. One master's (older) winner followed a program of running six days a week, roller-skiing three days a week, and bicycling twice a week. He also emphasized rest. Others say contestants should work on endurance first and then begin adding speed. And preparation for altitude is important.

Quad Ski Trail
Getting there: Take FR 239 to FR 453, turn right and go 1.9 miles to a cleared parking area on the right. A sign with a skier along with other small, colored arrows let

you know you're in the right place.

At any time other than Quad weekend, you can test yourself on the Quad ski trail. A tough course for serious athletes, it's mostly straight up and straight down—not for wimps. With a variety of tracks off in other directions, the trail climbs through ponderosas and Douglas firs, eventually reaching the high meadows on the mountain, in view of the radio towers on La Mosca. These meadows are great for skiing around the mostly open slopes.

Distance: Two to three miles, depending on detours.
Time: 4 hours.
Difficulty: Advanced and brazen intermediate skiers only.

3

Cabezon and Other Volcanic Plugs

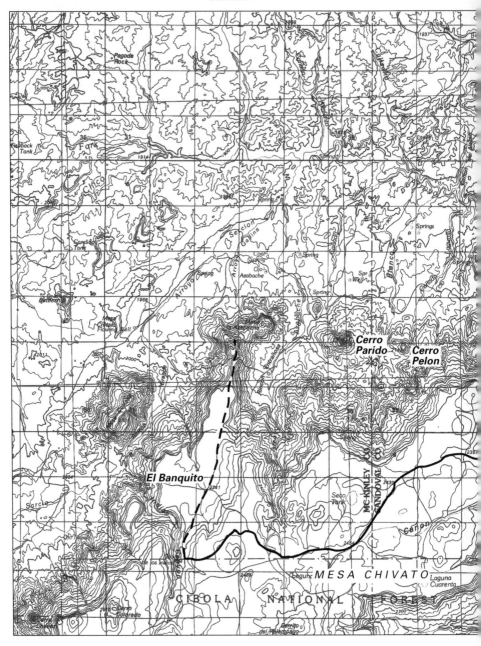

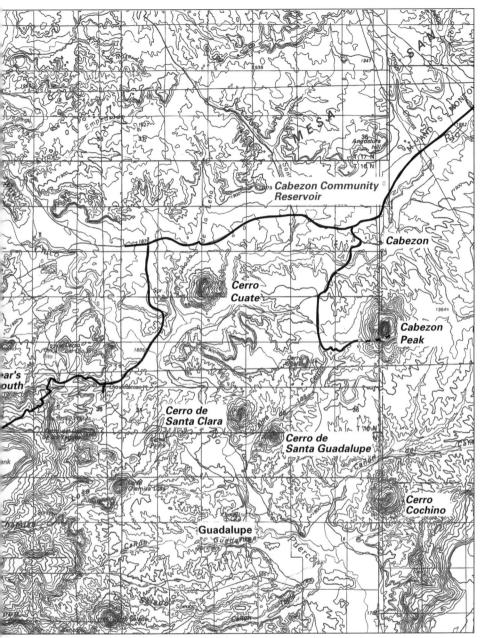

Cabezon and Other Volcanic Plugs

*The Rio Puerco starts in the shadow of the forested
Nacimiento Mountains, moves south through rolling
grasslands browsed by pronghorn antelope; gouges
between red and white rock mesas, towering volcanic
peaks, the colors bold and the land rugged; then widens
as the country becomes more gentle, sagelands dipping
gradually to the arroyo rims. It steals unnoticed under
the incessant rushing of wheels on Highway 66 and
finally opens into the quiet flow of the Rio Grande.*
                                    Michael Jenkinson, 1971

*(Pages 146–47)
Cabezon Peak.*

B etween Albuquerque's West Mesa and Mt. Taylor
is the broad basin of the Rio Puerco valley. Known
to few, the valley keeps its secrets well. Captain
C. E. Dutton in 1885 wrote that the valley "is a
medley of low cliffs or bluffs, showing the light browns
and pale yellows of the lower and middle Cretaceous
sandstones and shales. Out of this confused patchwork
of bright colors rise several . . . objects of remarkable
aspect. They are apparently inaccessible eyries of black
rock . . ."

Dutton's eyries are a little-known geologic wonder—
more than fifty volcanic plugs, or necks, that ring Mt.
Taylor like sentinels. Like Shiprock, in northwestern New
Mexico, they were formed when lava cooled and solidified in the throat of a volcano and erosion then wore
away the cinder cone.

Cabezon, at 7,785 feet, is the biggest of them all; bigger even than the better-known Devil's Tower, in Wyoming. A landmark visible for miles, it is also sacred to
Pueblo Indians and Navajos. Navajos call the plug Tsé
Naajiin ("black rock coming down"). Their creation story
tells how supernatural beings called the Hero Twins
killed an evil giant, cut off his head and tossed it to the
east, where it became Cabezon, Spanish for "big head."

The plugs can be seen just north of Laguna Pueblo.
Those with names include Celosa ("jealous woman"),
Negro ("black"), Tecolote ("owl"), Cerrito Negro ("little
black hill"), Don Basilio, Chato, Don Leonardo, Rincones
("narrow valleys"), two Santa Rosas, Lagunitas ("little
lakes"), Guadalupe, Cochino ("pig"), Santa Clara, Cuates
("twins"), Parido ("born"), Chavez, Alesna ("awl"),
Perdido ("lost"), Lobo ("wolf"), and Picacho ("peak").

As spectacular and nearly as high as Cabezon is Cerro
Alesna, located on the northwest side of Mt. Taylor, on
the Lee Ranch. Its crystallized center is reportedly a bun-
dle of five-sided columns so hard they ring when struck.
Three other plugs—Picacho, Tecolotito, and Tecolote—
are likewise formed by bundles of "devil's fence posts."

Third largest is Lagunitas Peak, twelve miles southwest of Cabezon. The ascent to its top is said to be through a hole in the rock.

Tecolote, three miles northeast of Cebolleta, once held a cluster of Navajo hogans. From Celosa Peak near Cebolleta Canyon, according to legend, a jilted Indian girl jumped to her death long ago. Celosa was also the signal tower for desperate Spanish colonists under siege by Navajos at Cebolleta. To summon their friends, the Lagunas, a messenger would wave a red blanket from Celosa. Lobo is embedded in a cliff at the rim of the plateau near Grants.

"Why look for a Devil's Tower? We are on bigger and better ones," wrote E. R. Harrington in 1938. "There are so many of them in sight that we look on them as commonplace. Perhaps that is why the Cabezon is not a national monument or why Alesna is not advertised in chamber of commerce literature . . . These great towers have looked down upon traders, mountain men, gold seekers and Indian war parties, and they now bask in the sunshine waiting for a new day when they shall receive the geological homage which is their due."

The rolling lands beneath the towers have gotten a different kind of attention. One writer suggested that the Rio Puerco valley be a monument to overgrazing.

The first settlers in the area arrived soon after the Spanish reconquest. In 1767 the Spanish governor approved the land grant of Miguel Montoya and his cousin Santiago, near Cabezon Peak. A year later Joaquín de Mestas Peralta got his grant north of Cabezon Peak on the condition that he treat the Navajos in the area with kindness. By the 1770s settlers were established enough to record a wedding and a baptism. A map of 1779 shows a village at the base of Cabezon Peak called Portería ("gatekeeper's place"), along with the Mestas and Montoya *ranchos.*

Almost from the beginning, however, the settlement lost livestock and crops to Navajo raids that grew more intense and more violent. The ranchos, on the eastern fringe of Navajo country, made easy targets for Navajo parties setting out to raid the pueblos and Rio Grande settlements. From the 1770s until the 1830s, settlers fled and returned repeatedly, until they finally gave up on the valley. In this period another grant, the Ojo del Espíritu Santo ("spring of the Holy Ghost") was issued in 1815 to Luis María Cabeza de Baca. It was the same grant issued in 1766 to the pueblos of Jemez, Zia, and Santa Ana. Baca argued that the pueblos weren't using the land because of Navajo raids; it began a land dispute that fumed until the 1930s.

In 1893 the three pueblos tried to reclaim their land, and attorney Thomas B. Catron defended the Baca descendents. The pueblos ultimately lost, and Catron, a

Guadalupe.

Republican political boss, became owner of the grant. Catron owned whole or part interests in thirty-one land grants and was once believed to own more land than any other individual in the United States.

The first American record of the valley was made by Lt. James W. Abert, in 1846. He wrote that the valley was wide, flat, and overgrown with varieties of artemisias and "coarse grass fit only for sheep and goats." The banks of the Rio Puerco then were ten to thirty feet high. The only trees were cedars on sand hills and cottonwoods in the riverbed. At that time the settlement at Cabezon was deserted. After Navajos were confined to a reservation, Spanish families returned and founded four villages: La Posta (1872), Casa Salazar (1867), Guadalupe (1874), and San Luis (date unknown). La Posta, at the foot of Cabezon, was later renamed Cabezon.

In the early 1870s, the Star Line Mail and Transportation Co. began running stages from Santa Fe through Peña Blanca, San Ysidro, Cabezon, Willow Springs, San Mateo, San Antonio Springs, Bacon Springs, and Fort Wingate. The stage road made use of an old trade route between Zuni and Jemez pueblos and a portion of the Great Navajo Trail between Navajo country and Santa Fe. One passenger described the stage as "small uncomfortable coaches that travel day and night at the rate of about 6 miles per hour." The fare was twenty to twenty-five cents a mile, and meals at the stage stations were one dollar. Old-timers in the area have told stories about an Indian attack on the stage between Willow Springs and Cabezon. They overturned and burned the coach, killed all the passengers except for one woman who escaped in the darkness, and took the mules. When the stage failed to show up on time the next morning, the stationmaster rode out and rescued the woman, who was hiding in the brush.

The Santa Fe Railroad at one point considered running its tracks through here but settled on the southern route instead. When the railroad was completed in 1881, it put the stageline out of business, but with a new road from Albuquerque to Cuba, Cabezon held on.

Travelers then risked more than Indian attacks. Although the settlers were quiet and hard working, the isolated Rio Puerco valley was a haven for rustlers, train robbers, and anybody who didn't want to talk about his past. It also drew gringo haters, who mostly came by their opinions after being cheated or abused by Anglos. Criminals along the Puerco, wrote trader Nathan Bibo, "became so wild that they would be riding through the little towns— threatening and bulldozing people, and nearly all inhabitants would be careful to remain inside their houses." In 1876, while rounding up scattered sheep, Bibo was accosted by one outlaw who demanded that Bibo get off his horse and enter a house filled with his friends. Bibo clobbered the bandit with his riding whip and galloped away, as the prone outlaw shot at him. The next day Bibo pulled his gun on a horse thief driving a stolen herd. The man pleaded for his life. "I am sorry to say we let him go," Bibo wrote, "because we could have saved the lives of nearly a dozen people who were killed by this one desperado within two years after that, before he was killed in Colfax County."

In 1884 local ranchers chased a band of rustlers led by Candido and Manuel Castillo into the canyons around Mt. Taylor. Unfortunately Don Juan Romero, a well-liked citizen, died in the fray. Deputy Sheriff Jesus Montoya and a group of local men, with help from a Navajo tracker, followed the Castillos to Española. In a gunfight in a store, the Cabezon men shot both brothers and their horses. Manuel was able to drag his brother into the night, where by chance he encountered a group of Penitentes. Penitentes are sworn to aid and protect each other, and the Castillos were Penitentes. They helped Manuel move his dying brother and later bury him. Then Manuel fled and was never seen again.

Cabezon was probably a hiding place in the late 1890s for train robbers. In one foray Cole Young, a member of Black Jack Ketchum's gang, held up the Atlantic & Pacific at the Rio Puerco bridge. A U.S. marshal happened to be on the train. As Young was shooting at the brakeman, the marshall fired and killed the outlaw. The rest of the gang escaped, likely into the Puerco valley.

Meanwhile Cabezon had become a trading center for Navajos and area ranchers. Renamed in 1891, it had a post office, blacksmith shop, general stores, four or five saloons, and three dance halls. One of the earliest merchants was young Richard Heller, who with a partner bought the struggling trading post in late 1888. Heller, a native of Czechoslovakia, was soon fluent in English, Spanish, and Navajo, and managed to charm the locals. Heller and his partner in 1894 provided most of the material and labor when residents built their church, La Iglesia de San José. His store carried necessities such as flour, coffee, sugar, and calico, along with wooden barrels of candy, wooden boxes of cookies and crackers, perfume, sewing notions, twists and plugs of tobacco, and tools. Like other New Mexico traders of his day, he often sold on credit and carried Navajo sheepherders and Puerco ranchers from year to year. Once a year he would take a wagon around to collect sheep or wool in payment, becoming an instant sheep rancher. At one time he ran sixteen thousand sheep and two thousand head of cattle. He sent as many as forty wagons loaded with wool to Albuquerque. On the south side of town, Marcelino and Perciliano Archuleta ran a large store and had their own electric generator. On the side they were bankers.

The area was then called the breadbasket of New Mexico. Buffalo grass was so tall, recalled a former resident, that the first sheepherders had to cut the grass with a scythe so their animals could graze. After the land was cleared for crops, wagon after wagon of wheat and corn left the area for Albuquerque. The people also grew corn, beans, and pumpkins.

Fiestas would draw people within a hundred miles for several days of music, dancing, gambling, and horse racing. Doors were open for food and refreshment. Sometimes tightrope walkers, clowns, and trained dogs would entertain. Musicians announced a dance by parading down the street as they played violins and guitars.

The Rio Puerco even then wasn't much of a river. Jemez Indian people called it Napota Pohu'u, or "dry mud with creek." Fr. Francisco Domínguez in 1776 wrote, "It is called the Rio Puerco because its water is as dirty as the gutters of the streets . . ." Still the 140-mile-long river was the only water around, and narrow as it was, it still carried a good head of water. Settlers built dams at Cabezon and San Luis after 1870.

With more farming and ever-larger herds, overgrazing changed the land forever. The Puerco became wider, and periodic floods wiped out fields and houses on its banks. By the 1930s the Puerco was more than two hundred feet wide in places and cut more than ten feet deep, with little water in it. Its silt each year would cover twelve thousand acres a foot deep. Ring grass and snakeweed had replaced the lush buffalo grass. In 1934 the federal government bought the Espíritu Santo land grant under a program to recover marginal lands. But

Pueblo and local Hispanic ranchers continued to squabble over grazing rights on the land. In early 1938, after two years of drought, the Hispanic stockmen were desperate and marched onto the grant with their livestock.

It was a brief victory. In those same years, the government under the Taylor Grazing Act forced local ranchers to reduce the size of their herds. People here still have bitter memories of forced slaughters.

Finally the thin land could yield no more. People left. Richard Heller hung on, and his fortunes withered with the Puerco grasses. He died in 1947. His wife Beatriz kept the store and post office open another year. For years afterward, former Navajo and Hispanic customers sought her out in Albuquerque to settle up debts to "Don Ricardo and Doña Beatriz."

The dance hall heard its last music in 1951.

Even deserted, Cabezon holds its romance. In the early 1970s producers of a television commercial rigged up an airplane propeller to blow tumbleweeds through the village for a shoot. Cabezon has also drawn people for the wrong reasons. Looters, vandals, and souvenir hunters picked at the deserted buildings like turkey vultures until Benito Lucero, who owns the land, closed the village and fenced it off. In the early 1960s, Lucero stopped three men from hauling off the church bell. It's still hidden for safekeeping.

Today when the Rio Puerco joins the Rio Grande, it provides only 6 percent of the big river's flow but 56 percent of its silt. Government range conservationists have reclamation plans for the area, but not much hope of recovery. The BLM has designated 8,159 acres here as Wilderness Study Area.

Cabezon Peak

Getting there: Take NM 44 from Bernalillo and turn left 18.1 miles from the San Ysidro intersection, at county road 279. A small sign will indicate the villages of San Luis and Cabezon. Motoring past San Luis, take a moment to appreciate the village's pretty church, and across the road, its Penitente morada. After about 12 miles, you can see to the south the ghost town of Cabezon. Admire it from the road. The old village is on private property, and because of years of vandalism, the owner doesn't take kindly to trespassers. At 12.3 miles from the turnoff take the two-track left toward Cabezon Peak.

Cabezon's vertical ribbed sides are as awesome as they are intimidating. What you see looking up at the plug is its nearly cylindrical core of basalt, about fifteen hundred feet in diameter and eight hundred feet high. The ribs represent a cooling pattern called columnar jointing. With its shoulders, the Big Head juts more than two thousand feet from the valley floor.

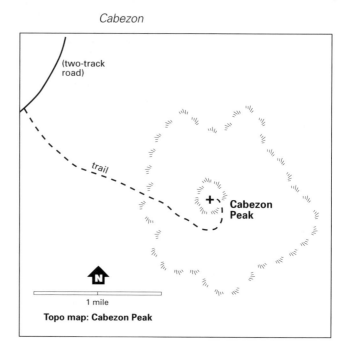

(two-track road)

trail

Cabezon Peak

N

1 mile

Topo map: Cabezon Peak

Surprisingly this is not a technical climb. Hiking around the plug in a southerly direction, begin ascending the plug's pedestal. In less than a mile, cross a fence and continue toward the base. About 0.2 miles from the fence, you can see a chimney or a bit of wall jutting from the plug, and this is where you begin the climb, over several hundred feet of scree (loose rock). If you look up at green rock, colored by moss and lichens, you've gone too far. The climb soon gets steep enough for monkey-style, hands-and-feet progress up the rock. A crude trail ascends through the chimney and angles up the rock. It's steep but there are ample handholds and footholds. I have to confess to moments of fear. Another half-hour or so of this climbing brings you to the rounded top of the giant's head.

The climbing of Cabezon is its own reward, but the views from 7,785 feet in elevation will take your breath away, if the ascent hasn't already. To the northeast are the Nacimiento Mountains, with Redondo Peak just behind. The Sandias are to the east. Mt. Taylor spreads out to the southwest, and Ladron Peak far to the south. To the northwest is the vast Chaco Mesa. Nearby three smaller volcanic plugs—Cerro de Santa Clara, Cerro Chato, and Cerro Cuate—jut from the rolling floor of piñon and grasses, and distant plugs are silhouettes in the blue haze of afternoon rain.

To locate the trail down, you should be looking out at the Sandias and a small stock pond.

Wildlife here includes mule deer, white-tailed deer, pronghorn antelope, coyote, bobcat, gray fox, and badger. The most commonly seen birds are golden eagles,

red-tailed hawks, sparrow hawks, horned larks, piñon jays, ravens, western meadowlarks, and Oregon juncos. Golden eagles are known to nest on Cabezon, as are red-tailed hawks, sparrow hawks, prairie falcons, and great horned owls. Reptiles include the collared lizard, eastern fence lizard, bullsnake, and western diamond-back rattlesnake.

Cabezon Peak is home to Wright's pincushion cactus, Knight's milk vetch, and grama-grass cactus, all on the state list of endangered species.

(Left) Climbing up through the Cabezon chimney. (Right) To the left of hiker the Bear's Mouth yawns; a volcanic plug forms the jaw, a lava cap the snout.

Distance: 2–3 miles; about a 1,300-foot ascent from parking, 2,000-foot ascent from valley floor.
Time: 5 hours.
Difficulty: Not a technical climb, but strenuous and tough on the knees. The BLM calls this climb "appropriate for both beginning and intermediate climbers."
Topo Map: Cabezon Peak.

Bear's Mouth
(See Cabezon Peak map, p. 144–45)
Getting there: Take NM 44 from Bernalillo and turn left on county road 279, 18.1 miles from the San Ysidro intersection. Pass Cabezon to your left. After you've traveled just over 22 miles on county 279, you will pass a camping area on your right. At 32 miles the road will fork; bear right (the left fork goes to Guadalupe). The road, BLM 1103, climbs Mesa Chivato. Park at the top, when the road levels out.

From the road up Mesa Chivato, which is part of Mt. Taylor's broad pedestal, you can see Bear's Mouth to your right, or northwest. A lava cap on the mesa forms the bear's snout, a jutting volcanic plug below is its jaw. There is no trail here. The idea is to hike along the rim to the plug. Whether you reach Bear's Mouth or not, the views here are worth the trouble. This area is so undeveloped, it's one of the few places where you can look out and imagine what New Mexico was like two centuries ago. You can see all of the northwestern quarter, it seems. The Navajos' Huerfano Mountain is a mound on the western horizon, Chaco Mesa is to the north, Cabezon rises regally to the east. Swallows play in the updrafts.

You may find it easier to parallel the rim, hiking north, and make your way to the rim from time to time for a look. We found an old two-track road through a long meadow that was heading more or less in the right direction and used it for a couple of miles. Trekking through the piñon and juniper here, you'll find collapsed brush structures remaining from Navajo piñon camps. This is one of their favorite gathering areas. And no wonder! Piñons here are big and numerous. Watch for high points along the rim—one of them is Bear's Mouth. Striations in the jaw plug are columnar jointing formed in volcanism. The snout outcrop is red lava, festively decorated in green, yellow, and orange lichens. West of Bear's Mouth is another plug, the mitten-shaped Cerro Parido.

After rains the vegetation is generous: aster, penstemon, lupine, globe mallow, Indian paintbrush, and beeweed. I was surprised to find aspens growing in a crevice near the rim.

Distance: 9.6 miles.
Time: 5–6 hours.
Difficulty: Somewhat challenging with no trail but the terrain isn't especially difficult.
Topo Map: Chaco Mesa Quadrangle.

El Banquito
(See Cabezon map, p. 144–45)
Getting there: Take NM 44 from Bernalillo and turn left on county road 279, 18.1 miles from the San Ysidro intersection. Pass Cabezon to your left. After you've traveled just over 22 miles on county 279, you will pass a camping area on your right. At 32 miles the road will fork; bear right. The road climbs Mesa Chivato. On top of Mesa Chivato, the road becomes rough and rocky. Unless you have a high-clearance or four-wheel-drive vehicle, you should stop here and walk. Or continue another .2 miles and park at the sign.

A sign will tell you El Banquito ("little bench") mesa is two miles away. It also means that you have two miles of fairly boring hiking on a closed road, before you reach the stunning topography that makes it worthwhile. Be

patient. Enjoy the sage, rabbit brush, and senecio. Overhead a golden eagle may grace the sky. And watch for
signs of bear and coyote in the track.

*View west from
El Banquito.*

Shortly the broad mesa narrows, and you can see the
volcanic plugs Bear's Mouth and Cerro Parido on the right
and Cabezon in the distance. In a half-mile you're on the
basalt cap of the bench and the northernmost point of
Mesa Chivato, like a peninsula surrounded by blue sky
instead of water. Lavender mesas rise in the distance,
and the necks, or plugs, of old volcanoes peer over the
edge. On the western side, the big pyramid-shaped plug
you can see is Cerro Chavez; the pointy one in the distance is Cerro Alesna, second largest of Mt. Taylor's
plugs after Cabezon.

Wildlife here was exciting. A rattlesnake let us know
it wasn't receiving guests. As we were gathering our
wits after that encounter, we looked over the edge to
see a doe elk and her calf browsing below.

This is a BLM Wilderness Study Area and may become
the Boca del Oso ("mouth of the bear") Wilderness.

*Distance: 5.3 miles, round-trip, from the El Banquito
sign.
Time: 5 hours.
Difficulty: Moderate.
Topo Map: Chaco Mesa Quadrangle.*

Volcanic Neck/Seboyeta/Marquez Tour
For a different outing, try the driving tour of the Seboyeta
shrine and Mt. Taylor's volcanic necks. Take I-40 to NM
279 and drive 13 miles to the ancient village of Seboyeta.

As you pass the village of Bibo, named for an early trading family, you will see the first neck off to the right—Cerro de la Celosa—and behind it, Cerro Negro.

Just north of Seboyeta, a pretty box canyon with a spring shelters a shrine to the Virgin Mary and to St. Bernadette of Lourdes. Before the brick altar and its statue, the faithful have placed candles and flowers. Nearby are wooden pews. There are two stories about its beginning. The more reliable version is that during one of many forays by the men of the village, the women promised that if their husbands returned safely, they would build a shrine in the cliff nearby. The shrine, called Los Portales, has welcomed many travelers and their relatives, who have wanted to give thanks for a safe return. The other story describes the shrine as a gesture by villagers grateful for their survival against Navajo raids.

For the plug tour, leave the village and take the unmarked paved road that runs straight as a ruler to the east, passing Celosa and Negro and angling to the north-

Cerro de la Celosa, where legend tells of a jilted young Indian woman throwing herself from its summit. The colonists of Cebolleta once watched for Navajo raiding parties from this plug and signaled for help from Laguna Pueblo people.

east. The industrial site to the right is the former Sohio uranium mine. The scenery turns pretty here—canyons and mesas, cactus and wildflowers. About fourteen miles from Seboyeta, the distant black thumbs of volcanic plugs keep watch like sentinels on the horizon.

Resist the urge to get out and hike. This is the Juan Tafoya Land Grant, which is private property. This grant, once 199,000 acres of mesas and rolling hills, now covers just 3,840. Like many other grants, it fell into the hands of outsiders. Adjacent is the Cebolleta Land Grant. You will pass Cerro Tecolote before arriving at the old village of Marquez. From here you can see the plugs Chato, Don Leonardo, and Rincones. Looking down on Marquez from this road, you can nearly see the place as it once was, a ranching community. This village began on an unknown date in the last century, when four families camped in a white cave. They withstood Navajo raids and built a village, which at one time numbered twenty-five families. It had a church, two schools, two bars, a post office (1901), a grocery store, and a dance hall.

159

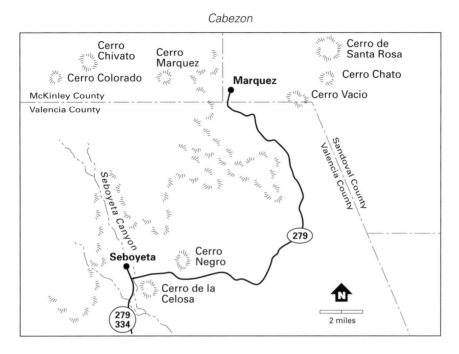

Cerro Chivato

Cerro Marquez

Cerro Colorado

McKinley County

Valencia County

Cerro de Santa Rosa

Cerro Chato

Marquez

Cerro Vacio

279

Seboyeta Canyon

Sandoval County / Valencia County

Seboyeta

Cerro Negro

Cerro de la Celosa

279 / 334

N

2 miles

Although some of the adobe houses are trying to return to the earth, others are maintained. The church shows someone's tender attentions, and a few families still live here.

This sleepy little place was nearly a uranium boom town. In 1977 two companies were building mines, and several more were exploring nearby. Lawmakers and promoters were thinking about building a road here from Rio Rancho or NM 44, to the north. Mineral exploration had polluted the Marquez spring, so residents were using a mining company's well. But they were looking forward to the return of relatives who could work in the mines.

One bit of early economic development I saw in those days was Florenzio Martinez's Cuatro Vientos Bar, which featured a bar, a juke box, a pool table, and a few chairs in a twelve-by-fourteen-foot shed. State environmental regulators, who came to look in on the mines, told bar customers they couldn't pitch beer cans into the arroyo anymore. And they told a would-be local developer that eight trailers on his land were too many.

Beyond Marquez, the road becomes impassable for all but four-wheel-drive vehicles. Apparently it's possible to drive from here to Cabezon, but going east from here we tried one terrible road after another and they all seemed to enter private property.

Church at Marquez before restoration.

4

Zuni Mountains

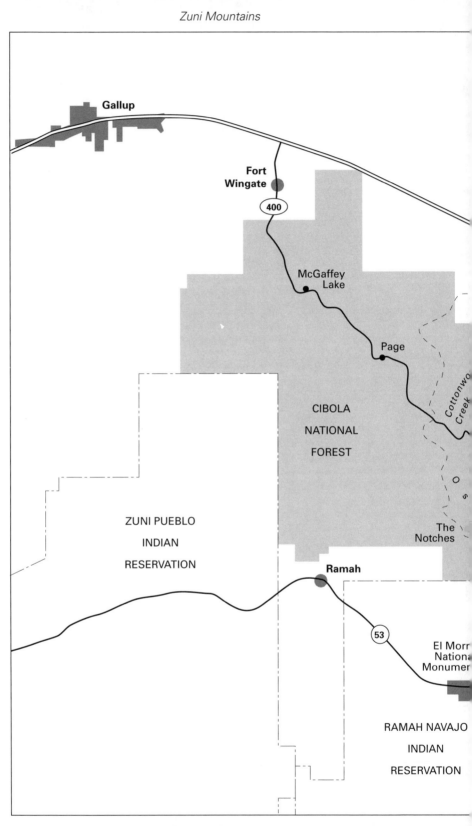

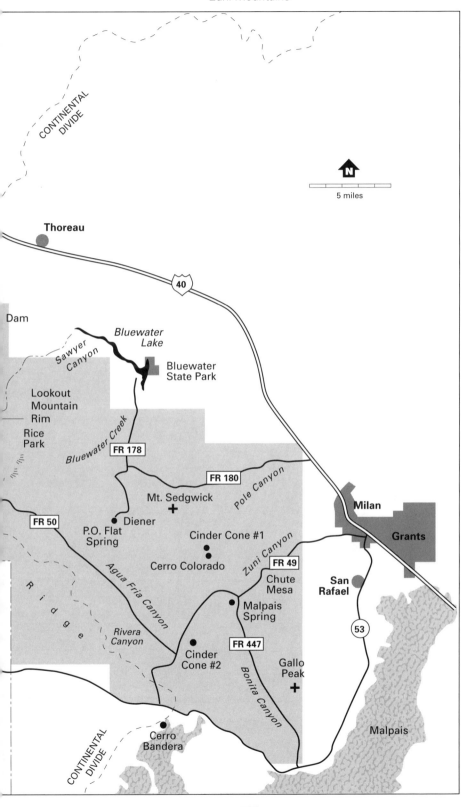

Zuni Mountains

(Pages 166–67)
Zuni Mountain
scene.

*Of the many volcanic regions I have explored, one of
the most interesting is in the Zuni Mountains of western
New Mexico, and along their slopes. All through the
range—whose tops are over 8,000 feet in altitude—are
scattered scores of extinct volcanoes; and their lava
flows have overrun many thousands of square miles. The
range is covered with a magnificent pine forest—a rare
enough thing in the southwest—partly growing upon
ancient flows and cut in all directions by later ones. The
soil everywhere is sown with jagged fragments of lava,
which makes travel irksome; and in the picturesque Zuni
canyon which traverses the range is a singular sight—
where the lava, too impatient to await outlet by a crater,
boiled out in great waves from under the bottom of the
canyon's walls, which are sandstone precipices hundreds
of feet high.*

Charles F. Lummis, 1908

*The Zuni Mountains and a large part of the Zuni Plateau
are densely pineclad; lofty pines rising from a variety of
scrub growth, including in favorable localities clumps
of small oaks. Small springs, little more than seepage
places, occur at not infrequent intervals in such forests,
and the park-like groves around them make the most
delightful camping places imaginable.*

Leslie Spier, 1917

As much as I love El Malpais and Mt. Taylor, I have
to confess that in the gentle beauty of the Zuni
Mountains, my heart leads my feet. In times of
pain and turmoil, this is the place that means
solace. Fortunately many will disagree. The Zunis lack
the ragged peaks, plunging mountain streams, the drama
of the Sangre de Cristos or the Gila. "Boring," my husband said, until I'd taken him to a few special places.

The landscape is rounded, the valleys broad. The Zuni
Mountains form a broad dome of 6,400 to 9,000 feet
stretching nearly sixty miles from Grants to Gallup. The
highest point is 9,256 feet at Mt. Sedgwick. Created by
uplift, erosion, and volcanic activity, the Zunis contain
some of the oldest exposed rock in northwestern New
Mexico (mostly granite) and are ringed and laced with
red sandstone cliffs. The Zunis also hide isolated volcanic cinder cones and their ancient lava flows. From
high points you can see the pink, piñon-studded sides of
Zuni and Bonita canyons to the northeast and the blue
pyramid of Mt. Taylor reaching across the horizon. To the
south the land rolls away, dipping long and green into
Agua Fria Valley and then folding into Oso Ridge, the

long spine that forms the Continental Divide in this part of western New Mexico. Stands of ponderosa pines cloak the hills. Tracks of wild turkey, bear, and deer punctuate the trails.

A hiker fifty years ago would have found a different world. Devastated by a half-century of logging and overgrazing that ended only in the 1940s, the pillaged mountains nursed hardly a tree or blade of grass. Erosion cut ugly arroyos, and wildlife was scarce. Today's stands of ponderosas, about the same height and a healthy distance apart among tall grass and wildflowers, give the Zuni Mountains a parklike beauty. They're also a monument to what Mother Nature and people can do in concert.

Railroad beds make good hiking trails. This one is in Rivera Canyon.

The government established Zuni National Forest on March 2, 1909, from portions of the Zuni and Navajo Indian reservations (Indian lands were returned in 1912; Zunis got additional lands from the forest in 1935). A 1909 study described the Zuni Mountains as a "high group" along the Continental Divide, with the western range, or Oso Ridge, separated from an eastern range by the upper Bluewater and Cottonwood Creek valleys. In December 1928 the Forest Service combined the Zuni divisions with four others—Datil, Mt. Taylor, Manzano, and Magdalena—to form Cibola National Forest, totaling 2.3 million acres. At present, the agency has 415,630 acres, or 649 square miles, in the Zuni Mountains.

Geology

Captain Clarence E. Dutton, surveying for the U.S. Geological Survey in 1879, declared that the Zuni Mountains weren't really mountains but rather a "broad elongate dome almost completely ringed by high inward-facing cliffs. . . . To the westward rises by moderate slopes a large and rather lofty mass, designated on the map 'Zuni Mountains,' though it seems to me more proper to call it a plateau . . . clothed all the way up with pines and juniper. The declivity is gentle and its surface is heavily timbered, so that the eye sees little else than a forest . . . The platform named Zuni Mountains . . . is not a proper mountain range."

During much of the Paleozoic era, a sea covering much of the area deposited limestones, sandstones, and shales. From the Ordovician to the Pennsylvanian periods, uplifts pushed dense limestones and conglomerates upward, which were later exposed through erosion. Unlike much of southern New Mexico, where Paleozoic deposits are twenty thousand feet thick, the sediment here is only about one thousand feet thick. During the Permian era, a sea crept north, with a shallow arm reaching present-day El Morro. As the water fluctuated, it left mixed limestone and gypsum, red muds and sands of the Abo and Yeso formations. A final movement of the sea reached just north of the Zuni Mountains and left the limestones and sandstones of the San Andres and Glorieta formations, which held large quantities of sea fossils.

The area was a low plain above sea level from Triassic into Cretaceous times. In the Triassic period, meandering rivers deposited the red, green, and purple shales, conglomerate, and sandstone that became the Chinle Formation. The land changed from forest to desert and back to forest. In the Jurassic period, winds deposited sand dunes to form the Zuni sandstone, and the sea advanced and left deposits of limestone and gypsum. The ring of rosy cliffs around the Zuni Mountains are Jurassic. In Late Cretaceous times, the sea advanced and retreated repeatedly across the Zuni Mountain area, leaving gray and black Mancos shale containing fossil clams and light-colored Dakota and Gallup sandstones. Slow-moving streams built deltas in the retreating and lush swamps, and lagoons followed the retreat, becoming today's coal deposits.

The sea retreated for good at the end of Cretaceous times, about seventy million years ago. As Cenozoic times began, forces lifted the earth's crust, pushing rocks into a broad dome that formed the Zuni Mountains, and running water began eroding the new slopes and cutting away canyons, until Precambrian granite saw the light of day. Mt. Sedgwick is composed primarily of this rock. Volcanic eruptions began to the south and northeast of the mountains during early Tertiary times. By Middle Tertiary times, lava flows and piles of ash had been deposited south of the Zunis. Mt. Taylor and the Jemez Mountains were active volcanos. In the Pleistocene era, as ice covered much of the United States and Canada, volcanoes poured out streams of lava. By the end of the Ice Age, the Zuni Mountain area looked much as it does now.

Meteors

Meteors are interesting geologic footnotes; the Zuni Mountain area has had at least three. In 1918, 1921, and 1929, people found fragments of the same meteor. The first was found near San Rafael and offered for sale to the Smithsonian; the second was found at a Breece Co. logging camp and offered to the Field Museum in Chicago. Then in 1929 Rodolfo Otero of San Rafael offered to sell the Smithsonian a 1,060-pound meteorite, and the museum bought it for $500. The location of Otero's find was described as "45 miles southwest of Grants in the Malipi lava" and also "in the Zuni Mountains," a description one researcher found conflicting. What he didn't know is that the Zunis contain lava flows.

A newspaper in June 1929 reported that a half-ton, iron meteorite was found on the Continental Divide, imbedded in "malapais rock," south of Grants. Getting the thing out of the Zunis proved to be a heroic effort. At one point the specimen rolled from its burro-drawn wagon and killed a man. At times three animals couldn't pull the weight. They did finally struggle into Grants and put it on a train for Washington, D.C. Geologists called it Grant. (Meteorites are all given names, usually for their location, and the hamlet of Grant had not yet changed its name to Grants; one fragment is known as Breece.) Grant was a cone-shaped, iron octahedrite, 21 inches from base to top. Parts of it now rest in the Field Museum of Chicago, the Smithsonian, and the University of New Mexico's Meteorite Museum.

A second meteorite called Bluewater, also an iron octahedrite, was found in 1946. It too reposes in the UNM Meteorite Museum.

In April 1893 a falling meteorite caused some excitement in the area. The *Gallup Gleaner* reported that a meteor streaked over Isleta, scaring residents into church. At Coolidge a group of people enjoying the evening air on the porch of Charles Paxton's store were startled to see it shoot close overhead. Paxton and a friend followed it on horseback, until they lost it near the Navajo Reservation. A Navajo later told Paxton where it fell, fifteen miles west of Coolidge. It slammed into the ground a foot deep, and Paxton dug it out and hauled it to his store. It was an egg shape about three feet long and weighing 300 pounds. It looked like iron.

Flora and Fauna

Pedro de Castañeda, chronicler to the Coronado expedition, performed the first biological survey in 1540. He observed a "very large number" of cranes, wild geese, and blackbirds in this area and a "great many" native fowl, such as wild turkey. He also saw "tame" eagles in the pueblos, probably intended for ceremonial use.

In inventories taken from 1902 to 1909, the U.S. Forest Service observed 41 species of birds, including buzzards, horned owls, swifts, and sparrow hawks. Turkeys were common in the timbered areas except in summer, and swallows were abundant. Common mammals were squirrels, chipmunks, mice, rats, porcupines, jackrabbits, cottontails, black and brown bears, and lynx. Coyotes were plentiful on the lower mesas. Mountain lions were infrequent, and antelope had disappeared.

Forest Service inventories in the 1930s described the San Juan coyote, a small, pale coyote found in the Zuni Mountains and around Gallup, Bluewater, and Ft. Wingate. The collared peccary, or javelina, a piglike animal, wasn't reported in the earlier survey but in this one was found in the Cebolleta Mountains, the San Mateo Mountains, and along the Continental Divide. The "big bronze wild turkey . . . is the aristocrat of North American game birds," the report said. Wild turkey and scaled quail were found in the Cebolleta Mountains, near Ramah, and in the San Mateo Mountains.

Thanks to a survey done for a controversial proposed power line, we have a lot of recent information about flora and fauna in the Zunis. The survey reported 42 species of birds in the higher mountains, 107 in the piñon-juniper areas, and 157 in riparian (riverside) areas. Birds you are likely to see include turkey vultures, scaled quail, red-tailed hawks, American coots, sandpipers, screech owls, great-horned owls, burrowing owls, common nighthawks, common poorwills, white-throated swifts, hummingbirds, northern flickers, flycatchers, swallows, jays, ravens, grosbeaks, bluebirds, wrens, and sparrows.

The Mexican spotted owl, said to prefer old-growth forest, is surprisingly common here. Another surprise is the northern goshawk, which is also abundant. It's unusual for the two to be neighbors, but the Zunis are the northernmost range of the owl and the southernmost range of the goshawk.

Mammals include shrews, cottontails, jackrabbits, squirrels, chipmunks, prairie dogs, antelope, mice, rats, porcupines, coyotes, black bears, raccoons, skunks, weasels, bobcats, mountain lions, mule deer and elk. There are also red, kit, and gray foxes and 20 species of bats.

Lizards include the northern sagebrush, eastern fence, side-blotched, tree, and short-horned; there are also skinks and whiptails. Snakes include the regal ringneck, the Graham patch-nosed, Sonora gopher, wandering garter, New Mexico milk, and Sonora Mountain kingsnake. There are black-tailed, prairie, and western diamondback rattlesnakes. (In 1915, the *Carbon City News* reported that a section crew at Perea killed the biggest rattler ever seen: "83 feet," with 140 rattles.) Fish include the Zuni Mountain sucker, the bluegill, and cutthroat and rainbow trout.

The Zuni Mountains get twenty to twenty-four inches of rain a year—twice that of the surrounding area. Half of it arrives from July through September, in afternoon and evening showers. Keep that in mind when planning your hikes.

Along with the ubiquitous piñon pines and one-seed junipers, the most common trees are ponderosa pines; alligator bark, Utah, and Rocky Mountain junipers; Arizona, Gambel's, and gray oaks; white and Douglas firs; and aspens. In the highest elevations are found subalpine firs and Engelmann and blue spruces. The most common shrubs are sagebrush, four-wing saltbush, mountain mahogany, rabbit brush, winter fat, Apache plume, and currants. Cacti include hedgehogs, barrel, cholla, and prickly pear. Wildflowers include Indian paintbrush, buckwheat, gilias, lupines, goldenrod, globe mal-

Navajo sweat lodge.

lows, verbenas, yarrow, asters, irises, bee balms, primroses, and vetches.

History

Zuni, Navajo, and Acoma Indian people have used the Zuni Mountains for centuries. Zuni Pueblo people hunted bear and deer here, foraged for plants, and gathered obsidian for points and tools. They also mined copper, turquoise, and blue paint. These mountains are sacred to the Acoma Indians, who believe the Rainmaker of the West lives here, and all three tribes have religious shrines and sacred sites here. Spaniards traversed the Zuni Mountains often to visit Zuni Pueblo but made no attempt to exploit resources or colonize.

The first American to take note of the area was James H. Simpson, a topographical engineer with the U.S. Army. Returning from an expedition into Navajo country in 1849, he detoured to record inscriptions at El Morro. Trying to catch up again with soldiers, Simpson and his companions picked up their trail near present-day Tinaja, rode north of Paxton Springs, and crossed the Continental Divide. He paused at the top of Oso Ridge in the Zuni Mountains, to admire the great mountain to the northeast, which he named Mt. Taylor. Then he passed down the Agua Fria Valley to Zuni Canyon.

In 1883 Adolph F. Bandelier took the same route, which came to be known as the Navajo trail. He wrote, "The road winds up to the top of the Sierra de Zuni, which is not a flat mesa, but a series of parallel ridges, therefore hill and vale . . . Beautiful pine trees compose the forest. It is not the low brush of the piñon and sabinos, but the dense stately timber, which I see now almost for the first time in New Mexico."

Logging and the Zuni Mountain Railroad

The Zuni Mountains in 1880 were black with timber. The thick stands had caught the attention of an entrepreneur or two, but with no way to ship timber, they mostly supplied local needs. When the Atlantic & Pacific Railroad began building west from Albuquerque, transportation was at hand, and the railroad had a mighty appetite for crossties. It wasn't long before logging and tie-cutting operations dotted the area. By 1889 Henry Hart and W. S. Bliss had mills, and the following year, *The Elk,* a Gallup newspaper, described Hart City, twenty-two miles southeast of Gallup. It had a well-stocked merchandise store, and "one of the best sawmills in the Zuni range" was shipping fifteen to twenty loads a day to Coolidge. The newspaper advised that there were "thousands of acres of fine timber and ranch lands which can be had for the taking as every other section is government land. Fine large valleys and parks abound in plenty . . ."

Large-scale logging got its start in 1890, with a short-lived operation by the brothers William and Austin Mitchell. On June 30, 1890, the financially ailing A&P railroad sold 314,668 acres of land and its timber to the Michigan lumbermen for about $1.50 an acre. In 1891 the Mitchell brothers incorporated the Zuni Mountain Railway Co. The A&P surveyed a route into the mountains and helped build a rail line. A year later work began on a mill thirty 30 miles west of Grants, which became the town of Mitchell (later Thoreau). To supply water to the mill boiler, they built a handsome rock dam south of Mitchell in Cottonwood Canyon. It still stands. In May 1892 the locomotive arrived. Operations had hardly begun when it derailed, forcing the mill to shut down until a new locomotive arrived in August. In September the Mitchells halted work without explanation. The cash-strapped A&P had probably not dropped its rates for timbering, as promised, and economic conditions soured as the Panic of 1893 set in.

It was ten years before anyone attempted large-scale logging again. Late in 1901 the American Lumber Com-

pany bought 292,625 acres from the Mitchell brothers for $1.1 million and forged new agreements with the Santa Fe Railroad, which had taken over the A&P. American converted from narrow gauge to standard gauge and extended the rail line past the rock dam and into Cottonwood Canyon over a pigpen trestle (a log-cabin-type bridge) and on to Sawyer, in the heart of the Zuni Mountains. In October 1903 the company shipped its first load of logs.

American harvested timber from Cottonwood Canyon to Oso Ridge to Kettner, the main logging camp. Loggers with two-man saws felled trees and skidded them to the tracks on a horse-drawn "big wheel," which was simply two 12-foot wooden wheels on an axle or wagon. Later a small-wheeled wagon called a "bummer" replaced the big wheels. Using skids and a chain, the teamster and lead team would "cross haul" a log onto the wagon. Eventually "steam donkeys" (loaders) were used. Pulling the cars were mainline locomotives and, on steep spurs, special logging locomotives like the Shay geared locomotive, a real workhorse. As loggers worked, section crews of Navajos or Hispanics built rail spurs into nearly every drainage along the main line and could lay about a half-mile of track a day, with the help of a locomotive.

American cut about 35 million board feet in both 1904 and 1905 and 50 million in 1906 and employed 250 men in the Zunis. At the Albuquerque mill, 850 workers turned the logs into cut lumber, doors, moldings, and boxes. American's sash and door factory was one of the nation's largest. At its peak, around 1910, the company produced

Logging operation, between 1885 and 1890. (Photo by Ben Wittick, courtesy Museum of New Mexico, 15600.)

Crew at Zuni Mountain Lumber and Trade Co. sawmill, about 1900. (Photo courtesy Museum of New Mexico, 130764.)

60 million board feet of timber, employed 700 loggers, and shipped 100 carloads of logs a day.

The headquarters camp of Kettner, named for a homesteader in the area, had a post office, a company store, a roundhouse, a two-story hotel with fifty rooms, and a cookhouse that could feed 700 loggers. It also had a school with 35 students, the children of loggers and ranchers. Not one stick remains of the camp today. In 1909 Sawyer, a rough camp a few miles away named for a company officer, became American's headquarters. The post office was moved from Kettner, and Sawyer also had a school and general store.

Saloons sprang up at the lumber camps, despite the company's efforts to discourage them. Loggers drank all they could hold, and the Kettner area became known for brawls and occasional murders. By all accounts life in the Zuni camps was bone hard. Hazel Fallon Rogers, whose mother was a lumber-camp cook, was born in Kettner and lived in every logging camp in the Zunis. She recalled traveling in snow up to the horses' bellies, and once their wagon overturned in the snow. Roy Heath, whose father ran a butcher shop in Sawyer, observed that in the logging camps, men worked ten hours a day. "Life wasn't very good."

In 1913 American Lumber suddenly halted all operations and went into receivership.

Thoreau

Mitchell was becoming a ghost town in 1896 when Richard Wetherill, who had discovered and explored the ruins of Mesa Verde, began excavating in Chaco Can-

yon for the Hyde Exploring Expedition. The expedition
built a store and three warehouses to store artifacts
and Navajo rugs for shipment east. By 1901 the road
from Pueblo Bonito to Thoreau was in almost constant
use by the expedition's wagons loaded with blankets,
hides, and wool. The trading enterprise flourished and
then declined, finally expiring with Wetherill's murder
in 1910.

Supposedly members of the Hyde Expedition renamed
the town Thoreau, but that's a subject of debate. Longtime residents have claimed that the town was named
for a bookkeeper of the Mitchell brothers, an army paymaster, or a railroad contractor. One said it was wishful
thinking on the part of local teachers, who tried to tie the
town to the great poet. Henry David Thoreau himself
never traveled west of Minnesota. On one thing everyone agrees: the pronunciation (Thuh-ROO) is unchanged
from the beginning.

With the railroad and logging, Thoreau boomed.
Three west-bound and three east-bound trains a day
arrived with goods and carried away lumber and livestock. Thoreau became the second largest shipping
point in New Mexico for cattle and sheep. It had a big
depot and a Harvey House, where a traveler could stay
for fifty cents and eat well for twenty-five or thirty cents.
Paydays on the first and fifteenth brought seven work
gangs to town. And tourists were starting to come
through. Trading posts continued to do a brisk business. Traders bought wool, piñons, lambs, and rugs
from Indians and paid them in scrip redeemable at their
stores. During a good piñon year, they might ship three
boxcar loads.

In 1918 a promoter named J. F. Branson bought land
north of the tracks, platted it, and sold lots. He also built
an opera house and garage. Two years later a resident
named Lulu Bimbo told a Gallup newspaper that a town-
site was laid out and lots were selling for one hundred
dollars. In 1921 the Gallup newspapers were excitedly
reporting an oil strike near Thoreau. And drillers were at
work in the Zuni Mountains, Ambrosia Lake, and Gallup.
The source of many of the reports: J. F. Branson.

Thoreau became quite a mecca, with a movie theater, soda fountain, two general stores, multiple gambling parlors, and a whorehouse. Its two hotels were
always full. Motorists from Gallup noted that the Elk
Hotel was "beautifully done up." Roads were so bad
then that it took two days to get from Gallup to Albuquerque. For fun there were dances. At "weight dances,"
a man paid a penny for each pound his partner weighed.
In "chalk and toe" dances, the women lined up behind
a curtain and had a number chalked on their toes. The
man with the corresponding number became her date
for the evening. And there were baseball games. One

time in 1927, the miners outside Gallup played a game of fat men against skinny. The fat guys won.

But not all the fun was so innocent. One night in 1924 three locals, a lumberjack, and a gambler were playing poker. In a scene that could have inspired Hollywood westerns, one local man shot the lumberjack in the neck. The gambler returned fire across the table, walked around to the other side, lifted his victim by an arm, and pumped in three more bullets. Incredibly the man survived. A neighbor lady cut a bullet from the lumberjack's neck with a butcher knife, and he returned to camp.

Thoreau's fortunes changed by the late 1920s. Logging shifted toward Grants, and the Depression settled in. Ranchers went broke, and Navajos lost their sheep to drought and overgrazing. Fires, often of dubious origin, consumed buildings. Much of the land returned to Branson. Thoreau was becoming a ghost town again when surveying began in 1935 for Route 66. After trader Homer Jones became the westernmost dealer for Phillips 66, Frank Phillips himself commissioned a Navajo rug with the Phillips 66 logo. Today the town survives on trade from the reservation and nearby I-40.

McGaffey

One of Thoreau's traders became a lumber baron. Amasa B. McGaffey in 1903 bought out the former Hyde store at Thoreau and with a partner operated a string of stores in American Lumber's camps at Kettner, Sawyer, Cold Springs, and Guam (Coolidge). In 1907 he contracted with the Santa Fe Railroad and American Lumber to cut crossties. Next he organized the Santa Barbara Tie and Pole Co. to cut ties and timbers north of Santa Fe. He hauled ties to his mill, floated the cut ties down the Rio Grande to a boom near Cochiti, and then hauled them by rail to a tie-treating plant in Albuquerque.

In 1910 he organized the McGaffey Co. and built a sawmill at Schuster Springs, in what was then a thickly wooded area of the western Zuni Mountains. On 24,000 acres near Fort Wingate, he began logging and soon acquired another 12,000 acres of timber in Zuni National Forest. In 1912 McGaffey built a railroad spur from Perea, on the Santa Fe Railroad, along Sixmile Canyon to Turkey Springs and into Train Canyon to his headquarters town of McGaffey (FR 547 today makes use of the old roadbed in places or parallels it). His logging camps were at Camp Ten and The Notches. Later on the railroad crossed Oso Ridge into the Dan Valley, near Ramah. During harvest season, area farmers used the line to haul wheat and potatoes.

McGaffey became the biggest and most genteel of the lumber camps. With as many as two hundred families at one time, McGaffey was a tidy, even pretty town, with rows of houses in the trees. It had a Catholic church, a five-room school with a hundred students, a general store, and a post office. "There was a whole complete town," said longtime Grants resident Red Prestridge, "with water system and with water spigots in the streets where you could bring your buckets to fill up with water, and an electric light system plant and a commissary where you could buy anything—a wagon, or a log wagon or horse's hay, dresses, shoes, whatever—and a post office." Sawmill workers once struck to protest high prices at the company store. A sheriff settled the dispute.

A measure of the citizens' aspirations to culture was the sixty-by-twenty-six-foot hall called the Alhambra, built in 1915 for dances, drama, opera, and "lectures on science," according to the *Carbon City News*. A. B. McGaffey and his wife hosted dances for their workers. And people came from all over the Zunis for the Fourth of July celebration, which had footraces, horse races, a chicken pull, and a dance.

McGaffey also had its wild side. Consider this newspaper item, dated 1915: "Sidney Hicks became intoxicated Saturday afternoon and tried to drive his yoke of steers into the butcher shop. He was prevented by the narrowness of the door. There have been other complaints of narrowness of the butcher's door lately."

Settlers

> *The curtains of night are pinned back by the stars*
> *And the heavenly moon lights the sky*
> *It's shining down on the Zunis tonight*
> *As it has in the years gone by.*
>
> *Casting its shadows in the valley deep*
> *And high on the mountain walls*
> *Guarding the shepherd as he sleeps*
> *In rhythm to the night bird's call.*
>
> *It will guide the weary cowboy home*
> *Down o'er the mountain trails*
> *And send its moonbeams to the valley it seems*
> *To dance to the coyote's wails.*
>
> *Cecil Moore, 1938*

Settlers spying the broad green valleys of the Zuni Mountains must have felt close to heaven. The soil was rich alluvium, the rainfall abundant. After the 1916 Homestead Act drew the first big wave of people, the Zunis became the breadbasket of western New Mexico. Farmers then called the Zuni Mountain rye crop the "finest in the world." By 1918 they were well enough established to organize a farmers association to test new varieties of wheat and oats, improve marketing, and study disease prevention. The state land commis-

(Above) Zuni Mountain homestead. (Right) Homestead at Page.

sioner observed a few years later that the Zuni Mountains produced the finest grain, wheat, oats, and barley he had ever seen.

They were also doing well with vegetables. One farmer brought a twenty-eight-pound cabbage to Gallup. The vast Page Valley, named for the Canadians Gregory and James Page who operated a sawmill in nearby Foster Canyon in the 1880s, held the best farms. Potatoes were worth seventy-five cents per hundred pounds to a Grants merchant.

Logging accelerated settlement, as logging companies or the railroad sold cutover timberlands, and the Forest Service offered grazing permits. In August 1915 the *Carbon City News* wrote, "rich timber and grazing districts offer almost untouched opportunities" in the Zuni Mountains. The Forest Service had grazing permits on the slopes of Mt. Sedgwick and offered, at reasonable rates, "logging chances" in the area. The McGaffey Co. advertised farmlands for lease in 1917, saying, "No crop failures. Finest land in the Zuni Mountains." That same year one newspaper reported that Zuni Mountain farms would double their crops, then mostly potatoes. The McGaffey Co. itself planned to cultivate four thousand acres, and land baron Silvestre Mirabal was planning to plant land owned by American Lumber. There were then seven thousand acres under cultivation.

In one typical transaction, John Garvin of West Virginia in 1906 acquired thirty thousand acres of near "primeval forest" south of McGaffey from the Santa Fe Railroad. In 1928 Garvin offered to sell thirty thousand acres of cutover land to farmers and stockmen. Rainfall,

he said, was 19 to 21.5 inches, compared with 13 inches in Gallup. Grain weighed forty to fifty-two pounds a
bushel, compared with twenty-six to thirty pounds in the
lower areas.

Activity increased as copper mining began around
Diener and operated from 1916 to the early 1930s. "It
was called tree copper—petrified wood turned to copper," recalled longtime resident Dovie Bright. "It was a
very high grade copper." In 1915 The Copper Hill Mining
Co. and area settlers built a road from Copperton, site of
several mines and mills, to Bluewater. Later, when the
defense industry needed fluorspar during World War II,
Navajo Fluorspar Co. operated three mines on the east
side of the Zuni Mountains from 1940 until 1952, when
foreign competition brought down the price.

Mining and especially logging were a godsend to
homesteaders. When homesteaders elsewhere began
to starve out, those in the Zuni Mountains were selling
meat, produce, and hay to nearby mines and logging
camps. Many found work there. Buck Moore, who had
been a freighter in White Oaks until gold mining petered
out in Lincoln County, moved his family here in a covered wagon in 1905. When American Lumber folded,
recalled his son Cecil, the company "sold off all their big
logging horses, stored all the equipment at headquarters
camp and made my father the caretaker." Moore began
hauling timber from the logging camps to the railroad
and also cut and sold ties as he homesteaded. His sons
Cecil and Roy Moore laid track for the Zuni Mountain
Railway. Cecil also homesteaded in the early 1930s,
traded cattle, ran a tourist attraction at the Ice Caves,

and operated the first sawmill and lumberyard in the Grants area. He was also quite a fiddler and a cowboy poet. He died at eighty-three, in 1985.

Cecil once described their life here: "I was from a family of eight kids raised on top of the Zuni Mountains, where we dry farmed and raised cattle and hogs. My father also worked for a large lumber company [American Lumber] while the rest did the ranch work. By lamplight we ate breakfast . . . and supper too. . . . Each kid had his part lined out by the parents—us older ones fed the horses, hogs and milked the cows, while the young fed the chickens, cats and dogs and put out water . . . My mother washed clothes twice a week, and the only running water we had was down under the hill in the creek. We had to carry water up this hill in buckets and tubs so she could wash on the rub board. She could use more water than a steam engine, and she always had a strap or a switch handy to see we did it."

One indication of prosperity was this item in the *Gallup Independent:* In 1923 Charles Berger bought a "radio outfit" for his farm near McGaffey. "Now the wilds of the Zuni Mountains are about to be filled with the operatic and scientific wonders of the world," the newspaper observed.

Today collapsed cabins and deserted farmhouses tell that the good times didn't last. As logging waned so did the markets for produce, and the shift from horses to trucks meant loggers didn't need grain. Small stockmen had trouble competing for range with big cattle and sheep companies. And the skies grew stingier with rain. By 1936 the farms of Page Valley had given way to sheep pasture.

Breece

In 1917 George Breece of West Virginia and his McKinley Land and Lumber Co. (later called the George E. Breece Lumber Co.) bought American Lumber's properties, which included the railroad and 242,478 acres of land. Breece had spent his life in the lumber business, working his way up from sawyer to superintendent. During World War I he used his expertise in the Army Signal Corps, which was lumbering to provide timbers for airplanes. When Breece returned to New Mexico in 1919, he had the rank of colonel, which became his moniker after that.

In July 1919 Breece had the Zuni Mountain Railroad's tracks rebuilt from Thoreau to Sawyer, and a hundred men began logging. The colonel began acquiring massive tracts of land and timber rights. Wheeling and dealing in the next two years, Breece acquired 739,974 acres of state land and timber rights to another 100,000 acres, sold 170,000 acres to Sylvestre Mirabal and bought the timber on Mirabal's land, and then bought 530,000 feet of timber in Cottonwood Canyon from the Forest

Service. (In the enabling act, the federal government gave the state 10 million acres of land for schools, some of it in the Zuni Mountains. The state then sold its land to lumber companies, so that they could "block up," or consolidate, their alternating sections.)

In 1920 or 1921, Breece moved the main logging camp from Sawyer to Las Tusas ("corn silk") Valley, south of Thoreau and west of Bluewater Reservoir. The new camp of Breece was soon a bustling place. In 1921 the company started up its Albuquerque mills.

The Santa Fe's rising freight rates in 1922 turned Grants into a boom town. To save twenty-nine miles on the trip to the Albuquerque mills, Breece's board of directors decided to build a new railroad from Grants into the logging areas. Construction began in early 1926 as Zuni, Navajo, and Hispanic laborers pushed new tracks through the lava into Zuni Canyon to Malpais Spring and then up La Jara Canyon into Agua Fria Creek near Paxton Springs. Cecil Moore recalled using twenty teams of horses to move dirt and a hundred men with picks and shovels to make the rock cuts. The new railroad began operating in 1927, but that year fire destroyed the company's roundhouse, at a loss of $150,000.

In 1928 Paxton Springs became Breece's new head-quarters logging camp and the terminus of its railroad. It had a large store, a school, a post office, and one hundred to three hundred residents. Paxton Springs was apparently named for an elderly woman known only as Mrs. Paxton, who lived there in the 1880s with her horse, dog, and cat. (Paxton Springs nearly had a darker history. In 1944 scientists with the Manhattan Project were looking for a test site for the atomic bomb. Their list included Paxton Springs, the area near Cabezon Peak northeast of Mt. Taylor, and the desert south of El Morro. They ruled them all out because of Indians living in the area and because it would be difficult to transport the ten-thousand-pound "gadget," as the bomb was called, over the area's poor roads. They chose instead the windswept Alamogordo Bombing Range.)

As Breece shifted operations east, he pushed the slumbering Grants into the twentieth century. On the west side of town, he built a roundhouse and homes for his workers, which came to be known as Breecetown. The old roundhouse still stands, behind the Diamond-G Hardware Store. A wonderful adobe building, it's now used as a warehouse. Across the street are some of the original company houses. Breecetown ballooned the town's population from under four hundred people to around four thousand and prompted Grants to get electricity and running water in 1929. The colonel also brought in a doctor who had once pitched for the Detroit Tigers. He practiced medicine in his living room, managed the Breece baseball team, and scouted for players.

"We played our first game at Thoreau," recalled Red Prestridge. "Had to use rocks for bases, and there were prairie dog holes. We had one baseball and two rubber baseballs exactly the same weight and size with the threads molded in them with 'Red Goose Shoes' printed on them, and one of them went down a prairie dog hole . . . so we got a home run. When Doc was here, he sent my brother Rex to the leagues three times."

Loggers

Loggers in the 1920s worked for $2.50 a day and lived in company houses or logging camps. "The thing was— Breece and McGaffey—we all had a job. We had money," Red Prestridge said. "It wasn't a lot of money. Store clerk could make up to $125 a month, and a store manager could make $425. I think if a man worked out in the woods as a log scaler or tie inspector he would make better money than in the store. Loggers who drove teams would get 45 cents an hour, worked 10 hours a day and made pretty fair money." Jose Abran Barreras said he made good money working for Breece—$500 a month in 1925—and bought a new Chrysler 60 for $2,000.

Breece contracted the logging, Prestridge said. "The colonel had verbal contracts that were better than one written. He lived up to his word." Each of about twenty contractors had an area to log with horses. "You would hardly ever get more than three miles from the railroad. That was about as far as a horse could carry the logs."

Breece was the first in the area to use logging trucks. Big Colton trucks hauled logs from Mt. Sedgwick to Malpais Springs, Prestridge said, but they broke down often. In about 1928 Breece bought road equipment and Ford and Chevrolet trucks that could haul about three thousand feet of timber. "But they still horse-logged until about 1934, 1935," Prestridge said. In the 1930s trucks gradually replaced rail for hauling logs.

Breece's camps were as rowdy as American Lumber's. "Violence seemed unrestrained," wrote Gary Tietjen. The most notorious killing was probably the murder of Ben Wales. In 1918 Wales lived at a place called Spud Ranch, near Kettner. One morning he came out of his cabin and was shot with a .22-caliber pistol. He struggled back inside, leaving blood all over the door as he shut it and pushed his bed against it. Then he lay down and died. "I don't know what they killed him for," an old-timer said later. "He never hurt nobody." Another neighbor wrote to a Gallup newspaper that Wales was "a good blacksmith and useful man to the community." The same year an unnamed culprit called the "Zuni Mountain Terror" was captured and brought to Albuquerque for Wales's murder. Five years later homesteader Buck Moore, who had found Wales's body, died in a shootout over a pig (see Zuni Mountain Hikes, Rice Park).

On the Fourth of July, 1929, a logger shot and killed a fellow logger, "Salkie" Noble, in a lumber camp south of Grants. The sheriff caught the culprit sleeping in the rocks at El Morro.

Prestridge recalled fights and moonshining in the area. "You see, it was in prohibition days, and a lot of fellows made moonshine liquor," he said. "I knew seven or eight of them, where their stills were. They would send revenuers out from Albuquerque."

End of the Line

By the late 1920s, Breece's logging proposals were becoming more ambitious, as the timber stands disappeared. Loggers had taken out millions of feet of timber, often cutting faster than timber could be shipped. McGaffey too was running out of trees and looking for new stands. Financing was difficult. After securing timber rights on the Navajo Reservation, he assigned them to a Texas company in 1929. Days later, on September 3 in Albuquerque, he boarded one of the nation's first commercial airliners for a hunting trip in California. The plane crashed high on Mt. Taylor, killing all aboard. The McGaffey operation was winding down when, in one last cruel turn of events, the assistant foreman died in a mill accident.

In 1934 the State-Federal Transient Service turned McGaffey into a camp for transients, who got housing and food in return for work. By 1936 McGaffey was becoming a summer resort, and the Game Protective Association of McKinley County had begun stocking McGaffey Lake.

By 1929 Breece's employee ranks thinned along with the trees, and hard times across the country added to the burden. As the 1930s opened, shutdowns were frequent and wages were cut. In January 1930 Breece's beautiful home in Grants burned to the ground, as he and his wife were preparing to move to Cloudcroft. Breece in 1931 leased and then sold his operation to Grants businessmen Carl Seligman and M. R. Prestridge, of the Bernalillo Mercantile Co. With Paxton Springs continuing as headquarters camp, the new owners began logging in the area with a hundred men on the payroll. They built new track from Agua Fria through Rivera Canyon into Valle Largo, where there was already a logging camp. Today the remains of two log buildings are visible at Agua Fria, along with a cold deck for storing and loading logs. Eventually, the line reached Tinaja in El Morro valley, which became another logging camp.

Locomotives pulled their last load in the fall of 1941, about when commercial timber ran out. Prestridge and Seligman sold the rolling stock back to Breece, but he never operated again; he sold his Albuquerque sawmill in 1942. In 1946 Prestridge and his brother Red logged on Mt. Taylor for four years, but it was the end of an era.

Breece sold the railroad to a Minnesota company. Its engine and loader had a device that would "pop the spikes out" of the tracks, break rails at the angle bars, and load them on a trailing car. "They just went to the end of the railroad and dragged it in with them," Prestridge said. "I think the greater part of that metal went to Japan before World War II."

Seeds of Recovery

When the last railroad whistle blew in the canyons of the Zuni Mountains, there was hardly a tree or blade of grass. Loggers had removed sawtimber in the first cut; trees too small for lumber were taken later for crossties and mining materials. The only conservation requirement in those days was to leave two trees an acre for reseeding, and they usually left the two worst. Then they sold surface rights to area ranchers, who overgrazed it. Tree cover and grasses disappeared, and the inevitable erosion lowered water tables and dried out wet meadows. The black-footed ferret was seen no more.

By 1940 Cottonwood Canyon, once a willow-lined trout stream, had become a small, intermittent stream subject to flash floods. Its vertical banks were ten to twenty feet high. Bluewater Canyon was in the same state. Both were ruined for fishing. Only a small remnant of the once plentiful deer, wild turkey, and bear could be found. Local communities petitioned the Forest Service to acquire Mirabal's 246,480 acres and Breece's 157,680 acres. A 1940 Forest Service report said that "Breece and Mirabal pine lands (are) so completely denuded as to require planting at about 60,000 acres . . . The private timber land owners in this case were seemingly committed to the philosophy of liquidating their investments at a profit [which] did not include such important factors as sustained yield of timber and employment; nor did they include provision for a residual stand for reseeding future cuts or to protect watershed values. Aside from the remaining virgin area—about 5,000 acres—the lands are barren of timber . . ."

A few had seen disaster looming years before. As early as 1894, a government official admitted that "our forestry laws are inadequate in themselves as well as feebly enforced." The government was then considering preservation of its timber belts, and European countries already had laws requiring reseeding and limited cutting. In 1902 the government required descriptions and bids for timber cutting on public land. Any other timber cutting was illegal, but the law was rarely enforced and the penalty was only the cost of timber. The Forest Service began to sell timber in New Mexico in 1905. Demand from sawmills dictated how much was cut, and as early as 1907 government timber managers worried about sustained yield.

Although Grants and Gallup had embraced logging and the jobs it provided, they weren't without a conservation ethic. American Lumber had considered reforestation with catalpa trees. In 1911 Gallup citizen W. R. Maloon announced that he would plant 1,750 yellow pines in one area of the Zunis and 3,500 more near Sawyer. In March 1916 the governor proclaimed arbor and bird day in the state, pointing out that trees had aesthetic as well as economic values. Breece gave lip service to the rules of forest conservation of that day and agreed to leave seed trees so that the timber supplies would not be depleted but "constantly replenish" themselves.

In 1925, foresters warned that timber was being cut faster than it could grow back naturally, and American Forest Week was declared. The New Deal years saw the first big push for sustainable-yield and conservation practices as well as for the regulation of private forests (Congress rejected the latter).

In a 1934 brochure, the Forest Service explained its mission: "The national forests are created in order to insure a perpetual supply of timber for homes and industries and to prevent the destruction of forest and vegetation cover . . . Cutting is allowed at a rate not exceeding the sustained yield of management units." Loggers were supposed to remove only "ripe timber," leaving young, fast-growing trees and enough big trees for seed production. Sustained-yield practices included tree planting on denuded areas and eroded lands. However, sustained yield didn't become law until the 1940s and didn't attract attention until 1960.

The Forest Service formed Zuni National Forest on March 2, 1909, and by 1934 the boundaries were about as they are today; but islands of private property made management difficult. Through trades and acquisitions, the agency began filling in, and by the 1970s, the Zuni Mountains portion of Cibola National Forest totaled 415,630 acres, or 649 square miles. Reseeding had taken place on its own by the 1970s, but the Forest Service identified 17,000 to 18,000 acres of clear-cut forest with good enough soil to grow trees again. Reforestation efforts got a shot in the arm with the 1974 Timber Stand Improvement Act. Trial and error proved that only ponderosa seed from the Zuni Mountains would take hold. Foresters ultimately became so discriminating that they collected seed only from the best trees in the Zunis and returned seedlings to the place of collection. From 1977 to 1987, the agency planted about 2,000 acres a year.

The Forest Service also joined other groups for habitat improvement. In 1986 the Forest Service, state Game and Fish Department, local water users, and Ducks Unlimited joined to build a dike and islands in the jewel-like Rice Park for ducks, deer, and elk.

There is still logging in the Zunis and on Mt. Taylor,

but at a fraction of the pace of the Breece days. As the Forest Service grows more conservative in its sustainable-yield estimates, even that amount of logging is likely to decrease.

Zuni Mountain Hikes

Hikes from FR 49

Chute Mesa

Getting there: Just south of Grants on NM 53, almost immediately south of I-40, turn right to the Zuni Canyon road. Soon after entering Zuni Canyon on FR 49, you will see the locomotive-shaped markers of the Zuni Mountain Railroad Tour (see next section). Stop at the second marker, and park.

This is Chute Mesa, so named because the loggers sent timbers crashing down its face to the railroad tracks below. For the hike up, find a two-track turnoff that was once a logging road just beyond the #2 railroad sign and begin walking up. The road angles gradually up the side of an adjacent slope.

In the late summer, afternoon rains encourage the sagewort to scent the canyon, and the slopes are loaded with the curlicues of mountain mahogany. About midway up white sandstone is nature's rock garden, holding yucca and cactus. Wild geranium and snakeweed are everywhere. Kathleen is pleased to find green gentian, which isn't known to grow here.

Near the top of the mesa, just over a mile from the bottom, the road dissolves into a confusion of forks and branches. The next move requires a little exploring. You can continue on what looks to be the most-traveled branch of the road, which brings you to a water tank. Find the berm near the tank and follow it back in the direction you've come. (There is a road directly below the water tank; that's *not* the one.) Near the end of the berm, look across what appears to be a rude limestone quarry with white rock rubble, and you should see a road. Another choice: From the muddle of forks, leave the roads and walk up to your left, watching for the berm and the scattered white rock and look for the old logging road in the trees that angles off to the left.

After a mile, this road brings you to a clearing—actually to the clear-cut mesa top, where the lumber arrived for its trip down the canyon side. A brief search along the edge should bring you to the chute, which is littered with tangles and curls of rusted cable. We find other rusted pieces, including the tooth of a peavey, used to hook and pull logs. A rock on the edge has a groove worn in it from working cables. From the top there's a fine view of Zuni Canyon and its volcanic flow along the

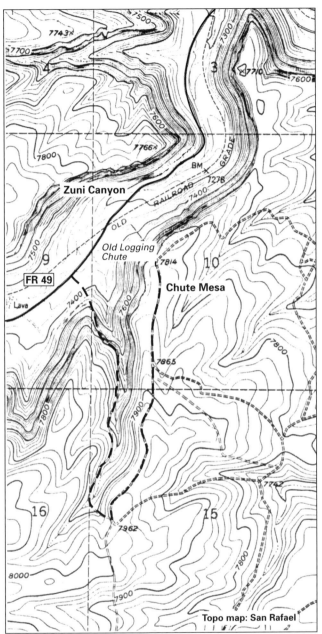

bottom. Reclining behind the opposite canyon wall is Mt. Sedgwick.

The fearless and hardy could scramble or slide down the chute with some difficulty. Normal folks and confessed wimps should hike down the way they came. On our trek down, Kathleen spots fresh bear tracks; by fresh, she means since we walked up. Then we see no more tracks. The bruin is possibly up the hill watching us.

189

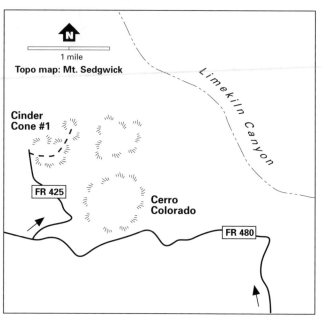

Distance: 4–6 miles, depending on how much exploring you do on top.
Time: 4 hours.
Difficulty: Not difficult, but some complaints from the knee.
Topo Map: San Rafael.

Unnamed Cindercone #1

Getting there: Just south of Grants on NM 53, take the turnoff to Zuni Canyon. From the Zuni Canyon road, or FR 49, take the right fork to FR 480 at Malpais Springs. At the windmill and water tank, turn right to FR 425. The red hill at the intersection is Cerro Colorado. Next to it, as you continue less than a mile down FR 425, is an unnamed, tree-studded cinder cone.

It's a short, steep scramble up loose lava to the top of this volcanic cone, where the elevation is 8,343 feet. In the late summer it's polka-dotted with wildflowers—scarlet gilia, flax, buckwheat. A cluster of hedgehog cactus nestles in the crotch of an ancient, twisted juniper. Another clump of the cactus bears its amber fruit, which the Navajos call heart-twister. Kathleen tastes one. It's like pear or kiwi, she says. Then she plants it next to a sheltering rock.

The top of this cone is littered with squeezes—the molten rock squeezed from the earth like a twist of toothpaste—and bombs, the rounded forms with a pointed end that were blown from the volcano and shaped by their plummet back to the ground. The evening primrose holds forth on top. An exotic-looking beauty, its defiant choice of a hostile landscape as home earns my respect.

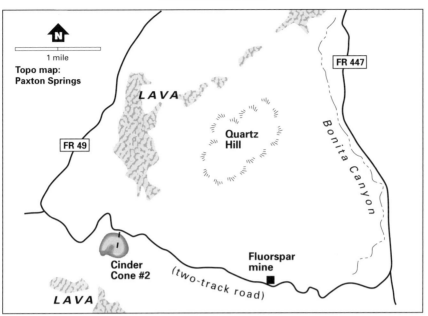

Like other volcanic cones, this one is crescent-shaped. Douglas firs enjoy the shelter and moisture of its bowl. This cone offers fabulous views of Mt. Taylor to the northeast and Mt. Sedgwick to the northwest. I always like getting to the top of something. Without thinking I always take a deep breath, drink in the view, and wish it could last forever.

Distance: Less than ¾ miles up and down.
Time: About an hour.
Difficulty: A brief but somewhat challenging scramble.
Topo map: Mt. Sedgwick.

Unnamed Cinder Cone #2/ Fluorspar Mines
Getting there: Just south of Grants on NM 53, take the turnoff to Zuni Canyon, which becomes FR 49. At Malpais Spring, turn left to FR 447. You will notice the remains of some stone and wood structures, all that's left of one Breece lumber camp. Nearby, on the right, a pile of old lumber tells you that a sawmill stood here. Turn right onto a four-wheel-drive track 2.9 miles south of Malpais Spring, and drive west.

Just over a mile in, you will see a fluorspar mine with its headframe still standing. The shaft has been filled in, but the hole is still about twenty feet deep. The corner post of the fence around the mine is an old rusted octagon rifle barrel. Continuing on, the road forks just beyond the old mine. Take the right fork past several test pits. Slightly over a mile from the first mine is a second, this one unfilled. Hang onto your kids and dogs! In another two miles, you will reach the cinder cone responsible for the

Headframe remaining from a fluorspar mine that operated during World War II.

Zuni Canyon flow—a brown mound with scattered trees and vegetation. On the cone's steep sides Kathleen finds penstemon, wild geranium, lambsquarter, trumpet flower (gentian), lupine, and wax currant. "It's a hummingbird's paradise," she says.

As you climb you can look into the pink, piñon-studded sides of Zuni and Bonita canyons to the northeast. From the top you see that this cone, like the others in the area, blew up and out one side, forming a crescent. The rim is studded with ponderosa pine and Douglas fir, yucca and Apache plume. Kathleen finds buckwheat and chokecherries at the crater's mouth. The occasional egg-shaped lava rocks are bombs spit out by the cone. Right next to the cone are three small cinder cones. To the south is the broad green band of the Agua Fria Valley and beyond it, Oso Ridge. You can see Bandera Crater and Cerro Alto (the taller cone) peeking over Oso Ridge.

Continue on the same road, and in slightly less than two miles, it meets FR 49. Turn right for the trip back out through Zuni Canyon, or left to exit through Oso Ridge on FR 50.

Distance: 1 mile.
Time: 1 hour.
Difficulty: Short, steep climb but not difficult.
Topo Map: Paxton Springs.

Mt. Sedgwick
(See Mt. Sedgwick loop tour map, p. 212)
Getting there: Take FR 49 and turn north (right) on FR

480. This is one of the most spectacular drives in the Zunis, although not for the timid. After 8.7 miles turn on FR 504, which forks after 2.3 miles to FR 504A. (You can also take the paved road from Thoreau to Bluewater Lake, which turns into FR 178, and turn onto FR 504.) FR 504A is a primitive road for four-wheel-drive vehicles. You can stop here and walk.

Mt. Sedgwick is the highest point in the Zuni Mountains, at 9,256 feet. In 1885 Captain C. E. Dutton of the U.S. Geological Service wrote, "It is not a mountain of large proportions, though sufficient to be a conspicuous feature of the plateau." Modest as it is, Sedgwick offers a dramatic view of Mt. Taylor, with Black Mesa reaching south. Looking to the right of Taylor and in the foreground, a red slash indicates Zuni Canyon. To the left, or northwest, are a line of red cliffs that reminded Dutton of Utah's Vermilion Cliffs. "Its brilliant color, its massiveness, the bold and absolutely vertical faces, the smoothness of the wall, all combine to make it a very striking object of contemplation," he wrote. Also visible are the dramatic walls of Bluewater Canyon.

Nobody knows how this mountain got its name. I found no homesteaders, railroaders, or ranchers here by that name. My money is on General John Sedgwick, a Civil War hero who fought in some of the fiercest battles in the East and died at the height of his fame. The nation mourned his death in 1864, according to his biographer. Because it was popular then to remember war heroes with statues, libraries, and natural features bearing their names, it's entirely likely that army officers then at Fort Wingate named the mountain for one of their own.

The scattered timbers of a wooden fire-watch tower sit in a heap near the top, reminders of more exciting times here. One of the fire lookouts, around 1920, was Lucy Jane Whiteside, who had a ranch at the base of the mountain. A Missourian who came to New Mexico for her health, she married Dave Whiteside in 1905, and they moved to the Zuni Mountains. They ranched at the base of the mountain, and he served as fire lookout and she as a fire fighter. In 1919 a reputed cattle rustler asked the Whitesides to take in a young woman he'd gotten pregnant. When Dave Whiteside refused, the rustler shot him in the back and then in the head. The murderer served a ten-year sentence and later killed himself.

After her husband's death, Lucy Whiteside took over his duties as rancher and lookout and continued fighting fires. She fought more than one blaze singlehandedly. Later she and her two daughters moved into Grants, where she became known throughout the area for her midwifery. For years she ran a hotel and cafe, which became a favorite haunt of railroad crews and, later, miners. One man remembered her kindness with a donation to build a library in her name. The Mother Whiteside

Memorial Library was dedicated in 1954. She died in California in 1958.

This tower was also the scene of a mishap in 1930, when fire lookout Van Parsons knocked a gun off the shelf while getting a drink from the water bucket and shot himself in the arm.

The road you just used was built from the sweat of needy people. In 1934 one of many government work projects in the area had twenty-five to fifty-five men laboring here. Chosen according to need, they were mostly paid in groceries and necessities, at the rate of fifty cents an hour.

Distance: 2 miles round-trip on 504A, or less if you drive up.
Time: 1–2 hours.
Difficulty: A somewhat breathless ascent; drive partway, and it's a good one to show little kids what a mountain top is like without an arduous hike.
Topo Map: Mt. Sedgwick.

Hikes from FR 50

FR 50 is the main road through the Zuni Mountains and is maintained most of the year for car travel. The turnoff is nearly opposite the Ice Caves off NM 53, south of Grants. You will pass the turnoff to the Zuni Mountain fire lookout. The scenery is lovely very quickly, especially in the early summer—tall ponderosa pines and distant mountains—and about the time you think it must be nice to be a rancher here, you'll pass the No Easy Life Ranch on the left. Crossing the Forest Service boundary from private land, look to the right to see a cinder cone, which is the source of the Zuni Canyon lava flow. FR 50 also includes a portion of the Zuni Mountain Railroad tour, and you'll see the locomotive-shaped signs 5 through 13. Turning into the Agua Fria Valley, you'll pass the slim remnants of two logging ghost towns, Cold Springs and Sawyer. The road follows Oso Ridge.

Rivera Canyon/Railroad Bed Loop

On this pleasant hike, you can follow an old bed of the Zuni Mountain Railroad to the biggest trestle I've seen here and enjoy the lovely Rivera Canyon. Watch for sweet clover, columbine, scarlet gilia, daisies, and purple asters. The rail bed and its trestles are some of the last built in the Zuni Mountains. They represent an effort by Grants businessmen who bought George Breece's operation in 1931 and tried to keep logging alive. They built track from Agua Fria through Rivera Canyon into Valle Largo, where there was already a logging camp.

You can start from either end of the loop, at Rivera Canyon or the railroad bed. Road and hike descriptions for both follow.

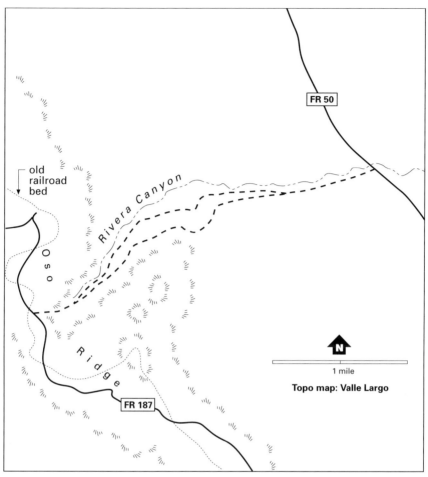

*Getting to Rivera Canyon: From NM 53 take FR 50, 6
miles to Rivera Canyon turnoff, which has no sign at this
writing. You will see a rude two-track, which follows a
fence a short distance along private land. You can park
here and walk, or if you have a four-wheel-drive, continue just over a mile until you reach an open meadow,
where a dirt track branches to the left.*

Follow the dirt track up the drainage. The trees get
bigger and prettier, and shortly you will see a sign identi-
fying Rivera Canyon. It's a lovely place of big oak trees
and singing birds. Continue up the road, which follows
the drainage. About 0.3 miles from the sign, the road
forks off. Leave the road and stay in the drainage. You'll
see a huge, five-foot stump—an example of what the
trees here were like once. About a mile from the Rivera
Canyon sign, the drainage will meet the railroad bed,
identifiable from its berms and remaining ties. Follow
the bed until you reach the starting place of the upper
loop, at FR 187. Return to Rivera Canyon by the railroad
bed.

Getting to the railroad bed: From FR 50, turn toward the Oso Ridge Lookout. Instead of going to the lookout, take FR 187 and go 2.9 miles to a small clearing on the right, where downed logs, berms, and old tracks hint at past human activity.

Locate the old railroad bed in the clearing from its berm, which looks like an earthen dam. Follow it along a fence 0.4 miles until you come to an old railroad trestle, the largest I've seen in the Zuni Mountains, followed shortly by a smaller trestle. The bed tends to fade in places, but follow the berms or watch for the rotted

Rivera Canyon railroad trestle.

wood that once formed ties. In places the ties are still intact, and you'll notice that the old railroaders used round logs, flattened on top with an adz. You can also tell what gauge the rails were. The packed rock around and under crossties, called ballast, distributed the weight of trains and allowed water to drain.

Continue on the railroad bed just over 1.5 miles, until you can see a red sandstone outcrop across a broad meadow. Leave the roadbed and head across toward the outcrop. When you encounter a road, take it back in the direction you've come, toward Rivera Canyon. Return by Rivera Canyon.

Distance: 3.5 miles.
Time: 1.5 hours.
Difficulty: Roadbed requires a bit of high stepping over old ties and some scrambling across arroyos; not difficult.
Topo Map: Valle Largo.

Cottonwood Canyon

Getting there: Take FR 50 to FR 483 and turn right (north). From this point you will need a high-clearance vehicle. Or you can hike 2.5 miles through the broad valley along Lookout Mountain Rim to the mouth of Cottonwood Canyon.

This is a pretty hike right away, although it should be renamed Aspen Canyon for the aspens that line the creek here. Keep that in mind for fall hikes! Follow a two-track over an old railroad bed into the canyon. It soon turns into a decent cattle/game trail. There are also sandstone outcrops here to keep the scenery interesting. Growth is generous: tall grasses, willows, ponderosas, firs. You would only know this is an old railroad bed if you have sharp eyes. Occasionally you might spot fragments of big timbers that once formed trestles.

At about 2.7 miles, the trail turns again into a two-track. A patch covered with cinders tells you that you've arrived at Rock Dam. The finest relic of the railroad days, it's made of huge (four-feet by three-feet) blocks of sandstone. Expecting an ugly rubble dam, I found this

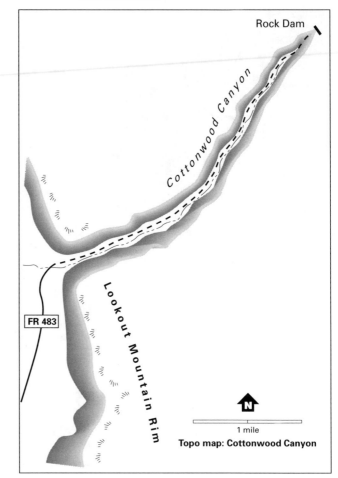

Topo map: Cottonwood Canyon

dam as pretty as a Roman aqueduct. My husband, trained as an archeologist, found that a bit of a stretch, but he did agree that it was a handsome construction.

On either side of the dam is a healthy riparian area; we startled a kingfisher. Crossing the dam we found more old railbed and followed it north for a view of Las Tusas Valley.

The beauty of the canyon belies its harsh use. The Zuni Mountains' lumber boom got its start right here, when a short-lived logging operation in 1891 built a rail line from present-day Thoreau into these mountains and a year later built this dam to supply water to the lumber-mill boiler. Operations halted soon after. Ten years later a second company bought the property, converted from narrow gauge to standard gauge, and extended the rail line farther into the canyon over a pigpen trestle (a log-cabin-type bridge) and on to Sawyer and, later, along the Agua Fria Valley to Paxton Springs. Ultimately, under a third owner, the Zuni Mountain Railway was fifty-five miles long.

However, by 1940, this place was nearly barren. Cut-over land had been sold or leased to ranchers, who over-grazed it. Without tree cover and grasses, erosion low-ered water tables and dried out wet meadows. Cotton-wood Canyon, once a willow-lined trout stream, had become a small, intermittent stream gouged by flash floods. Its vertical banks were ten to twenty feet high. Looking at this wonderful little canyon today, it's hard to believe. These mountains have a remarkable ability to heal themselves, given time.

The dam on Cottonwood Creek was built in 1891 to supply a lumber mill boiler.

Distance: 6 miles, round-trip.
Time: 4–5 hours.
Difficulty: Moderately easy.
Topo Map: Cottonwood Canyon.

Continental Divide/The Notches (See Continental Divide, p. 219)

Hikes from FR 178 or 180

Pole Canyon/Limekiln
Getting there: Go west on old Route 66 (NM 122) from Milan, and when you see the sawmill and tipi burner, turn left. The road appears to head directly for the saw-mill, but passes it and becomes FR 180. From the Forest Service boundary, continue 2.5 miles and turn left oppo-site a gate. You will see ruins in the distance to your left. Go down the track 1.3 miles to the ruin and park. (Just as we parked, a buck popped out of the brush. As we watched him saunter up the hill, two more racks sur-

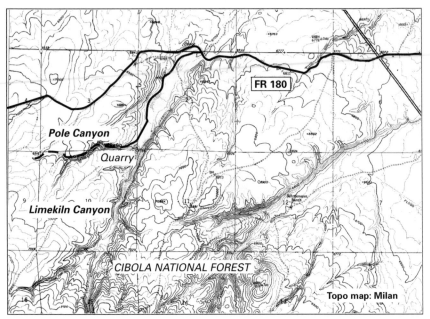

FR 180

Pole Canyon

Quarry

Limekiln Canyon

CIBOLA NATIONAL FOREST

Topo map: Milan

(Pages 200–201) Ruins of a lime-kiln that operated during the 1920s. (Opposite) Pole Canyon.

faced, and his friends joined him at a safe distance.)

Crossing the arroyo there, you can take a look at the old limekiln. This place operated in the 1920s. Return to this arroyo and hike west into it; it will quickly deepen to a canyon. There is either no trail here or a rude cattle trail. The creek here is seasonal. We encounter pools and no running water, but there's evidence all the way of fast water and flash floods. The birds are thick here and in the many side canyons. At the end of the summer, they find ample New Mexico olives. The canyon also holds Apache plume, beeweed, Indian paintbrush, skunk-bush, and the occasional ponderosa pine.

This is a somewhat magical place. I find myself looking up at the canyon rim expecting to see—what? Indian hunters? Hobbits? The canyon deepens. A red-tailed hawk screeches at us, sounding for a moment like a mountain lion.

After a mile the canyon turns back into an arroyo that meanders across a broad meadow. Following the brushy arroyo visually, you will see Mt. Sedgwick on the other side and in the foreground, the walls of a canyon, which is the continuation of Pole Canyon. You can either follow the arroyo or make a beeline across the meadow for the canyon, just over a mile away. Entering the canyon, you pick up a two-track road that winds through jagged lava and ends in about a quarter mile. From here you bush-whack up the creek bottom. It can be tough going here, but there are rewards. Coursing water over time has smoothed the rough basalt in the canyon bottom until it's as slick and blue-black as a raven's wing. A lava flow here, curving against the original canyon walls, has nar-

rowed the passage, ending in an abrupt lava wall. Beyond the wall, Virginia creeper climbs to create a curtain of hanging gardens.

At 3 miles we climb out of the canyon to the left, find a two-track road, and follow it nearly back to FR 180. In the fresh mud, turkey tracks are etched like peace symbols. A chimney rock watches over this end of the canyon, which ends at 3.5 miles. We return on the two-track, and discover that we could have avoided bushwhacking in the canyon bottom (but missed the pretty stuff) by finding a game trail up the south side of the canyon to the two-track. You can search out this little trail between two formations of smoothed, black basalt.

Distance: 6.1 miles.
Time: 5.5 hours.
Difficulty: Level country, some boulder scrambling and bushwhacking; moderately challenging.
Topo Map: Milan.

Rice Park

Getting there: The easy route is to take exit 53 south from I-40 to NM 612, which becomes FR 178, and drive 9.4 miles to FR 569. A more interesting route is to take old Route 66, or NM 122, west from Milan to the lumber mill and take a left. The road rounds the mill, turns into FR 180, and heads toward the Zunis. Stay on 180 15.4 miles, until you reach pavement at FR 178 and turn right, toward Bluewater Lake. The road follows spectacular scenery in Bluewater Canyon and Bluewater Creek, before it bends around the lake and continues west. After about 8 miles, take FR 569 left to Rice Park. This road dead-ends. Just before the dead end, turn right on a two-track. Stay on the two-track to a small reservoir.

In their guide to camping, the Boy Scouts' Zuni chapter, Order of the Arrow, calls this "one of the most beautiful areas in the Zuni Mountains." The Boy Scouts are right. This is a lovely mountain valley. In 1986 the Forest Service, in cooperation with Ducks Unlimited, the state Game and Fish Department, and local water users, built a dam, created islands and marshland, and seeded the valley with grain for wild ducks and migrating birds. This is a great spot for birds—and mosquitos.

The Boy Scouts report seeing wild turkey, Abert's squirrels, blue jays, and deer; and bear have been killed here in recent years.

Rice Park is such a pretty place, it seems an unlikely spot for a murder; but in the spring of 1923, homesteader Buck Moore died here in a fracas over a pig. Tom Mace, who was lumberman George Breece's livestock caretaker, had borrowed a boar from Moore and

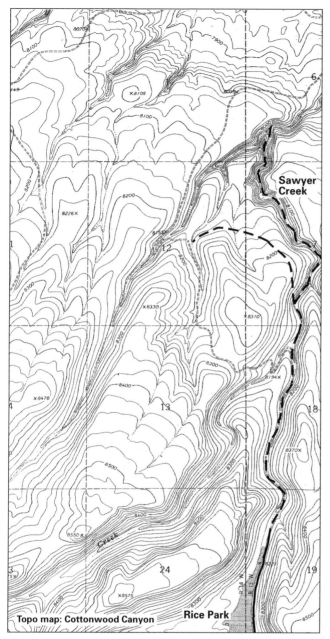

Topo map: Cottonwood Canyon

Sawyer Creek

Rice Park

returned it. The animal got loose and returned to Mace's place, so he shot it. Mace was a fighter and hell raiser, and the two men hadn't liked each other since Moore ran Mace out of his camp.

Moore drove a team into Camp 8, left it standing near a corral, and entered the camp store. When he came out, Mace was leaning against the corral fence, with both hands on his hips. "I killed your hog," he hollered. "I know you did, and I have come to make you pay for

Rice Park.

him," Moore said. Mace said he had no money. Moore drew a gun from his belt, but held it at his side, pointed to the ground. He demanded that Mace go to the company office and arrange to pay for the hog.

The two men had slowly walked toward each other. Mace turned with his left side toward Moore and grabbed Moore's gun hand, as he drew his own gun from a hip pocket and fired twice into Moore's stomach. Then he put two more bullets in the dying man. Mace guarded the body until the authorities came to arrest him and wouldn't let anybody, including Moore's wife, touch the body. He pleaded self-defense and served five years in the penitentiary.

Moore left a wife and eight children. His family said he never carried a gun and never had one at home. They didn't know where he got a gun that day. Old-timer Fats Tietjen once told the story and was asked if the nearest town had a doctor. "No," he said, "you died back then."

Below the dam follow a road down the valley. At about 1.3 miles, you come to a side canyon. Go north (right). You have two choices here.

Choice #1: Follow an old railroad bed (clue: scattered ties, raised bed) along the slope on the left side. This will take you up and over the top of a mesa (about 2 miles) and into the next canyon. Lots of thirty-foot ponderosas now grow where logging trains once ran. For a beautiful view, find a place to look into Sawyer Canyon. The giant ponderosas and Douglas firs of the canyon bottom bely the fact that the canyon was probably logged, because the tracks ran right through here.

Choice #2: Stay in the canyon bottom and hike north

along a cattle trail that's surprisingly hikable. A couple of volunteers with an afternoon to spare could turn this into a great trail. You will soon be in the enchanted forest, a lush place with such a variety of plant life it doesn't even look like the Zuni Mountains, my husband sniffs. The yarrow is thick and the wild iris looks happy. There's also wild rose, lazy susan, aster, aspen, and willow. We find a stump plundered for bugs by a bear and later on a big mound of bear scat. You can hike as far up as you want, but the brush gets thicker. We made it about 1.3 miles, nearly to where the canyon ends, before turning back.

Distance: 3–4 miles on either route.
Time: 5 hours to do both.
Difficulty: Moderate; some bushwhacking.
Topo Map: Cottonwood Canyon, Pine Canyon.

Hikes from NM 53

Gallo Peak

Getting there: From I-40, drive south on NM 53 16 miles to the turnoff for FR 447, opposite the Zuni-Acoma Trail. Drive about 5 miles up Bonita Canyon (a gentle place with lots of good car campsites) and park in sight of Gallo Peak.

Gallo ("rooster") Peak marks the western boundary of Laguna Pueblo aboriginal lands. Acomas called it Ram Peak. It is also a geologic tutor that offers its layers for instruction. At the base of this mesa are the early shale and sandstone deposits of the Abo Formation and above that the Yeso Formation, both transported here by streams over a floodplain. The Yeso reaches about halfway up the mesa; the upper portion was laid out by advancing and retreating waters, which also left gypsum and limestone.

The next layer, which forms most of the top half of the mesa, is Glorieta sandstone—once beach, sandbars, and sand dunes. Finally the sea left a topping, now San Andres limestone, which caps Gallo Peak.

Hike across the flat, following the drainage, and head toward the saddle between Gallo and the mesa to the west. I've heard of people climbing straight up Gallo, but wouldn't recommend it. Continue up the drainage until you reach the top of the saddle and then hike toward the top of the peak. There is a faint trail here. The grades here are more gentle (they're gentler still on the north side of the peak), but you'll still have to do some bush-whacking and scrambling over loose granite near the top.

On our way up on a Christmas Day, my husband found a pick and shovel beside a rock—the tools of a discouraged prospector, perhaps? The shovel carried the label: "Union Fork & Hoe Co. Razor Back—only shovel with a back-

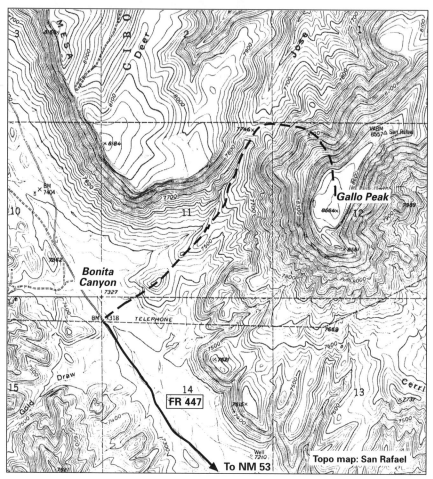

(Pages 208–9)
Gallo Peak

bone." He tucked them back under the rock for some future archeologist.

Gallo Peak, elevation 8,664 feet, is the tallest mesa in the area. The top offers one of the best views of the malpais, which the horizon appears to hold in a tormented bowl.

Distance: 2–3 miles.
Time: 4–6 hours.
Difficulty: A tough scramble over steep slopes in places, bushwhacking in others.
Topo Map: San Rafael.

McGaffey Lake

Getting there: If you stay on FR 50 all the way through the Zunis, for the scenic tour, you'll reach McGaffey Lake. You can also take NM 400, just east of Gallup.

This six-acre lake near the old logging town of McGaffey is stocked with rainbow trout. In 1992 the New Mexico Department of Game and Fish and the

Forest Service spruced the place up, adding a floating fishing dock and improving wildlife habitat. The dock is a convenience for fishing, but it also saves wear and tear on the shoreline.

Biking and Skiing

The Zuni Mountains, with their level-to-rolling surfaces and profusion of old logging roads, are ideal for biking and cross-country skiing.

Biking

■ FR 50, the main road, guarantees a pretty ride with little traffic. Once you're here, you can pick your side roads.

■ A long and pretty tour is the loop of FR 49, FR 480, and FR 50.

■ Quartz Hill, just outside Zuni Canyon, is framed by old logging roads.

■ FR 187 takes you to the Oso Ridge fire lookout and then parallels Oso Ridge, for nice views.

Another way to bike through the Zunis is on the Zuni Mountain Classic Bike Tour each September. The Zuni Mountain Coalition started this event as a protest against planned power-line construction through the area. This isn't a race, but a tour for the entire family. For more information check area sporting-goods shops or contact the ZMC at PO Box 888, Ramah, NM 87321.

Skiing

With the exception of FR 50 and FR 49, most of the bike tours mentioned here are suitable for skiing.

Mt. Sedgwick Loop (Skiing and biking)

Getting there: Take FR 49 to FR 480. After 8.7 miles, turn on FR 504. (You can also take the paved road from Thoreau to Bluewater Lake, which turns into FR 178, and turn onto FR 504.)

Park at the cabin and ski (or bike) down 504, which forks after 2.3 miles to FR 504A. Ski to the top of Mt. Sedgwick, the highest point in the Zuni Mountains at 9,256 feet. For a short tour, you can return the way you came. Or you can continue down FR 504 for an utterly pleasant glide down an aspen-filled valley. This road intersects with FR 178, which tends to be busy, so ski along the side until you reach FR 480, at Post Office Flat. Yes, there was once an unofficial post office here, for loggers and homesteaders. Continue on FR 480, a curving, rolling ribbon of white that returns through long aspen meadows to the starting place.

We did this loop by accident. Intending only to ski in and out, we were lured by the other half of FR 504 and a

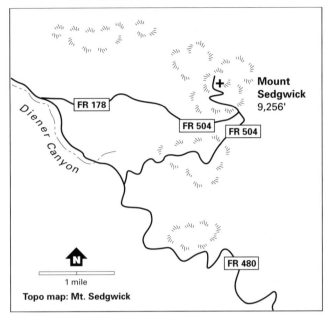

FR 178

Diener Canyon

FR 504   FR 504

+ **Mount Sedgwick**
9,256'

FR 480

N

1 mile

Topo map: Mt. Sedgwick

notion that the road linked to another somehow, a short
ways away. Stupidly, we hadn't brought the map. Sure
enough it all linked up, but at a greater distance than we
thought. We found the car in the dark.

Distance: 9.2 miles (including Sedgwick).
Time: 6–7 hours.
*Difficulty: Easy to moderate (except for coming up and
down Sedgwick).*
Topo Map: Mt. Sedgwick.

Zuni Mountain Historic Auto Tour

In 1990 the Forest Service, using railroad buff Vernon
Glover's tome *Zuni Mountain Railroads,* organized its
self-guided auto tour of the area's railroad-logging landmarks and environment. Visitors can pick up the agency's brochure and match descriptions with locomotive-
shaped signposts. I've included the tour here, along
with my own expanded explanation of stops on the
tour. The sixty-mile route has eighteen stops, beginning at Zuni Canyon, continuing through the pretty
Agua Fria Valley, and coming out at Bluewater Lake.
The signs aren't always easy to see, so keep an eye
out for them.

Stop 1, Milepost 5.6: Forest Service Boundary.
Welcome to Zuni Canyon, one of my favorite canyons. In
the last century, Captain C. E. Dutton of the USGS
wrote, "From Grant Station may be discerned a cañon
deeply incised into the sloping flank and descending

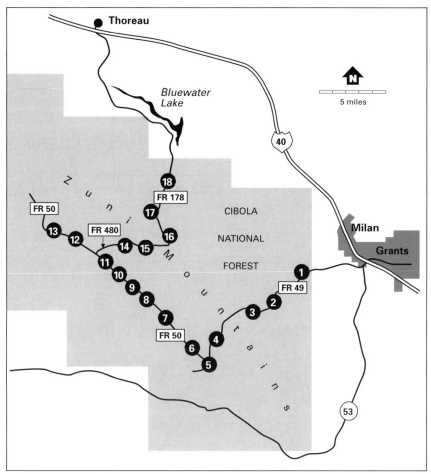

towards us with a very tortuous course . . . The cañon steadily deepens and at length becomes quite pleasing. Its depth increases until the upper end is reached when suddenly it emerges into open country. The walls swing at right angles, to right and left, and we find ourselves in the heart of the plateau. The country now before us is by no means smooth. Just at the upper opening of the cañon, strangely enough, is a stream of basalt, rough, clinkery, black and forbidding . . . In front of us the country is much obscured by the forest of great [ponderosa] pine trees but so far as can be seen it is a medley of low rolling hills, like the rolling prairie of Iowa . . . Passing around the lava beds and penetrating into the granitic area, we find the country heavily forested, covered with abundant soil and green with luxuriant grass and herbage."

Next Stop 4.4 miles
Stop 2, Milepost 9.7: Chute Mesa.
Look to your left and see, on the south side of Zuni Canyon, where workers dropped logs down a natural

chute to railroad cars waiting below. On top of the mesa horses and, later tractors, dragged logs to the edge. Because of damage to the logs, the lumber companies eventually used a cable system. You can hike to the top of Chute Mesa (see Hiking, p. 188).

Next stop: 1.4 miles
Stop 3, Milepost 11.1: Malpais Springs.
The road you were just on was first built to this point in 1934 by government works-project laborers. In the late 1920s, Breece Lumber Co. had a camp near here of movable houses and tents. They cut a channel through the lava rock from the spring to the west; nothing remains of the camp. Opposite the railroad sign is a gate, which is the entry to the area. The piles of jagged, loose lava hint that this was a volcanic vent, and the rough, black piles form themselves around a pond (during wet seasons) or a marsh (during dry seasons). The thick, tall grasses and globe mallows contrast with the basalt for a nice walk—but watch for snakes.

La Jara Trestle. (Opposite) Cold Springs.

Next stop: 2.5 miles
Stop 4, Milepost 13.5: La Jara Trestle.
Walk down the road from the railroad sign to find the remains of a railroad trestle, or Bridge 17, the seventeenth bridge from Grants. Like trestles built today, the timber supports are squared beams, not logs. On your way in, you'll pass a nice spring, which has been fenced in by the Forest Service to keep cows from trampling the springhead. The chest-high clover there must keep the bees happy. After La Jara Bridge, turn onto FR 50.

Next stop: 3.4 miles
Stop 5, Milepost 16.7: Set-Out Tracks.
Nothing remains of it, but on this spot were the set-out tracks, where the smaller Shay or Climax-type engines from the woods could be replaced by mainline locomotives. Railroad grades also extended from here to Paxton Springs and Agua Fria Springs and up the Agua Fria Valley.

Next stop: 3 miles
Stop 6, Milepost 19.5: Young trees.
The Forest Service refers to this field of baby ponderosa pines, planted here in 1984, as a plantation. It represents some of the agency's efforts to restore the woodlands cut in the last century. Between 1979 and 1989, the Forest Service planted 8,900 acres of seedlings.

Next stop: 1.2 miles
Stop 7, Milepost 20.3: Cold Springs.
The valley northeast of here had the coldest water in the Zuni Mountains. This plus the tall grass made it a natural draw for the U.S. Army's exploration parties and later for people from the nearby logging town of Sawyer. The two collapsed log buildings and other remnants you see are on private land, so admire them from the road. They were once used in ranching and in 1931 to feed men and teams of Breece Co. horses.

Next stop: 1.9 miles
Stop 8, Milepost 23.3: Fields.
This is one of many areas cleared by homesteaders who came here from 1916 through the 1920s. Because the soil was rich and rainfall abundant, the area was the breadbasket of western New Mexico for a time. Dryland farms grew quality rye, wheat, oats, and barley, as well as vegetables, much of which was sold to nearby mines and logging camps. Potatoes were worth seventy-five cents per hundred pounds to a Grants merchant.

Next stop: 1.5 miles
Stop 9, Milepost 24.8: Continental Divide.
The great divide is on your left (south) along Oso Ridge. In this area the divide forms along the Chain of Craters on the Ramah Navajo Reservation and El Malpais and follows the lava to Cerro Bandera, where it crosses the road to Oso Ridge. It continues west and north through the Zuni Mountains to the village of Continental Divide and Mt. Powell, on the Navajo Reservation. You've been driving along Oso Ridge for a few miles now.

Next stop: 2.1 miles
Stop 10, Milepost 26.9: Geology.
The Forest Service would like you to pause here to learn about the geology of the Zuni Mountains. See previous geology information. Continue past the turnoff for FR 480 (the Forest Service's tour map is incorrect).

Next stop: 3.9 miles
Stop 11, Milepost 29.6: Camp Nine.
This is the site of the ninth of American Lumber Company's ten camps. From 1901 to 1913, the company's railroad moved deeper into the mountains from Cotton-

Trestle at Sawyer used to elevate trains to transfer coal to tenders.

wood Canyon, to the south, through the Agua Fria Valley here. Occupied for just a few years, Camp Nine consisted of a few cabins, a well house, some barns, and other outbuildings. Nothing remains.

Next stop: 0.9 miles
Stop 12, Milepost 30.5: Sawyer.
From the road you can't see anything, but cross the fence to the north, and you will find the remains of Sawyer, which was named for the president of American Lumber. It served as a main logging camp, first for American and then for Breece, from 1909 to 1921. Imagine as you look at the four collapsed log homes that two hundred people—including sixty children—once lived here. Remains of hogans and sweat lodges indicate that Navajo workers lived here too. The most interesting relic is a long, low, collapsed trestle, which was used to elevate carloads of coal for easier transfer to tenders.

The camp had a big general store, a two-room school (operated during the winter), a saloon, and a boarding-

house for single men. A post office operated here from
1909 to 1916, with mail arriving on horseback. A priest
celebrated mass once a month. The town faded away
when Breece relocated the main logging camp to Bluewater Lake and moved most of the buildings. Sawyer,
like most logging camps, was rowdy and lawless. Saloons proliferated nearby, even though the companies
discouraged them. One old-timer recalled that "a Mr.
Tuck of Gallup lived there but won't talk about it. His
father was killed there."

Next stop: 0.5 miles
Stop 13, Milepost 31: Virgin forest.
This is one of few stands of virgin timber left in the Zuni
Mountains. In the fifty years after 1892, loggers removed
800 million board feet of timber. By the early 1940s, the
mountains were all but stripped bare. Loggers in those
days were required to leave just two trees an acre, and
they usually left the two worst. Nearly all the forest
you've driven through is less than fifty years old and
recovered on its own or with reseeding by the Forest
Service. Turn around and return to the turnoff for FR 480
and turn left.

Next stop: 5.3 miles
Stop 14, Milepost 36.3: Quartz Hill.
This is some of the oldest rock visible in the Zuni Mountains. You can see a vein of quartz in the Precambrian
granite.

Next stop: 1.9 miles
Stop 15, Milepost 38.2: Post Office Flat.
This meadow and corral are the site of a small cabin that
served as an unofficial post office for loggers and homesteaders. The area is a wildflower garden with wild irises, yellow columbines, asters, and sunflowers, among
others. Near here was Copperton, established at the
turn of the century. At one time it had four mining companies, a sawmill, a dairyman, a general store, and a
boardinghouse. Its post office operated from 1901 to
1911. In 1916 a man was mysteriously burned to death
at his campfire, as he was moving a mill to Copperton.
Despite the inquest held at Sawyer, nobody ever learned
how he died or why. From FR 480, turn onto FR 178.

Next stop: 1.7 miles
Stop 16, Milepost 39.9: Diener.
Copper mining began here in 1916 and operated to the
early 1930s. "It was called tree copper—petrified wood
turned to copper," recalled longtime resident Dovie
Bright. "It was a very high grade copper." The camp of
ten cabins here never was home to more than ten or
twenty California miners. Its post office operated from

1916 to 1931. "When I first visited there," recalls an old-timer, "there were ore cars on the track, a head frame, shuttles and a shaft from the top of the mountain down into the mountain . . . Farther down the canyon there were homes and wells and a smelter." The mill burned in the 1930s, but its brick foundation is still visible on the hillside across the flat. One of the two collapsed shafts now serves as a planter for an opportunistic aspen tree.

Next stop: 2.3 miles
Stop 17, Milepost 42.2: Mirabal Mines.
You can't see any of them from here, but this area hosted a small mining boom after 1918, when Moise Mirabal located mining claims here. They apparently paid off, because other mining companies also staked claims. During World War II, these hills produced a thousand tons of fluorspar, a flux used in making steel that was in high demand by the defense industry. Fluorspar mines closed in 1952, when foreign competition brought down the price. Some silver and copper were also mined here. This is a popular camping spot today.

Next stop: 3 miles
Stop 18, Milepost 45.2: Bluewater Creek.
This is one of the loveliest places in the Zunis and a favorite of fishermen. The creek feeds Bluewater Lake and is also riparian habitat. It's hard to believe that by 1940, clear-cutting and overgrazing had turned Bluewater Creek into a small, intermittent stream subject to flash floods and ruined for fishing. It's now managed carefully by the Forest Service. From here follow FR 178 16 miles to I-40, at Thoreau.

Distance: 60 miles.
Time: 2–3 hours.
Difficulty: The tour is over good gravel roads, so that a four-wheel-drive vehicle isn't necessary. However, if it starts to rain, the roads get slick and treacherous. Exit quickly!

The Continental Divide
The Continental Divide is a long spine from Alaska to South America. It is both an idea—the point where water runs either to the Pacific or the Atlantic Oceans—and a real place of forbidding mountain ridges. To pioneers the divide was a barrier and a hazard to wagons, livestock, and human life. In our time it has captured the imagination of hikers, who count a trek along The Great Divide among the great outdoor challenges.

In 1966 the Bureau of Outdoor Recreation recommended a border-to-border Continental Divide Trail among a system of national scenic trails. Pieces of the trail existed in places, some of them built in the 1930s by the Civilian Conservation Corps. In 1968 Congress passed the National Trails System Act, which recommended study of the Continental Divide, and in 1978 it gained official trail status. The Forest Service has coordinated the trail effort of some 1,500 miles through five states. New Mexico has the longest portion of the trail, at 790 miles.

In New Mexico the divide begins in the San Luis Mountains of the bootheel and follows the Animas Mountains before it crosses the desert into the Burro Mountains and the Pinos Altos Range. It angles through the Black Range, turns west before the Plains of San Agustin, and continues north through the Tularosa Mountains and the Mangas Mountains. In this area the divide forms along the Chain of Craters on the Ramah Navajo Reservation and El Malpais and clings to the lava to Cerro Bandera, where it crosses the road to Oso Ridge in the Zuni Mountains. It continues west and north, through the Zuni Mountains to the village of Continental Divide and Mt. Powell, on the Navajo Reservation. It crosses the Jicarilla Apache Reservation and tops out at Chama and Cumbres Pass.

"Though there is scarcely a mile that is not in—or in sight of—mountains, the divide touches more sharply contrasting terrain in New Mexico than in any other state," wrote Michael Robbins in *High Country Trail— Along the Continental Divide.* Curiously Robbins wrote about precious little of that sharply contrasting terrain. The hiking narrative begins dutifully in the bootheel and takes the reader into the Gila. After a long digression on prehistoric Indian culture and Navajo crafts, Robbins is suddenly in Chama, having skipped over most of the divide in New Mexico.

In *The Great Divide,* Stephen Pern at least noted the Zuni Mountains, where he spent two and a half days "picking my way along the slabby rocks of the Oso Ridge." He called the Zunis "a confusion of hogbacks and parallel troughs running up towards Route 66. . . . I kept stubbing my feet, unused to the irregular surface, pine needles and fragments of crinkly lichen in my socks. The forested ridge was broad and gave little sense of elevations, though sometimes I caught flashes of pink through the trees . . . and below me on either side of the ridge, a hint of wet, boggy valleys."

Because the divide passes through Indian Reservations, private land, and developed land and is in places inviting only to mountain goats, the trail will be for the most part near the Continental Divide and not actually on it. However, the trunk route branches into numerous side trails, picnic grounds, and campgrounds.

At this writing a strong possibility is for the trail to follow NM 117 north to La Ventana, continue along La Rendija drainage into El Malpais National Conservation

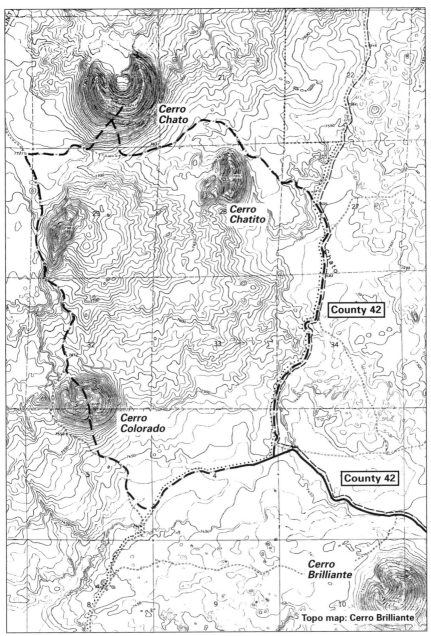

Area, pass through the Chain of Craters, follow county road 42 to NM 53, cross the Zuni-Acoma trail back to NM 117, and follow it to Grants. It would cross I-40 and enter the Mt. Taylor area and then use Forest Service roads to pass through the Ignacio Chavez and Chamisa wilderness study areas to Sandoval County road 279.

For those who would like to experience the real Continental Divide, here are two hikes or, if you combine them, one long trek.

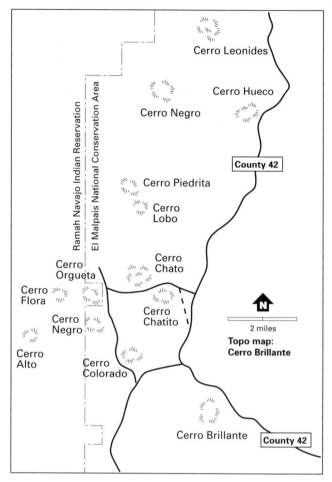

Cerro Leonides

Cerro Hueco

Cerro Negro

Ramah Navajo Indian Reservation

El Malpais National Conservation Area

County 42

Cerro Piedrita

Cerro Lobo

Cerro Chato

Cerro Orgueta

Cerro Flora

N

2 miles

Topo map: Cerro Brillante

Cerro Negro

Cerro Chatito

Cerro Alto

Cerro Colorado

Cerro Brillante

County 42

Chain of Craters Loop

Getting there: On NM 117, drive 34.5 miles south and west and turn right on county road 42. About 10.5 miles down the county road, you will be opposite Cerro Brillante ("bright hill"), a large cinder cone. In less than two miles, the road will fork; leave 42 and take the left fork. Drive up the road 0.3 miles and park.

You can make the short hikes to climb Cerro Brillante and Cerro Colorado from here, but this tour will describe a loop from Cerro Colorado to Cerro Chato ("snubnosed").

The Chain of Craters is a series of thirty volcanic cones that stretch for twenty miles from north to south in a half-moon from Cerro Bandera, near NM 53, across El Malpais to Cerro Brillante. They make up a portion of the Continental Divide. All can be seen in a drive along county 42. The craters range in size from a few feet to hundreds of feet above the surrounding plain. The highest crater on public land is Cerro Chato, at 8,247 feet. Cerro Alto is larger, but is on Ramah Navajo land and closed to the public.

Violent eruptions of thick magma from deep inside the earth created these cones 110,000 to 200,000 years ago, when volcanic debris exploded from vents and built up steep-sided slopes. Lava then breached one side and poured out along channels. As a result most of these volcanoes are crescent-shaped. They're composed of basaltic ash and cinders, and the tops are littered with lava "bombs"—rounded clinkers that took their shape as they shot from the earth and sailed through the air.

Most are in an 18,300-acre area on the western side of El Malpais, in the National Conservation Area, and have a web of tracks and roads connecting them. Mountain bikes are legal here, but bikers disagree on whether this is a good place for biking.

Vegetation includes forests of ponderosa pine, piñon, alligator juniper, and other juniper. Shrubs include oak, gooseberry, gray horsebrush, sage, snakeweed, rabbit brush, and mountain mahogany. There are lots of wildflowers, including Indian paintbrush, pingue, creeping mahonia, and buckwheat. Grasses are Arizona fescue, mountain muhly, june grass, blue grama, bottlebrush squirreltail, and mutton grass. Wildlife you're likely to see here includes mule deer, antelope, coyote, and bear.

From your parked car, continue hiking down the road. In a half-mile you will be opposite Cerro Colorado ("red hill"), named for its reddish cinders. On the right is a faint two-track that leaves the road and joins another road angling off from the first. This road past Cerro Colorado is little used, because it's trying to become an arroyo. It is one of several meandering among the craters; consider it your trail.

About 1.5 miles from parking is the base. We made a slight traverse up the sides, scrambling over loose cinders. The sides in early fall are covered with verbena, four o'clocks, and globe mallow. In about a quarter-mile, we're on top. The wildflowers are thick among the clinkers. To the southeast Brillante looms over a flat called La Vega ("the meadow"). To the west the biggest cone is Cerro Alto ("high"), while Chato and its little brother Chatito are to the northeast.

Climb down toward the northeast and follow what was probably a lava channel now filled with grass, ponderosa pines, and tall piñons. You should encounter the road again. Continue on it for another mile or so, until Chato comes into view. The road forks. Take the right fork toward Chato, which is just over 4 miles into the loop. You can see that Chato is tallest and steepest on the road side. Walk along its flank and come up the shorter side—you may encounter a giant alligator juniper—and find yourself on one end of a horseshoeshaped mountain crowned by big ponderosas. From here you can see many of the other craters in the chain and a distant, bluish Mt. Taylor.

Return the way you came and catch the road again,

which passes between Chato and Chatito. In less than a mile, the road will fork. Take the right fork along Chatito and toward Brillante. When the road angles away from Brillante, leave the road and hike cross-country toward Brillante, eventually intercepting county road 42. Near here and just off the road is a collapsed cabin. This was the homestead in 1929 of J. W. Worley. In 1942 he sold the place for ten dollars to the Carrica and Moleres families, but the owners never proved up, and the land reverted to the BLM.

Continue on 42 until the road forks, about a mile from the homestead; leave 42 and take the right fork. Take a second fork to the right soon after, back to the road you began with. With a little luck, your car is nearby.

Distance: 9.2 miles.
Time: 6 hours.
Difficulty: Brief but challenging scrambles up and down the craters; otherwise not difficult.
Topo Map: Cerro Brillante.

Oso Ridge/The Notches

Getting there: Turn right off NM 53 to FR 50. Just past Sawyer take FR 482 (at this writing, the sign for it is missing), which angles off to the left. This road continues about 5 miles. Near the gate, before FR 482 narrows, is a small road down the hill that leads to the Big Notch, identified by a downed sign.

Where FR 482 ends, walk up Oso ("bear") Ridge. The slope here is undemanding, and within a half mile, you're on top. From here you can hike as far as you want along Oso Ridge. You have good views in both directions, including the distant white cliffs of El Morro to the right. Because the rise is more gradual on the El Morro side (right) and more dramatic on the Notch side (left), the views will be better on the left. The terrain is pretty even but stony. There is an occasional faint trail—either for game or fire fighting. We saw signs of deer, elk, and bear, so the place earns its name.

Big Notch and Little Notch are chinks in Oso Ridge. Zuni Indian legend says they were created when Salt

Cerro Chato, one of the Chain of Craters.

225

The Chain of Craters area is surprisingly lush with grasses and trees.

Old Woman was fleeing and knocked two chunks out of Oso Ridge. One of the Zuni-Acoma trails passed through here. The place was a logging camp of the McGaffey Co., which built railroad tracks into this area of the Zunis in 1912 and later crossed Oso Ridge into the Dan Valley, near Ramah.

Southeast of here, a mile or so away, the names of features hint at a grisly past. Muerto ("corpse") Well, Muerto Spring, and Muerto Canyon may describe the place where an early settler befriended hapless travelers whom he killed and robbed, hiding their bodies in a well. Local legend has it that he grew wealthy from his treachery.

Distance: A few miles to 15 miles.
Time: A few hours to two days.
Difficulty: Not difficult.
Topo Map: Kettner Canyon.

El Morro Valley

The broad, high valley that frames El Morro is not a true valley, say geologists, but rather a high plateau surrounded by mountains. Whatever it is, it's one of the more spectacular places in western New Mexico.

In 1857 Lieutenant E. F. Beale of the army's camel brigade observed, "Timber of both pine and cedar is abundant, and everywhere the richest grass covers the ground . . . One would have to deal in superlatives altogether to describe the beauty of the country through which we passed this morning." Author-adventurer Charles Lummis wrote, "the plateau dips into a handsome valley, guarded on the north by the wilderness of pines and on the south by a long line of those superb mesas of many-colored sandstone which are among the characteristic beauties of the southwest. Through this valley ran an ancient and historic road—not hard to trace, for so many generations has it been abandoned—from Zuni to the Rio Grande."

The area was once home to ring-tailed cats, black bears, mountain sheep, beavers, muskrats, and possibly wolves. In the wooded uplands were bobcats and an occasional mountain lion. Anasazi people lived here, followed by Zunis and Navajos. Settlement by outsiders began with Hispanic herdsmen from San Rafael and Cubero, who eventually had four villages. One of the most remarkable and unheralded subchapters of New Mexico history is that of the Mormon settlement here. Because of their penchant for records, letters, and diaries, much information remains in Mormon archives. Finally from 1916 to the 1930s, a last wave of newcomers arrived to homestead.

In the 1930s the Atchison, Topeka & Santa Fe Railroad stimulated settlement by advertising sections of farmland in the area near Tingle, Atarque, Fence Lake, and El Morro. "Many fine people are coming in on account of that," wrote a WPA writer. "The WPA and the county commissioners built a good road down to that country last summer [1938]." When settlers arrived in the area, it was thick with piñon, juniper, and grama grass, but by the 1940s, the original vegetation had given way to sage and rabbit brush in overgrazed areas and to tumbleweeds and sunflowers on abandoned farmland. Arroyos had cut into sloped land, dunes had formed from

wind-borne topsoils from dry-land farming, and irrigated land was loaded with alkali. Human occupation and exter-mination campaigns by government and farmers reduced prairie-dog populations and predators by the 1940s, although coyotes still haunted the sleep of shepherds.

Tinaja

As Navajo and Apache raids abated in the 1860s, herders from Cubero and San Rafael began to move their live-stock to the broad valleys south of San Rafael. Around 1866 Pablo Candelaria and his brother-in-law, Jose Maria Marez, moved from Santa Fe to ranch in an area north of El Morro on a much-used wagon trail through the Zuni Mountains. They called their new home San Lorenzo, but the place was later renamed Tinaja ("earthen vat"), for a nearby Indian ruin that resembles a giant bowl. In 1870 Epitacio and Jesus Mazon moved into the area and eventually became sheep and cattle barons with vast tracts of land, at one time owning some twelve thou-sand sheep and twelve hundred head of cattle. Epitacio reportedly used a Mormon settler's headstone as a doorstep. When he died in 1900, he left a hundred-thou-sand-dollar fortune. Leopoldo Mazon was a millionaire, known for the fine cut of his clothes. He never wore western garb.

(Pages 228–29)
El Morro Valley

Tinaja became a center for Hispanic settlement and a stopping place for travelers. One old-timer recalled that Tinaja "was a Spanish town built with a plaza in the cen-ter" and had a dance pavilion. Settlers raised cattle and sheep and grew fields of corn, beans, and chile. Soon other villages grew along the well-used wagon trail: Las Norias, Pinitos, and Atarque.

Lorenzo Garcia and his family moved from Cebolleta to the new village of San Rafael but he died in 1881, dur-ing a raid by Geronimo's band. In 1882 his oldest son, Juan, moved the family to Jaralosa Canyon and settled at a natural lake, where they built several dams. He named the place Los Atarques ("the dams") and opened a store. The place became the village of Atarque. It had a post office from 1910 to 1955. In 1916 the *Carbon City News* described Atarque as a "Mexican settlement of many years in the middle of a stock grazing region" and a town of adobe houses shaded by cottonwoods.

In the 1940s most land in the area was controlled by a wealthy Texan with little tolerance for the Hispanic res-idents. Ownership of the village passed to Juan's youngest brother, David. When he died in the early 1950s, wrote a former village teacher, "the rancher who owned the land around Atarque made it so rough on the people they had to leave, so no one lives there now."

Tinaja is also deserted. Outsiders settled among the *rancherías*, and because many of the Hispanic settlers had never gotten title to their lands, they lost them to ruthless outsiders. By the 1920s few were left. Tinaja rallied briefly as the last of the lumber camps and died in 1940.

Savoia

The first Mormons here were probably A. M. Tenney and R. S. Smith, who settled on little Cebolla Creek in 1874. They named their settlement Cebolla ("onion"), which came to be called Savoia. When their mission was completed, they returned to Utah, and Lorenzo H. Hatch took over their site. In 1876 Hatch was directed by the Mormon church to leave St. George, Utah, and go work among the Zuni Indians. He got a left-handed recommendation from a U.S. marshall: "We of this territory have found men of Mr. Hatch's peculiar belief to make a valuable addition to our territory."

On September 7 Hatch found Zuni Valley to be a promising place. Several thousand people in four pueblo villages cultivated big fields of corn, wheat, and hay and owned thousands of sheep, goats, horses, donkeys, and cattle. Even the peaches were good. He traveled another twelve miles to Fish Springs, stopped for the night, and the next day began surveying for an irrigation ditch. The Zunis, called "Lamanites" by the Mormons, were friendly to the newcomers, but didn't want them so close. Hatch obliged by moving fifteen miles farther, where his camp was eighteen miles west of Tinaja (then San Lorenzo). The Mazons welcomed Hatch and his party. A week later the industrious Mormons were selling butter, cheese, and milk to soldiers at Ft. Wingate "at good prices," one wrote—fifty cents a pound for milk and cheese. Before long Zunis and Navajos invited the Mormons to settle in the Savoia Valley.

The newcomers, with their antlike discipline, organization, and work ethic, were a typical Mormon colony. While the taming of the West may have been otherwise serendipitous, the Saints, as they called themselves, were nothing if not deliberate. During general conferences, a church official would call from the pulpit designated individuals to found new colonies, and name the leader. Everyone was chosen carefully for the skills and equipment they might bring to the job. More difficult assignments were called "missions," and the missionaries couldn't leave their assignments without a release. After an organizing meeting, the colonists sold their property and loaded their possessions into wagons for the often arduous journey to a new land.

Arriving at a site, they paused to dedicate it with prayer and then fell to work erecting a stockade. Here they all lived with some protection and could sally forth each day in organized groups to dig irrigation ditches, plant crops, and build fences, roads, and houses—all at their own expense. The church would seed them with modest stocks of food. To get through the first winter in Savoia, one family got twenty-five pounds of flour, five pounds of sugar, five pounds of grease, and an old cow that gave a quart of milk a day.

In November the Mormon church sent Luther Burnham and Ernst Tietjen to locate among the Navajos. Tietjen had married his second wife a day before leaving for Zuni. The entire group settled at Savoia, "a lovely little valley in the pines," as Nettie Hunt put it, with a good spring. They began building the first cabin in January. After hauling logs to Ft. Wingate to be cut into lumber, they erected a ten-by-twenty-five-foot, two-room abode, adding more cabins in the spring, as they planted crops. One family sent their twelve-year-old son the twenty-five miles to the fort for mail once a week.

As other Mormon settlers arrived, the men built a stockade house. They dug a narrow, deep trench, lined it with upright pine poles, and filled it in again, leaving room for a door. A wagon cover became the roof. Here the settlers lived, sleeping in their wagons, until they had homes.

Released from his mission in September 1877, Hatch left, and the Burnham and Tietjen families became the first Mormons to stay in New Mexico for good. Tietjen brought his families to the valley in 1877 by oxcart. Along with their belongings, they also carried a load of poplar trees. Burnham's two families also joined him there in 1877. In the first two winters, settlers struggled to avoid starvation and sickness. "We used red roots and pig weeds and greasewood and sourdock for greens, seasoned with salt and pepper and vinegar. We gathered sego lily bulbs and cooked them in milk gravy," recalled one pioneer. Other families hunted tiny wild potatoes and onions. School lunches were parched corn.

After one long winter, Henry George's family had just a loaf of bread remaining, which they agreed to save for the baby. George managed to kill a porcupine, and after two and a half days of cooking, the animal was tough but edible. They followed with prickly pears. When a neighbor sent word he could loan some flour, George, weak from starvation, struggled over and back, helped up each time he stumbled in the snow by the thought of his children starving to death.

In late 1877 and the winter of 1878, a smallpox epidemic broke out in the settlement, and for nearly two months it took every healthy person to minister to the sick. The small settlement lost many to death and departures. Their Indian neighbors wanted to help, but the Mormons warned them away. At one point three Navajos crossed the mountains in four feet of snow and stopped short of the Hunt cabin. "Mother well remembers when one day they heard a call and looked out and there was their good friend Indian Charley, with his pony loaded down with quarters of venison tied to his small Indian saddle. These he cut loose and let fall in the snow and told Grandfather to give all the sick people some of it and tell them it would help them get well."

Despite warm relations between the Mormons and their Indian neighbors, the little village died in 1880. Apache raids in Arizona and New Mexico were driving off settlers, and the Savoia residents also feared their Navajo neighbors. At one point, Navajos gathered in the Zuni Mountains, above Savoia, "and were in a dangerous mood," wrote Luther Burnham's daughter. The reason, Mormons suspected, was that other Anglos—in particular the officers at Ft. Wingate—had fanned bitter sentiment against the Mormons' polygamy. Navajos also may have believed the Mormons were to blame for the smallpox epidemic. Burnham risked his life to attend a council meeting and talk the Navajos out of making war on his village. Still, enough threat remained from renegades that the church called in its outlying settlements. The Savoia pioneers retreated to a tent city at St. John, Arizona. Later only Tietjen returned.

Ramah

Tietjen asked for reinforcements, and a group set out from Sunset, Arizona, in 1882. They settled three miles from Savoia, at the new village of Navajo, later called Ramah from the Bible and the Book of Mormon. The Tietjens joined them, moving from Savoia. The first of the new arrivals showed up in June and within three days were planting melons, potatoes, and beans. Tietjen already had a reservoir underway, using Navajo labor and a scraper made from scrap iron taken from the Ft. Wingate dump. There was a second reservoir at Savoia and a third at Savoyita Canyon. Colonists forged an agreement to build a community reservoir; each family would receive stock reflecting the work they did. They found a limestone quarry and contracted to burn limestone to make mortar for a rock culvert in the dam.

They surveyed their land and divided it into blocks, leaving a large block in the center for a church, meeting house, and school. Drawing lots each colonist got a homesite in the community and farm acreage. Stock grazed in a common pasture, watched over by herdboys. Ramah settlers followed the church's colonizing procedure to the letter, with one significant difference: They didn't build a stockade; apparently they felt safe among the Zunis and Navajos.

Homes were log cabins with dirt floors. During the first summer the door was a quilt, and white factory cloth, a kind of cheesecloth, covered ceilings and window. A fireplace was both stove and heating source. A braided cloth wick stuck in grease, called a "bitch," was the lamp.

The following year the industrious colonists raised a

mind-boggling variety of crops: currants, cherries, strawberries, gooseberries, onions, carrots, beets, lettuce, radishes, beans, watercress, cucumbers, pepper grass, cabbage, sage, salsify, parsley, rhubarb, peas, wheat, oats, popcorn, and melons. Together they raised 1,340 bushels of oats, 387 bushels of barley, and 1,096 bushels of wheat.

The Mormon colonists might have enjoyed the fruits of their labors but for what they termed "the polygamy persecution." In the mid-1880s the government confiscated church properties and jailed church members and many, including some Ramah pioneers, fled to Mexico. One church leader advised that "one who has gone to the pen feels a thousand times better than one who has gone back on his wives . . . I am not a criminal only as the law has been turned to make me one." Other Mormon men, complained the *Gallup Gleaner* in 1894, abandoned their wives and children to poverty. This unfortunate period "left wounds so deep and bitter that they lasted till the third and fourth generations," Gary Tietjen wrote.

This wasn't the last of their trials. After grasshoppers destroyed crops three years in a row, from 1888 to 1890, Mormons bought a sawmill and moved it to the Zuni Mountains, but in 1891 it burned. By 1894 the dam was completed, and the Mormon farmers had three hundred acres of crops under cultivation. Three years later, however, the dam failed, and in the next two years, drought parched the farms anew. In the winter of 1896–97, sickness was rampant. As the Mormons suffered and labored to make their land fruitful, they couldn't correct one fatal flaw: The land wasn't theirs. They were squatters on railroad land, and when the Atlantic & Pacific Railroad sold its land in large blocks, the colonists couldn't afford to buy it. The new owner was Cebolla Cattle Co., and its operator, a Ft. Wingate army captain, ordered them off by March 15, 1889. With the second eviction notice, the settlers appealed to the church for help and got a loan of $6,400 to buy the land. The Mormons paid $10 an acre; the cattle company had paid 44 cents.

In 1890 the church released the people to go elsewhere, but they stayed. The dam washed out again in 1905, and the church loaned $2,000 to rebuild it in 1907. In 1908 typhoid fever afflicted the population. And yet the settlers didn't seem to dwell on their troubles. One pioneer wrote that "our people are not overblessed with this world's goods, as this land is not naturally the most desirable spot on earth . . . but the Saints who have stayed at their posts feel well, and we can see that God is blessing us."

For fun they danced, sometimes having to take turns because the rooms were so small. Pioneer Annie Burge recalled learning to waltz in the street to the sounds of a harmonica. "There was a panther that came around sometimes, though, and when we heard him scream, we would all scamper home." The colonists also put on plays and held candy pulls. And in winter there was ice skating and sledding.

Over time the mission "to bring enlightenment to the Navajos and Zunis" faded, and the settlers toiled in their other pursuit, "to make the desert blossom as a rose." The church encouraged them to treat their Indian neighbors well, and many were good friends, helping each other build houses and visiting back and forth. Some became fluent in Navajo. Evidence of abuse was viewed as an "un-Mormonlike attitude" and could mean severe discipline from the church. "In every case that I can call to mind of trouble with [Indians]," wrote one settler, "the white man has been the aggressor."

In 1916 Ramah was "only a little berg with one store in the town and two others close by that trade principally with the Indians," according to the *Gallup Independent*. But its citizens were known as good farmers. One Ramah farmer sold three wagonloads of cabbage to Gallup merchants, and each cabbage weighed from 3 to 12 pounds. One year Ramah merchants shipped 250,000 pounds of piñon nuts. Local farmers were in the habit of turning out their hogs in pine forests to fatten on piñons. The valley's pinto beans were selling for 12 cents a pound, potatoes for 6 cents.

In that period the Ramah Reservoir Co., fearing an attempt to blow up the reservoir (newspapers didn't speculate on the motive) placed a guard at the site, but they needn't have bothered. During a drought year, the reservoir went dry.

Real wealth remained elusive. In 1919 two companies drilled for oil here and in the Zuni Mountains. It was an "open secret among people around Ramah," the *Gallup Record* insisted, that the area had a spring that flowed with pure oil. But the oil was as elusive as the gold of Cibola, and in 1921 the newly formed Ramah Chamber of Commerce was promoting dairy and wheat farming. By 1937 the village that refused to die had about 315 people, fifty homes, five stores, a post office, a church, and a school. Today Ramah survives as a farming and ranching community, with the church at its center, as always.

Ramah Navajo

Navajos may have been living in the Ramah area as early as the 1600s, and Spanish communications refer to them frequently after 1672. They likely grazed their sheep in the Zuni Mountains in the summer and grew crops in the lush valleys south of the mountains. In the fall they collected piñons at the edge of the malpais.

After the Long Walk and their release from Fort

Sumner, in 1868, seven families returned to the area to find others on land they once enjoyed. In the 1880s big cattle companies crowded them off their mountain grazing lands, Mormon settlers occupied the valleys, and thousands of acres were given to railroad companies. By 1917 Navajos lost the use of land belonging to lumber companies and the railroad, as it was leased or sold. And with a new homestead law, settlers were claiming government land. Some Navajos homesteaded, but in any conflict with newcomers, Navajos usually lost. Their only defender for years was the trader at Ramah. It was in his best interests to protect Navajos, who kept him supplied with wool, pelts, and piñons, in return for high-priced merchandise. Still it was the trader who kept them from losing everything. In the late 1920s, he managed to bring in the Indian Service Administration, which invoked the Dawes Act of 1887. Most Navajo families got 160-acre plots, although much of it was in the malpais.

This pool at El Morro drew Indian and Spanish travelers for centuries.

In the 1930s the Navajo Tribe recognized Ramah as a chapter, and it continues as an independent-minded Navajo island.

El Morro Valley Hikes

El Morro National Monument
Getting there: Take NM 53 south and west 43 miles from Grants, or NM 32 south and east from Gallup.

Imagine going to a place in the East where you could find the autographs and comments of George Washington, Columbus, and Ulysses Grant etched into the wall. El Morro ("the bluff," or "castle"), with its collection of significant graffiti in sandstone, is such a place. In 1855 U.S. Attorney W. W. H. Davis wrote, "What a field for sober reflection this rock presents to the mind, with its inscriptions, hieroglyphics and ruined villages! It is a mute but eloquent historian of the past."

Besides being a remarkable historical monument, El Morro's lone trail is one of the most scenic in the state and one of my long-standing favorites. The trail begins at the visitor's center, where you need to sign in and pay your fee.

El Morro's two-hundred-foot castle of white sandstone shelters a basin of water that drew Indian and Spanish travelers for centuries before the first American saw it. The names they left etched into the rock are also inscribed in New Mexico and western history, hence the place's second name, Inscription Rock. The pool may have been an oasis for travelers, but by the 1930s park personnel for whom it was the sole water supply complained that after boiling, the water "jells and has to be eaten in chunks with knife and fork." Its scent was "reminiscent of a sewage disposal plant gone sour." Park rangers didn't get well water until 1962.

El Morro holds the nation's oldest graffiti.

Just past the pool begin the signatures. The oldest name is none other than Don Juan de Oñate, the first governor of New Mexico under Spain. Returning from exploring the Gulf of California, he carved this inscription: "Passed by here the Adelantado Don Juan de Oñate, from the discovery of the Sea of the South, the 16th of April of 1605." This was 15 years before Pilgrims landed at Plymouth Rock. In 1629 Franciscan friars carved the monument's only poem: "Here arrived the Señor and Governor/ Don Francisco Manuel de Silva Nieto/ Whose indubitable arm and valor/ Has overcome the impossible/ With the wagons of the King our Lord,/ A thing which he alone has accomplished/ August 5, 1629 that one may well to Zuni pass/ And carry the faith." Don Diego de Vargas signed the stone register in 1692, as he reconquered New Mexico following the Pueblo Revolt. He wrote, "Here was the General Don Diego de Vargas who conquered for our Holy Faith, and for the Royal Crown, all of New Mexico at his own expense, year of 1692." The last of the Spanish inscriptions is dated 1774.

Charles Lummis wrote that Spaniards didn't leave their names behind out of bravado or vanity. "They were piercing an unknown and frightful wilderness . . . a wilderness which remained until our own times the most dangerous in America. They were few—never was their army more than 200 men, and seldom was it a tenth of that amid tens of thousands of warlike savages. The chances were ten to one that they would never get back to the world . . . What they wrote was rather like leaving a headstone for unknown graves; a word to say, if any should ever follow, 'Here were the men who did not come back'."

The first American army officer to visit El Morro was Lieutenant J. H. Simpson, with the artist R. H. Kern. In September 1849 a trader they encountered on the road urged them to see the bluff. A surprised Simpson wrote in his journal about "a mass of sandstone rock, of a pearly whitish aspect . . ." They marveled at the inscriptions, "some of them very beautiful . . . inscriptions of interest, if not of value, one of them dating as far back as 1606, all of them very ancient, and several of them very deeply as well as beautifully engraven . . ."

Simpson ordered a halt so that he and Kern could immediately begin copying the petroglyphs and writings. It took two days and was time well spent; some of the markings are no longer visible. Simpson dubbed the place Inscription Rock, and the name stuck. His was the first English entry. Another American notable was Lieutenant E. F. Beale of the army's camel brigade. Lummis called El Morro "the most precious cliff, historically, possessed by any nation on earth, and, I am ashamed to say, the most utterly uncared for." He complained that El Morro's unprotected face held more and more contemporary graffiti by vandals who had even defaced the old inscriptions. Eventually the government listened, and El Morro became a national monument in 1906. The Park Service removed the modern names in the early 1920s and considered a coating of paraffin to preserve the etchings.

Trailside signs inform you about the plant life, which includes lemonade sumac, one-seed juniper, narrow-leaved and broad-leaved yucca, four-wing saltbush, Rocky Mountain juniper, and pale wolfberry. Birds seen in the area include piñon jays, spurred towhees, swallows, swifts, owls, red-shafted flickers, prairie falcons, wild turkeys, quail, killdeers, hummingbirds, woodpeckers, fly catchers, wrens, bluebirds, warblers, blackbirds, tanagers, and sparrows.

The trail winds around the north side of the butte and begins a traversing climb to the top. To the north is a fine view of Oso Ridge and the Zuni Mountains. The two dips you can see are The Notches. From here also is a good view of the ruddy cliffs that nearly ring the Zuni Mountains. These were formed in the Jurassic period, as winds dropped their sandy load to form sand dunes that ultimately became Zuni sandstone. You pass North Atsinna Ruin and look into a striking box canyon whose white columns enclose a park of grasses and ponderosa pines along with a sandstone pillar. From here you see that the bluff is actually U-shaped, and the trail makes a horseshoe around the canyon and takes you to a second site. Anglos call this pueblo Atsinna, the name Zuni people gave to the rock and its pool. It means "where pictures are on the rock."

Zunis call the site Heshoda Yatht'a.

One of many Anasazi villages built on mesas, it once had 875 rooms for a possible population of between one thousand and fifteen hundred. Outside walls were three stories high on the northeast and one story on the south-west, to protect from wind while absorbing the sun's warmth. Atsinna had a typical round Anasazi kiva, as well as a square kiva more common to Mogollon people, one indication of change in this period of time. The pueblo was probably built in 1275 and occupied until 1350, when the people withdrew to areas around pre-sent-day Zuni Pueblo.

The trail, cut into the rock here, winds around the mesa top before dropping down through a juniper and pine for-est. The stone steps you're marveling at were carved not by prehistoric Indians but during a government works pro-ject in 1934.

In 1921 a Gallup man nearly died when he didn't heed the usual warnings to stay on the trail. As his friends hiked back down the trail, he decided to climb down through a crevice. He slipped and skidded to the very edge of a 250-foot precipice, where he held on for his life. His friends urged him to hang on while they got help. It took two hours, but nearby sheepherders were able to lower a camp rope and rescue him.

Distance: 2.3 miles.
Time: 2 hours.
Difficulty: The uphills and steps cut in rock make this trail a bit challenging in places. As a three-year-old, my son loved this trail and could manage it easily.

(Left) Box canyon at El Morro. (Above) Atsinna ruin.

241

Ramah Lake.

Ramah Lake

Ramah Lake is a fifty-acre lake just outside the town, surrounded by red cliffs—one of the prettiest settings in the state. Fishing here, from the shore or by boat, is good for both trout and bass. Ramah Lake is also considered one of the state's small lakes suitable for canoeing.

Bluewater Valley

About four miles from Grants, I found the Agua Azul in bad condition, the bottoms all over flowed . . . The overflow of the Agua Azul at this time is a phenomenon which occurs usually . . . It explains why these fertile bottoms were not built upon by the aborigines. The latter had no means to check the inundation any.
Adolph F. Bandelier, March 25, 1883

Indian people say that long ago, "before the lava came," there was a great lake in this valley. From the Indian name for the place, Spaniards called the area north of the Zuni

Mountains Agua Azul. W. W. H. Davis, U.S. attorney for New Mexico Territory, in 1855 refers to Agua Azul, and the name was used well into this century. The first settler was a Frenchman named Dumas Provencher, who had a farm near the present Bluewater Lake in the early 1870s and a store and sawmill at San Rafael. Provencher operated stage stops here and at Cebolleta, Salazar, and San Rafael, on the stagecoach route from Santa Fe to Fort Apache. He was assassinated in San Rafael during a village election.

When the Atlantic & Pacific Railroad rendered stage stops obsolete, it created Bluewater anew in 1880 and 1881 and advertised in local newspapers for settlers. Provencher had sold his operation by then to the Acoma Land and Cattle Company, which in 1882 sold the property, the 7HL Ranch, to James M. Latta, a railroad contractor. In 1883 Latta organized the Zuni Mountain Cattle Co., with headquarters at Bluewater, and ran as many as ten thousand head from the Continental Divide to Bluewater. But as the government began breaking up public lands and the railroads claimed their alternating sections, big cattle companies found themselves hemmed in. Drought was the last straw. In February 1894 Latta sold the ranch for $3,000 to four partners led by the Mormon pioneer Ernst Tietjen, of Ramah.

Tietjen was then a brokenhearted man. In 1889 his beloved young daughter had died tragically in a house fire. His wife Amanda never recovered from the loss and died four years later. On the advice of Brigham Young, Jr., Tietjen acquired the Latta property, which gave him a chance to leave the place of painful memories. His partners were fellow Ramah pioneer Frihoff Nielson and two non-Mormons—W. F. McLaughlin, the trading-post operator at Fort Wingate, and his wealthy father-in-law, J. S. Van Doren. The latter two put up most of the cash.

Within two weeks Tietjen and Nielson had picked the spot for a reservoir at the confluence of Bluewater and Cottonwood creeks, and the four men formed the Bluewater Land and Irrigation Co. Using twenty-five teams and scrapers, they built the first earthen dam nine miles from the town of Bluewater, at the entrance to Bluewater Canyon. It was 150 feet wide, 260 feet long, and 42 feet high. Bluewater Valley, with its deep alluvial soil, held great promise. In the following year, the company built twenty-one miles of fence, dug thirty-one miles of ditches, and planted two thousand acres to oats, barley, wheat, corn, alfalfa, onions, carrots, sugar beets, melons, cabbages, and orchards. The Tietjen and Nielson families moved into the former 7HL ranch house, occupying opposite ends.

The dam and its promised irrigation water drew a flock of Mormon and non-Mormon settlers, and a new community, called "Mormontown" (later Bluewater), began forming in 1896, three miles west of the railroad town of Bluewater. One bride who came here in 1895 wrote, "My bridal mansion was a dirty little tent. There were harnesses, saddles and sacks of feed in one end of the tent. In the other end of the tent was an old government cot that Tom had picked up in the dump. We hauled water from the mouth of the canyon. I took work in a boarding house which the company was building just west of the railroad station. I was paid $16 a month and worked from four in the morning until six at night."

Relations were rocky between the Mormons and the "outsiders," and Tietjen and Nielson quit the company in 1902, getting a settlement in water rights. When they didn't receive the promised water, they sued, and the litigation lasted for years.

In March 1905 the dam washed out, damaging farms and washing out the railroad tracks. Old timers have said a hired vandal blew up the dam after an argument among the former partners; another account blames the cattle company's watchman for the act. When confronted he "left the area in a hurry one night rather than chance to

*Bluewater
Reservoir.*

hang on a tree," wrote Gary Tietjen in *Mormon Pioneers
in New Mexico.*

Trouble between the irrigation company and the Mormon settlers continued, and disputes over water flared.
The company's new local manager "was determined to
make the valley into a cattle ranch rather than a farm and
Mormons were just as determined to have it the other
way. Every now and then, the disputes erupted into
armed battles with pitchforks or guns," Tietjen wrote.

The company built a more expensive and elaborate dam
in 1907, but it washed out again two years later, again halting railroad traffic for days. Before long weeds took over
fields once expected to be a garden spot. Irrigation canals
dried up. The only things growing were feuds and lawsuits.

The peacemaker turned out to be an attorney for the
Santa Fe Railroad, Captain W. C. Reid. After one faction
appealed to Reid, he managed to unite all the factions,
persuaded the legislature to organize a new irrigation
district, and sold $360,000 in bonds to investors. Then
he monitored construction in the summer of 1926 of a

modern, reinforced concrete dam 90 feet high and 500
feet long. Seven miles long, the lake would hold fifty-
three thousand acre-feet of water.

"With irrigation, there is no better farmland anywhere,"
wrote the *Gallup Independent*. This project would irrigate
ten thousand acres. Excited locals made plans to build a
sugar-beet plant and creamery. That never happened, but
the Bluewater Valley became a rich, green patchwork of
orchards, barley, potatoes, vegetables, and three cuttings
of alfalfa each season. Nearby, limekilns were operating,
and lumber was available from mills, noted the project's
attorney, William A. Keleher. Tietjen died in February 1925,
before he could see his dream materialize.

In 1929 the governor signed legislation, termed a
"gift bill" by its critics, to loan Bluewater $25,000 for irri-
gation. There was no provision for interest or security.

The reservoir didn't end the farmers' misfortunes
here, however. A water shortage in the 1930s reduced
irrigated acreage to some three thousand to four thousand acres, which were producing fruit, oats, peas, and

*Bluewater
Canyon below
the dam.*

alfalfa. And in 1934 a grasshopper plague scoured every blade of vegetation for hundreds of acres.

In those years 160 people lived in Mormon Bluewater. "Within the last five years, several Norwegian families have settled on farms adjoining those of Mormon families," according to a WPA writer. "The Norwegians and Mormons get along splendidly, as do the Mormons and the Anglos living near the railroad. However, the Mormons and the Spanish-Americans who live in the town at the railroad do not mix at all—not even at school." Hispanic children were segregated at school, but because their parents were outnumbered in the community, they couldn't do anything about it. However, on a county level, "politicians press the Mormons whenever possible."

In 1939 Ralph Card and Dean Stanley bought four hundred acres near Bluewater and experimented with lettuce, cauliflower, broccoli, carrots, cabbage, potatoes, onions, and peas. Carrots became the leading cash crop from Grants to Bluewater, and a new industry sprang up. Navajo fieldhands were paid in company scrip. The carrot boom wilted in the late 1950s, just as uranium companies were buying land and water rights to fuel a new boom.

The reservoir also launched recreation in the area. In 1930 local sportsmen meeting in Bluewater said they were determined to end the dynamiting of fish. A month later the Game Protective Association met and held a dance at Bluewater, with the goal of opening Bluewater Lake for recreation. By 1936 the lake was stocked with trout, bass, perch, and crappie, and visitors could rent boats from a sportsmen's club. In 1937 the state of New Mexico bought 160 acres along the twenty-five-mile shoreline to develop for recreation.

This peaceful-looking place has not been without some notable crimes. For years an old cross could be seen along the railroad tracks near the old Bluewater Station. In 1894 two conductors found the body of a young, well-dressed man shot through the head near the Bluewater switch. Two days later the body was still there, so a freight conductor and fireman buried it. The thought of the unmarked grave apparently troubled workers, so a month later they built a mound of stones and erected a cross of telegraph poles, on which they inscribed, "To the Unknown Dead— Postal Telegraph Gang—June 18, 1894."

In August 1925 the body of Stella "Cactus Kate" Oliver was found in some rocks near Bluewater. The eighty-five-year-old woman from San Francisco was well known in mining and construction camps around the West. In Winslow, where she camped for three weeks, she had flashed sacks of diamonds, silver, money, and Liberty Bonds, apparently the proceeds of selling her restaurant in California. She was last seen in the company of a young man.

Bluewater Canyon

This is one of the most spectacular canyons in New Mexico.Bluewater Creek is one of the few perennial trout streams in the area and the growth is lush—cottonwoods, willows, and grasses, along with piñon, juniper, ponderosa pine, and Douglas fir. Songs of the canyon wren echo from sandstone walls that rise five hundred feet.

However, the canyon can only be hiked in pieces. Most accessible and a favorite for fishing is the portion south of the lake, along FR 178. You can also hike a short way along Bluewater Canyon from a trail at the campground on the north side of the lake, but you soon run into Navajo checkerboard land. Most promising for future hiking is a three-mile stretch of Bluewater Canyon northeast of Navajo lands on BLM land declared an Area of Critical Concern in 1981. In all likelihood, the BLM will develop a trail here. Inquire at the BLM office about hiking. It's worth a visit.

Bluewater Lake

Getting there: Take NM 412 south from the I-40 exit at Prewitt, to reach the northeastern portion of the lake. Take NM 612 south from the I-40 exit at Thoreau to reach the southeastern side.

Today Bluewater Lake is a twelve-hundred-acre lake popular for boating and fishing. I've always liked Bluewater, because it's one of New Mexico's few lakes surrounded by hills and trees. There are campgrounds on both sides of the lake.

Rainbow trout and channel catfish are stocked here, and crawfish also flourish. (My son, then three, learned to count with those crawfish, when we lived here briefly.) In the late 1980s, Bluewater Lake boasted the state-record rainbow trout, which was thirty inches long and sixteen pounds, and a typical catch is twelve to sixteen inches long. Periodically drought reduces lake levels to the twenty feet of water rights owned by the state, and fishing enthusiasts have had to be content with somewhat smaller fish. The best time to fish here, according to one expert, is just after the ice breaks and just before winter, with September and October being the best months.

Appendix: Campgrounds

For more information contact the Mt. Taylor Ranger District at 1800 Lobo Canyon Road in Grants, or call (505) 287-8833.

Mount Taylor
Coal Mine
Location: NM 547
Units: 17
Water: Drinking
Open: April–September

Lobo Canyon
Location: FR 239 and 193
Units: 9
Water: None
Open: April–September

Zuni Mountains
McGaffey
Location: NM 400, south of Fort Wingate
Units: 40
Water: Drinking

Ojo Redondo
Location: FR 480
Units: 20
Water: None

Quaking Aspen
Location: NM 400
Units: 20
Water: Drinking

El Morro
El Morro National Monument
Location: 43 miles south and west of Grants on NM 53
Units: 9
Water: Drinking

Bluewater Lake
Bluewater Lake State Park
Location: 7 miles south of I-40 on NM 412
Units: 100, plus primitive camping

Water: Drinking
Facilities: Showers, 14 sites with electricity, playground

Location: 10 miles south of I-40 on NM 612
Units: 13, plus primitive camping along lakeshore
Water: Drinking

Commercial Parks

Acoma Trading Center RV Park
Location: 20 miles east of Grants off I-40 at exit 102
Facilities: Full hookups, trading post, restaurant

Cibola Sands RV Park
Location: One mile south of I-40 on NM 53
Facilities: Full hookups, tent sites

El Morro Lodge and RV Park
Location: ¾ mile east of El Morro on NM 53
Facilities: Full hookups, cabins, cafe, gasoline

Grants-West RV Park
Location: Prewitt exit off I-40
Facilities: Full hookups, indoor pool, TV lounge, tent sites

Inscription Rock RV Park
Location: Two miles east of El Morro National
Monument on NM 53
Facilities: Full hookups

Lavaland RV Park
Location: Grants exit 85
Facilities: Full hookups

St. Bonaventure RV Park
Location: I-40 exit 53 at Thoreau
Facilities: Full hookups, cable TV, gift shop, grassy tent
spaces, laundry, wheelchair access

Bibliography

Books

Armitage, Merle. *Stella Dysart of Ambrosia Lake.* New York, N.Y.: Duell, Sloan and Pearce, 1959.

Bandelier, Adolph F. *The Southwestern Journals of Adolph F. Bandelier 1880–1882.* Ed. Charles H. Lange and Carroll L. Riley. Albuquerque: University of New Mexico Press and Santa Fe: The Museum of New Mexico Press, 1966.

Barela, Josephine. *Ojo Del Gallo.* Santa Fe, N.M.: Sleeping Fox Enterprises, 1975.

Boy Scouts, Zuni Chapter, Order of the Arrow. *Where to Go Camping in the Zuni Mountain District.* 1990.

Boyette, Ray. *Homesteading in the Thirties.* Santa Fe, N.M.: Sleeping Fox Enterprises, 1974.

Bevan, A.W.R., and Hutchison, Robert. *Catalogue of Meteorites.* London: British Museum, 1875.

Davis, W.W.H. *El Gringo or New Mexico and Her People.* Santa Fe, N.M.: Rydal Press, 1938.

Dobie, J. Frank. *Apache Gold and Yaqui Silver.* New York, N.Y.: Little, Brown & Co, 1939.

Dodge, Bertha S. *The Road West, Saga of the 35th Parallel.* Albuquerque, N.M.: University of New Mexico Press, 1980.

Foster, Roy W. *Southern Zuni Mountains.* Socorro, N.M.: New Mexico Bureau of Mines and Mineral Resources, 1971.

Gallegos, Robert. *Ambrosia Lake: Poems.* Grants, N.M.: Southwestern Alternatives, 1982.

Hayenga, Brad, and Shaw, Chris. *The New Mexico Mountain Bike Guide.* Albuquerque, N.M.: Big Ring Press, 1991.

Heath, Roxanne T. *Thoreau, Where the Trails Cross.* Thoreau, N.M.: R. T. Heath, 1982.

Howell, Anabel. *Ninety Miles from Nowhere.* Peralta, N.M.: Pine Tree Press, 1987.

Jenkinson, Michael. *Land of Clear Light.* New York, N.Y.: E. P. Dutton & Co. Inc., 1977.

Lange, Charles H., and Riley, Carroll L. *The Southwestern Journals of Adolph F. Bandelier 1883–1884.* Albuquerque, N.M.: University of New Mexico Press, 1970.

Lummis, Charles. S*ome Strange Corners of Our Country.* New York, N.Y.: The Century Co., 1908.

Lummis, Charles. *Tramp Across the Continent.* New York, N.Y.: Scribner, 1892.

Mabery, Marilyne. *El Malpais National Monument.* Tucson, Ariz.: Southwest Parks and Monuments Association, 1990.

McNitt, Frank. *Richard Wetherill: Anasazi.* Albuquerque, N.M.: University of New Mexico Press, 1966.

McPherson, Robert S. *Sacred Land Sacred View.* Charles Redd Center for Western Studies, Brigham Young University. Salt Lake City, Utah: Signature Books, 1992.

Meriwether, David. *My Life in the Mountains and on the Plains.* Norman, Okla.: University of Oklahoma Press, 1965.

Moore, Cecil. *Hole in the Wall: A Collection of Cowboy Poetry.* Socorro, N.M.: Orville Moore, 1990.

Pearce, T.M. *New Mexico Place Names: A Geographical Dictionary.* Albuquerque, N.M.: University of New Mexico Press, 1965.

Pern, Stephen. *The Great Divide.* New York, N.Y.: Viking, 1988.

Rittenhouse, Jack D. *Cabezon: A New Mexico Ghost Town.* Santa Fe, N.M.: Stagecoach Press, 1965.

Rittenhouse, Jack D. *Outlaw Days at Cabezon.* Santa Fe, N.M.: Stagecoach Press, 1964.

Robbins, Michael. *High Country Trail: Along the Continental Divide.* Washington, D.C.: National Geographic Society, 1981.

Sherman, James E. *Ghost Towns and Mining Camps of New Mexico.* Norman, Okla.: University of Oklahoma Press, 1975.

Simmons, Marc. *The Little Lion of the Southwest, a Life of Manuel Antonio Chaves.* Chicago, Ill.: Swallow Press, 1973.

Simpson, James H. *Navajo Expedition.* Norman, Okla.: University of Oklahoma Press, 1964.

Tietjen, Gary. *Encounter with the Frontier.* Los Alamos, N.M.: Gary Tietjen, 1969.

Tietjen, Gary. *Mormon Pioneers in New Mexico: History of Ramah, Fruitland, Luna, Beulah, Bluewater,* Virden and Carson. Los Alamos, N.M.: Gary Tietjen, 1980.

Vogt, Evon. *Modern Homesteaders.* Cambridge, Mass.: The Belknap Press of Harvard University Press, 1955.

White, Leslie A. *The Acoma Indians. Forty-Seventh Annual Report of the Bureau of American Ethnology.* Glorieta, N.M.: The Rio Grande Press Inc., 1929–1930.

Winslow, Richard Elliott III. *General John Sedgwick.* Novato, Calif.: Presidio Press, 1982.

Government Reports
Baker, Robert D. and Maxwell, Robert S. "Timeless Heritage/ A History of the Forest Service in the Southwest." U.S. Department of Agriculture. August 1988.

Dutton, C.E. "Mt. Taylor and the Zuni Plateau." U.S. Department of Interior Annual Report. 1886.

Kelley, Klara. "Archeological Investigations In West-Central

New Mexico." Vol 2, *Historic Cultural Resources.* U.S. Bureau of Land Management, Las Cruces District. 1988.

Glover, Vernon J., and Hereford, Joseph P. "Zuni Mountain Railroads." U.S. Forest Service, Southwestern Region. September 1986.

Holmes, Barbara E. "American Indian Land Use of El Malpais." Prepared for U.S. Bureau of Land Management by the Office of Contract Archeology, University of New Mexico. Albuquerque, N.M. 1989.

Laboratory of Anthropology. "Archeological Site Survey." Museum of New Mexico. Santa Fe, N.M. Surveyed for U.S. Bureau of Land Management, Albuquerque District. May 21, 1989.

Landgraf, John L. "Land-Use in the Ramah Area of New Mexico." Papers of the Peabody Museum of American Archeology and Ethnology, Harvard University. Vol. 42, No. 1. Cambridge, Mass. 1954.

Mangum, Neil C. In The Land of Frozen Fires/ El Malpais / A History of Occupation in El Malpais Country. Southwest Cultural Resources Center Professional Papers No. 32. Santa Fe, N.M. 1990.

Maxwell, Charles H. "El Malpais." U.S. Geological Survey. Denver, Colo. 1982.

Maxwell, Charles H. "Geologic Map of El Malpais Lava Field and Surrounding Areas, Cibola County, New Mexico." Department of the Interior, U.S. Geological Survey. 1986.

Otero, Kim. Untitled planning studies for proposed transmission line. Prepared for Public Service Co. of New Mexico by Dames and Moore, consultants; submitted to U.S. Forest Service, Cibola Ranger District. 1991.

Tainter, Joseph, and Gillio, David A. "Cultural Resources Overview, Mount Taylor Area." U.S. Forest Service. 1980.

U.S. Department of Interior, Bureau of Land Management. "El Malpais National Conservation Area Chain of Craters Wilderness Analysis Report/ Environmental Assessment." Albuquerque District Office. July 1991.

U.S. Department of Interior, Bureau of Land Management. "El Malpais National Conservation Area General Management Plan." 1991.

U.S. Department of Interior, Bureau of Land Management. "El Malpais National Conservation Area General Management Plan Draft." Rio Puerco Resource Area. Albuquerque, N.M. April 1990.

U.S. Department of Interior, Bureau of Land Management. "El Malpais National Monument and National Conservation Area Background Information." December 1987.

U.S. Department of Interior, Bureau of Land Management. "New Mexico Statewide Wilderness Study," Vol. 2. Santa Fe, N.M. 1986.

U.S. Department of Interior, National Park Service. "El Malpais National Monument General Management Plan/

Environmental Assessment/ Wilderness Suitability Study." El Malpais National Monument, N.M. January 1990.

U.S. Forest Service. "The National Forests of Arizona and New Mexico." U.S. Department of Agriculture, Southwest Region. 1934.

U.S. Forest Service. "Cibola National Forest, Mt. Taylor Ranger District." Albuquerque, N.M. 1975.

U.S. Forest Service. "Continental Divide National Scenic Trail Plan." Denver, Colo. 1985.

U.S. Forest Service. "Zuni Mountain Historic Railroads/ A Self Guided Motor Tour." Cibola National Forest, Mt. Taylor Ranger District. Grants, N.M. Undated.

Winter, Joseph C., editor. "High Altitude Adaptations in The Southwest." Prepared for U.S. Forest Service by Office of Contract Archeology, University of New Mexico. 1983.

Wozniak, Frank E., and Marshall, Michael P. "The Prehistoric Cebolla Canyon Community: An Archeological Class III Inventory of 320 Acres of BLM Land at the Mouth of Cebolla Canyon." Albuquerque, N.M. Prepared for U.S. Bureau of Land Management by Office of Contract Archeology, University of New Mexico. 1990.

Articles

Abarr, James. "It Could Happen Here: New Mexico Carries Seeds For Future Volcanic Blast." Albuquerque Journal Impact Magazine, June 10, 1980.

Abarr, James. "The Cavalry Post that Wouldn't Die." Albuquerque Journal Impact Magazine, March 2, 1982.

Albuquerque Journal. "WWII Bomb Found in El Malpais." June 15, 1990.

Anyon, Roger. "Thousands of Years of History." Experience Zuni New Mexico. The Zuni Area Chamber of Commerce, 1989.

Armstrong, Ruth. "West of Albuquerque and East of Zuni." Century, April 20, 1983.

Atkinson, A. "White Pueblo." Gold!, Summer, 1977.

Beebe, Katharine. "Quad Training Demanding Like Mount Taylor." Albuquerque Journal, November 21, 1990.

Beebe, Katharine. "Quadrathlon Wicked Winter Event." Albuquerque Journal, January 23, 1991.

Bergman, Edna Heatherington. "San Estevan Rey, Acoma." Century Magazine, December 16, 1981.

Bryan, Howard. "Off the Beaten Path." Albuquerque Tribune, February 11, 1954; June 6, 1957; December 12, 15, 1960; September 13, 1962; October 17, 1963; March 11, 1965; September 9, 14, 21, 1965; April 5, 1966; December 9, 1971; June 26, 1984.

Carbon City News. 1893, 1915–1917.

Clark, Neil. "Magic of the Malpais." Saturday Evening Post, April 20, 1946.

Dyroff, Bill. "Bluewater Lake Fully Recovered as Fishery." Albuquerque Journal, July 19, 1984.

Dyroff, Bill. "Athletes Tackle Skyscraper." Albuquerque Journal, February 11, 1988.

The Elk. Gallup, N.M. 1890–1891.

Ewald, Judy. "Rumors of Riches." Grants Beacon, March 22, 1991.

Fellers, Charlotte. "Proposed trail route not actually along divide." Gallup Independent, June 25, 1992.

"Flow Sheet." Newsletter of Los Amigos del Malpais. January, May, June, August, September, October, December 1990; March 1991.

Frentzel, Martin. "Quality of Life in the Wild Improving." Albuquerque Journal, October 22, 1992.

Gallup Gleaner. 1894–1895, 1917–1918.

Gallup Herald. 1918–1927.

Gallup Independent. 1915–1930.

Grant Review. 1934.

Harbert, Nancy. "El Malpais Hike: A Rugged Tour." Albuquerque Journal, November 2, 1989.

Harrison, Clark. "Perpetual Ice Caves of New Mexico." Rocks and Minerals, September 1940.

"High-powered rush for uranium claims." Life, September 17, 1956

Highway 53 Express. Thunder Hooves Publishing. Pine Hill, N. M. Summer 1990.

Historical Program, Fort Wingate Centennial. Fort Wingate Ordnance Depot. Gallup, N.M. August 25–29, 1969.

Jenkinson, Michael. "Ghosts of the Rio Puerco." Frontier Times. April–May 1971.

Julyan, Bob. "Naming Names." Quantum. University of New Mexico. Albuquerque, N.M. Winter 1993.

Lee, Floyd W.D. "History of Ranch of the Fernandez Sheep Company New Mexico." The Westerners Brand Book. May 1950.

Looney, Joe. "Mexican spotted owl endangers timber sales in Zuni Mountains." Cibola County Beacon. August 19, 1992.

MacClary, J.S. "Perpetual Ice Under Lava." Natural History. 1936.

McCutcheon, Chuck. "Sweat, Dreams Nurture Trail." Albuquerque Journal. May 12, 1991.

Morrissey, David H. "Almost Ground Zero." Albuquerque Journal. February 11, 1990.

New Mexico Historical Review.

"Bond-Sargent Company" by Frank Grubbs. January 1962.

"Coolidge and Thoreau: Forgotten Frontier Towns" by Irving Telling. July 1954.

"Early Navajo Geography" by Frank D. Reeve. October 1956.

"Historical Geography of the Middle Rio Puerco Valley, New Mexico" by Jerold Gwayne Widdison. October 1959.

"Navajo-Spanish Diplomacy, 1770–1790" by Frank D. Reeve. July 1960.

"The Navajo-Spanish Peace: 1720's and 1770's" by
Frank D. Reeve. January 1959.

"The Seboyetanos and the Navajos" by C. C. Marino.
January 1954.

New Mexico Magazine.

"America's First Guest Book" by John MacGregor.
March–April 1970.

"Baby Volcanoes" by F. Louis Hernandez. May 1968.

"Bandera Crater" by Betty Woods. April 1969.

"Camera Touring New Mexico . . . Exploring the
Malpais" by Wayne Winters. September 1951.

"Cebolleta/ Peaceful Village Grew From Violent Past"
by Juana and Bill Wilson. November 1990.

"Desert Ice Box" by E.R. Harrington. July 1940.

"Devil's Towers" by E.R. Harrington. October 1938.

"El Malpais: A Black and Broken Sea" by Ruth Armstrong. November 1983.

"F.O.B. Grants" by Cy Rouse. April 1944.

"Hot on the Trail" by Douglas Preston. June 1991.

"Laguna's Big-Name Cities" by Luke Lyon. August
1978.

"Lava Beds" by Betty Woods. October 1946.

"Lava Grotto." January 1969.

"Lost Adams Diggings" by E. Poage. April 1950.

"The Mail Bag" by George K. Congdon. July 1947.

"Mountain Men Make Last Stand in Gila" by M. H.
Salmon. September 1990.

"Malpais Country" by Kit Carson. August 1964.

"Malpais Mystery" by J. Wesley Huff. April 1947.

"Mothers of Cebolleta" by Ann Nolan Clark. February
1937.

"Natural Arches of New Mexico" by Rodman E. Snead.
February 1979.

"New Mexico's Craters of the Moon" by H.W. Stowell.
April 1933.

"New Mexico's Explosive Landscape" by Robin
McKinney. February 1978.

"Rivers of Fire" by H.L. James. September 1968.

"Seboyeta" by Betty Woods. February 1948.

"The Wandering Fort of Bear Springs" by Jim Rhodes.
March 1979.

"The Uranium Boom" by R.R. Spurrier. May 1955.

"The Yellowcake Makers" by Doyle Kline. September
1980.

"To The Top of Mt. Taylor" by Philip Ober. July 1957.

"Uranium Boom at Grants" by Wayne Winters. May 1951.

"War Mines at Grants" by Fremond Kutnewsky. February
1943.

"Town Out of the Past" by Henry T. Gurley. April 1957.

"Payoffs for many in giant uranium jackpot." Life.
December 10, 1956.

Peña, Abe. "San Rafael Recalls Some Wild Times." Cibola
County Beacon. March 21, 1991.

Peña, Abe. "Ambrosio Lake: From historic stock pond to uranium kingdom." Cibola County Beacon. August 28, 1992.

Peña, Abe. "From Chaves to Lee: story of the San Mateo land grant." Cibola County Beacon. September 11, 1992.

Robinson, Sherry. "Village of San Rafael Spans History from Coronado, Kit Carson to Present." The Reporter. June 10, 1976.

Ruppe, Reynold J. "The Archaeological Survey: A Defense." American Antiquity. January 1966.

Shoemaker, John. "The Mount Taylor Volcanic Field: A Digest of The Literature." New Mexico Geological Society, Eighteenth Field Conference.

Winsor, Sue. "Centennial." Grants Daily Beacon. April 30, 1982.

Interviews

Byron and Ina Aldridge and Lewis Bright. Transcript of Los Amigos program, Grants, N.M. September 13, 1987.

Dovie and Lewis Bright. Interview by Sherry Robinson. Grants, N.M. August 1990.

Esther Brown. Interviewer unknown. Transcript. Special Collections, Grants Branch, New Mexico State University. March 1976.

Kent Carlton, National Park Service, El Malpais National Monument. Interview by Sherry Robinson. January 18, 1991.

Mark Catron, U.S. Forest Service, Mt. Taylor Ranger District. Interview by Sherry Robinson. January 18, 1991.

John Gruener. Speech to Los Amigos del Malpais. April 20, 1991.

C.G. Gunderson. Interview by Sue Winsor. Transcript. Special Collections, Grants Branch, New Mexico State University. June 11, 1976.

Lee Martinez. Interview by Sue Winsor. Transcript. Special Collections, Grants Branch, New Mexico State University. June 8, 1976.

Salvador and Bennie Milan. Interviewer unknown. Transcript. Special Collections, Grants Branch, New Mexico State University. May 1976.

Vidal Mirabal. Interviewer unknown. Transcript. Special Collections, Grants Branch, New Mexico State University. April 17, 1984.

Manuel Padilla. Interview by George Dannenbaum. Transcript. Special Collections, Grants Branch, New Mexico State University. February 9, 1984.

Red and Marvel Prestridge. Interview by Sue Winsor. Transcript. Special Collections, Grants Branch, New Mexico State University. May 5, 1976.

Sue and Jim Savage. Interview by Sherry Robinson. Grants, N.M. October 21, 1989.

Theses and Papers

Foster, H. Mannie. "Mormon Settlements in Mexico and New Mexico." Master's thesis, University of New Mexico, 1937.

Gruener, John. "El Malpais Lava Tubes: Analog to Lunar Lava Tubes." Paper presented at "Space '90," Albuquerque, N.M. April 1990.

Lindsey, Alton A. Photographic Comparison of the Grants Malpais Vegetation. Informal report to U.S. Bureau of Land Management, 1981.

Moore, Cecil. "The Kid of Yesteryear and the Kid of Today. Special Collections, Grants Branch, New Mexico State University, n.d.

Osborn, Neal L. A Comparative Floristic Study of Mt. Taylor and Redondo Peak New Mexico. Ph.D. Thesis, University of New Mexico, 1962.

Miscellaneous documents. Authors unknown. Special Collections, Grants Branch, New Mexico State University. 1982–1986 (some dates unknown).

Riffle, Nancy L. The flora of Mt. Sedgwick and vicinity. Master's thesis, University of New Mexico, 1973.

Schroeder, Eugene. Mammals of Mt. Taylor, Valencia County, N.M. Master's thesis, University of New Mexico, 1961.

Shoemaker, John. Mount Taylor Volcanic Field: 18th Field Conference. New Mexico Geological Society, 1967.

Spier, Leslie. "The Zuni Region." The American Museum of Natural History. 1917.

"Tinaja." Author unknown. Special Collections, Grants Branch, New Mexico State University, March 1976.

WPA Writer's Project.
"The Adams Diggings" by E. V. Batchler. Nov. 19, 1938.
"Bluewater Lake and Dam" by Drake Delong. September 24, 1936.
"Buried Treasure" by L. Raines, n.d.
"The Church of the Golden Bell" told by Thomas Fallon to Elizabeth Morgan. 1935.
"The Story of Adam's [sic] Diggings" by L. Raines. 1936.
"Place Names"
"National Forests"
"Volcanoes and Lava Beds"
"National Monuments"
"Mountains"
"Canyons"
"Caves"
"Lakes and Dams"
"Spanish Trails"
"Outlaws"
"Conservation"
"Frontier Stories"
"McKinley County Places of Interest"
"Valencia County Places of Interest"

Correspondence

Postmaster (name unknown), Atarque, N.M. Letter to U.S. Work Projects Administration in Santa Fe, October 4, 1940.

Mrs. Frank Childers, Paxton Springs, N.M. Letter to Charles E. Minton. October 13, 1940.

Index